# LEADERSHIP
## IN EARLY CHILDHOOD

The pathway to professionalism

4th edition

# JILLIAN RODD

Open University Press

Open University Press
McGraw-Hill Education
McGraw-Hill House
Shoppenhangers Road
Maidenhead
Berkshire
England
SL6 2QL

email: enquiries@openup.co.uk
world wide web: www.openup.co.uk

and Two Penn Plaza, New York, NY 10121-2289, USA

First published 2013

Copyright © Jillian Rodd 2013

A catalogue record of this book is available from the British Library

ISBN-13: 978-0-335-24680-9
ISBN-10: 0-335-24680-X
eISBN: 978-0-335-24681-6

Library of Congress Cataloging-in-Publication Data
CIP data applied for

Published simultaneously in Australia and New Zealand by Allen & Unwin

Internal design by Brittany Britten
Indexes by Jillian Rodd
Typeset in 9.5/13 pt Plantin by Midland Typesetters, Australia
Printed by Phoenix Print Media, Singapore

**The McGraw·Hill** Companies

*Dedicated to the one I love,*
*my late husband,*
*Gerry Gray,*
*1948–2007*

# CONTENTS

# FOREWORD

In times of rapid change the role of leader can become a topic of whispered debate, anxious conversations or loyal declarations. It is often discussed by policy makers as a panacea for effective reform or a stumbling block for progress; by whole communities as the stuff of reputation and quality; and among early years professionals as simultaneously inspiring and unpredictably complex. In changing times everyone wants to talk about whose job it is to navigate our collective efforts towards a hopeful future.

Early childhood education and care across the world is in a state of flux. National governments are driving changes which seek to respond to the growing body of evidence that early engagement with children and their families delivers strong outcomes for whole communities. Alongside this, educators have, with increasing clarity, joined with families and policy makers to demand more concerted efforts to offer quality services to every child. But it is far from smooth sailing. These reforms take place among the challenges of the twenty-first century, which see us collectively grappling with global economic pressures that demand the careful use of limited resources and the multi-faceted needs of workers, families and communities.

It is into this multi-layered landscape that Jillian Rodd has produced a much welcomed new edition of *Leadership in Early Childhood*. When complex questions about the shape and nature of the sector are being asked, those who are charged with the responsibility to find the answers look for guidance, for tested strategies, and for the sound advice that speaks to the unique context of their work with children and families. Once again, with a deep and respectful appreciation for her reader, Jillian has offered a book full of sound advice, accompanied with practical approaches grounded in the contemporary theory of leadership and early childhood education and care.

Reflecting on my own career in early childhood, there have been key people, ideas and texts that have offered me clarity and confidence. For me they continue to be strong moorings in choppy seas, providing a sense of what is possible, informing the decisions I should make and helping me to formulate the principles for which I am prepared to take a stand. I first read Jillian's book at a time when I was about to give up on this fine profession. Things were changing, and the early childhood professional I imagined I would be was not my daily experience. Taking on a leadership role, I muddled my way through until a wise mentor gave me a copy of the second edition of this book. It was then that I realised two things: that thinking about leadership in early childhood was not just the business of academics but could be realised in the everyday work of children's services; and that I was deeply interested in becoming a more effective leader. Accordingly, I have since reciprocated by giving Jillian's book to a number of emerging leaders as they take on the essential role of leading others in the pursuit of quality.

The familiar reader will find changes in this edition that usefully inform their understanding of contemporary leadership in early childhood service provision. Jillian's attention to leading collaboratively in Chapter 8 will be well received by those who are working in the growing number of integrated early childhood sites where diverse perspectives need effective solutions. Similarly, the emphasis on quality leading in changing times (see Chapters 10 and 11) makes this text essential reading as we progress towards providing quality services for all children.

The new reader will be introduced to the fundamentals of leadership in early childhood education through an easily accessible collection of insights echoing and exploring their own experiences of leadership. From the plethora of leadership commentary, Jillian presents us with carefully selected theories and insights, balanced with practical examples and the voices of leaders working across the sector. Chapters that discuss the personal qualities of leaders and the art of communication in meeting our own and others' needs are critical in our shared ability to become leaders who inspire others, nurture ourselves and take decisive action.

This book speaks to all who have high expectations of our capacity to understand and deliver transformative services to young children and their families. It is another powerful tool in the repertoire of our sector's leaders, equipping emerging leaders to explore the possibilities of taking on a vital role.

*Catharine Hydon*
*Early Childhood Consultant*
*Dip Teaching (Early Childhood);*
*MEd (Early Child Education)*

# PREFACE AND ACKNOWLEDGEMENTS

The continuing interest surrounding leadership in early childhood encouraged the preparation of this fourth edition, which is the product of my own experience in early childhood. This book also reflects the opportunities I have had to work with gifted women and men who are dedicated to this important profession. The structure and content of the book have been revised and updated in the light of research, literature and helpful feedback. However, the basic intent remains the same: to offer insight into the nature of leadership, as well as the associated skills and responsibilities that are essential for enacting effective leadership in early childhood contexts.

Several people were instrumental in the production of this edition: Lizzy Walton, Associate Academic Publisher at Allen & Unwin, who finally pressed the right button to ignite my motivation and energy to write another edition; David Wright, an insightful early childhood leader and true friend, whose encouragement supported me through my loss and grief; Gerry Gray, my late husband, ever my rock and guiding star, who whispers to me on the wind and waves when I can't find my way alone. This edition would not have been written without his whispers on the waves of Waikiki and the winds of Barepta.

## Disclaimer

Every effort has been made to acknowledge the source of material that is not original in this book. However, many of the terms and concepts are so commonly used that the original source is uncertain. The author and publisher would be pleased to hear from copyright holders to rectify any omissions or errors.

# INTRODUCTION

*Leadership within early childhood has been and continues to be one of the major issues for debate. There is an identified need for strong leadership at government level and within local communities.*
DIRECTOR, EARLY LEARNING CENTRE

## THIS CHAPTER EXPLORES

- the role of leadership in early childhood
- the changing context of early childhood service provision
- early childhood educators' need to identify with professional leadership

In the twenty-first century, visionary and ethical leadership is proving to be a critical professional issue for early childhood educators around the world. Leadership continues to be of paramount importance for improving quality service provision for young children and families, and for early childhood to be recognised as a credible profession with unique expertise that is different from yet equal to other professions.

*The early childhood profession needs visionary and effective leaders so it can best position itself to meet future challenges.*
EARLY CHILDHOOD LECTURER

Leadership in early childhood is embodied and enacted in the experiences and environment provided for young children; the relationships between adults and those between adults and children; meeting and protecting the rights of children and adults; and working collaboratively to meet the needs of all concerned with young children's experiences in early childhood services. The challenge of effective leadership is to improve quality by helping early childhood communities to look beyond current circumstances, to forecast and to discover any need for creativity and innovation in service provision and to work towards making change happen in work with and for children and families.

*Young children need good leaders.*
PRIMARY ADVISER

Early childhood refers to a developmental period ranging from birth to approximately eight years of age. In many countries, two independent systems continue to provide care and education for young children, with staff employed in a range of services in one or both of the systems. The restructuring of early childhood training courses and awards, and the trend towards the provision of coordinated, integrated, multi-professional services for children and families in many countries have begun to overcome the artificial dichotomy that historically has differentiated care and education.

Unfortunately, terminology has maintained this unproductive division, with differing labels used to describe the roles, positions and jobs undertaken by those working in the range of early childhood services. Given the diversity and inter-changeability of terminology and structures, descriptors typically employed in international contexts are used in this book. Specifically, the term 'early childhood educator' or 'educator' refers to those who work directly with young children and their families in any early childhood context (Australian Government Department of Education, Employment and Workplace Relations, 2009). The term 'leader' generally refers to those responsible for the administration and operation of an early childhood service. The use of gender-neutral terminology is prioritised.

Leadership increasingly is being seen as a critical role and responsibility of early childhood educators, regardless of their initial qualifications—especially as service provision becomes more complex to meet the diverse needs of young children, families and local communities.

*Leadership is important as early childhood services have many responsibilities to many different people—different staff, families and children.*
PRE-SCHOOL DEVELOPMENT WORKER

*This brings increasing responsibilities because graduates are expected to rise to leadership roles and responsibilities.*
SENIOR LECTURER, EARLY CHILDHOOD EDUCATION

Ongoing changes in the provision and delivery of services for children and families require those who work in early childhood to be responsive continually to accelerating demographic and social change—for example, economic adversity and uncertainty, changes in family structure and employment patterns, child and family poverty, immigration and social justice issues.

*The current political agenda with ongoing initiatives has affected many services and what they offer.*
HEAD TEACHER, EARLY EXCELLENCE CENTRE

Early childhood remains high on the political agendas of governments in many countries, and early childhood educators are expected to respond regularly to new initiatives. The increase in inter-agency liaison and multi-disciplinary collaboration as a way of more effectively meeting the needs of children and families has demanded that early childhood educators work in ways that may be unfamiliar to them. Early childhood educators have led the inclusion of children with special needs into mainstream services, and many are exploring different pedagogies—for example, the Te Whariki curriculum in New Zealand and the Reggio Emilia pre-school approach in Italy, with a view to responding to identified needs and improving local services.

Currently, early childhood practice is grounded in inclusive, collaborative inter-personal relationships and respectful communication based on dialogue, exchange and reciprocity between educators, families and community members. Sustaining such a foundation requires strong leaders of high calibre and considerable courage who are capable of leading and meeting the interpersonal professional challenges of inclusive, collaborative, integrated, multi-professional teams.

Changing socio-political and contextual demands have precipitated an expansion of flexible services for children and families, with the ability to provide sensitive and skilled leadership highlighted as a key function. Research continues to reveal that the leadership style and performance of leaders of early childhood services—even when not the main focus of investigation—impact upon practice and policy, and determine the development and implementation of relevant and innovative services (Dunlop, 2008). This book addresses the fundamental question of how early childhood educators enact leadership as a means of ensuring responsive, high-quality services for young children and families.

It is beyond the scope of this book to describe and evaluate the range of initiatives, frameworks and targets that have been introduced by governments in many countries to guide and mandate early childhood practice and qualifications—for example, Australia's Early Years Learning Framework and England's Foundation Stage and Early Years Professional Status qualification. However, there have been times when early childhood educators have reacted negatively to what they consider to be arbitrary decisions or selective information about how best to achieve government goals for education in general and early childhood in particular. The paucity of the contribution by recognised early childhood experts to the development of some of these initiatives continues to raise concern about the appropriateness of their rationale and foundation.

Nevertheless, different initiatives have been, and will continue to be, endorsed and adopted at different times—the wheel turns regularly in education. Crucially, leadership and its enactment in early childhood remain independent of government frameworks and guidelines because the foundation of such leadership is embedded in the needs and expectations of young children, families and educators, which are relatively constant over time and unaffected by government prescriptions and fashionable trends.

Change—a hallmark of contemporary society—impacts greatly on early childhood services, making leadership—which is a necessary condition for effective change—worthy of greater attention by early childhood theorists, researchers and governments. The fundamental question of what is meant by 'leadership' in early childhood still has to be answered in a way that is meaningful and credible for educators.

*We, in early childhood, need to have conversations with each other about what it is we expect of our leaders ...*
SENIOR LECTURER, EARLY CHILDHOOD

Although politicians continue to call for better leadership from those charged with the responsibility for the provision of education for all members of society, attention to the importance of leadership in early childhood is relatively recent. When demands associated with rapid change in early childhood are raised, little if any reference is made to the presence (or absence) of leadership that facilitates the systematic implementation of appropriate change. In fact, the vast majority of government initiatives and frameworks provided as guidelines or mandated curricula for those who work in early childhood make scant reference to *how* their implementation should be introduced and supported. Such initiatives depend on skilled leadership for acceptance, compliance and sustainability, yet the centrality of such leadership is acknowledged rarely in supporting documentation. Experience confirms that early childhood educators can be resistant to new ideas and change. Therefore, the need for effective, active, and socially and politically astute leaders who understand the vital contribution of leadership to achieving quality provision has become even more pressing.

*It would appear that only a small number of early childhood educators build leadership/advocacy into their positions; consequently there is not a strong united voice that communicates to the wider community.*
DIRECTOR, EARLY LEARNING CENTRE

Although there are small pockets of research interest and activity—for example, in Australia, New Zealand, Finland, Norway and Britain—the subject of leadership in early childhood attracts few researchers (Dunlop, 2008). Despite the potential for exercising leadership in early childhood, existing research findings and professional publications have yet to focus early childhood educators' attention on evolving conceptualisations about leadership—a result of the changing world of leadership in general and the nature of leadership in early childhood in particular. This may be attributed in part to the apparent vagueness and haziness about what is meant by leadership in early childhood and its practical relevance. A commonly accepted definition of leadership for early childhood has yet to be constructed from systematic debate about the properties of, opportunities for and barriers to leadership.

A crucial component of leadership is choice. Regardless of how extensively a person is trained in leadership, or how deeply they are thrust into a position of leadership, it is essential that they make a conscious choice to accept that role (Kouzes and Posner, 2007). For a variety of reasons, many early childhood educators do not choose a leadership role. Low rates of pay, low status, poor working conditions, lack of understanding of employment rights and the repetitive, physically demanding and stressful nature of the work act as inhibitors to aspirations to leadership.

In addition, the majority of educators are not yet comfortable with, and choose not to respond to, the leadership demands of their work, including the managerial and supervisory aspects of working with adults (Ebbeck and Waniganayake, 2003). Unfortunately, in both early childhood training and practice there is an obvious emphasis on management at the expense of leadership, producing a sector that generally is over-managed and under-led. Leadership appears to be a phenomenon that remains an enigma for many in early childhood.

Early childhood educators around the world continue to conceptualise the professional role as one where the focus is on an ethic of care (Cameron and Moss, 2011) and interaction with children and families. Many have been slow to appreciate the need for a professionalised identity for their work (Lloyd and Hallett, 2010). Some are motivated to improve early childhood's status in the professional community, but many still regard activities that might contribute to the achievement of these goals—such as management, marketing, influencing policy, lobbying, public speaking, fundraising and research as conflicting with their own ethos of care and service. They identify minimally with attributes that underpin the instrumental, professional and entrepreneurial dimensions of leadership, remaining more comfortable with caring attributes that denote patience, warmth, capacity for nurture and energy.

Unless there is a more active and strong identification and recognition of the leadership role, as well as a broader conceptualisation of the professional role and associated skills, early childhood will not be able to meet its increasing need for competent leaders, educators, administrators, supervisors, mentors, researchers and advocates.

## Reflections on leadership in practice

I have always been passionate about the principles of good early childhood practice. I was fortunate to have had two head teachers who were sympathetic to my views and allowed me autonomy in my nursery. I was given further responsibility in the school—Key Stage 1 Coordinator and then Early Years Coordinator—and later became a member of the Senior Management Team. So I gradually learned new roles and took -on more responsibility. Now I lead a team of eight early childhood teachers who support children and families in the county.
EARLY EDUCATION TEAM LEADER

Although professionalism and professional self-confidence have grown, early childhood educators still need to develop a clearly delineated understanding about the breadth and depth of their leadership roles and responsibilities, and their relationship to the complexity of leading early childhood practice. Improvement in understanding and leading practice comes from scrutinising, questioning and reflecting upon traditional and accepted practice. For early childhood educators to gain a better understanding of and greater confidence to engage in leadership roles, more extensive professional discourse in supportive, non-threatening and non-judgemental arenas is essential.

The development of leadership in early childhood continues to be a critical challenge. If the provision of inclusive, socially and culturally responsive, coordinated and integrated services for young children and families is to be successful, it is unacceptable to rely on colleagues from other disciplines such as teaching, social work or nursing to provide leadership models and initiatives that can be borrowed and adapted to the needs and contexts of early childhood services. If early childhood is to achieve professional status equivalent to that of similar or related occupations, it is necessary to identify, nurture and train those who will emerge as leaders from *within* the profession. Empowerment within early childhood has to begin with people who identify with, feel comfortable in and choose the leadership role at service level, and who will progress to leadership—perhaps at government and policy levels. The basis of such empowerment lies in building an understanding about the vital role of leadership in early childhood and the skills required from the 'grass roots' up.

It is clear that the up-and-coming generation of early childhood leaders needs to be drawn from educators who are:

- passionate and committed
- politically astute and active
- emotionally intelligent
- ethically mature
- professionally integrated as leader-educators, and
- authentic, transparent and congruent.

With the current trend towards complex multi-disciplinary and integrated services, contemporary early childhood educators will continue to be challenged to perceive associated changes in their roles and responsibilities as opportunities to learn, develop and apply their considerable expertise to leadership in the range of services for young children and families that will emerge in the future.

Contemporary literature about leadership in early childhood currently focuses on pedagogical leadership, distributed leadership and leadership practice. While acknowledging the importance of pedagogical and distributed leadership, this book examines the practical skills that underpin effective leadership in early childhood contexts in the twenty-first century. Professional and practical capability in leadership in early childhood is the foundation of enhanced quality and practice in early childhood services.

# PART I

## DECONSTRUCTING LEADERSHIP

Considerable research has established leadership as a critical issue for every organisation in today's challenging and constantly changing world. Leadership is a broad term that is used to describe a vast range of activity in relation to organisational administration and management. Contemporary leadership is acknowledged as being essentially holistic, subtle, complex, multi-faceted, sometimes invisible and therefore difficult to pinpoint, identify and observe in context.

While it is useful to deconstruct leadership into various component parts—especially for those who are unfamiliar with what it encompasses—it is also important to keep in mind that effective leadership comes from integrated sophisticated thinking, genuine understanding and skilled action. Effective leadership creates synergy and is more than the sum of its parts.

This section introduces the concept of leadership and aims to illuminate some of its intricacies in the early childhood context.

Chapter 1 discusses the challenge of defining leadership, contrasts it with management and briefly outlines some key concepts that have influenced the development of current understandings of leadership in early childhood.

Chapter 2 identifies some of the personal qualities, attributes and characteristics associated with effective leadership and examines their influence on followers in early childhood.

Chapter 3 presents some current theories and models of leadership and explores their relationship to career development in early childhood.

# CHAPTER 1

# UNRAVELLING LEADERSHIP IN THE EARLY CHILDHOOD SECTOR

*Leadership is best defined as a process of engagement: the leader engages fellow professionals in best meeting the needs of children and families ... in early childhood there is an expectation that leaders will be consultative in their approach.*

LECTURER AND RESEARCHER

## THIS CHAPTER EXPLORES

- the challenge of defining leadership
- key concepts related to leadership
- differences between leadership and management
- why leadership works in some situations and not others
- leadership applied to the early childhood context

Despite the leadership role being addressed to at least some degree in pre- and in-service training programs, early childhood educators in many countries reluctantly identify with the concept of leadership as part of their professional responsibilities. This disinclination to see themselves as leaders is an interesting phenomenon because, historically, traditionally and currently, they are trained to demonstrate high levels of autonomy and independence in practice and policy. This requirement for independent decision-making and problem-solving skills stems from the physical isolation of early childhood services. With little access to immediate support and backup, early childhood educators develop autonomous styles and skills for meeting the demands of their situation, which in other work environments are referred to as leadership. The lack of an agreed and accepted definition of leadership in early childhood has contributed to an observed unwillingness to connect with this role, and it needs to be addressed.

## Defining the challenge of leadership

Leadership is a process and responsibility that requires attention to multiple roles, functions and people in ways that align with and promote commitment to shared values and vision. The literature reveals that there are many different definitions of leadership. It can be enacted in various ways and takes many forms. However, regardless of definition, the principles and skills underpinning effective leadership are generic—that is, context free. The key concepts in most definitions of leadership are:

- influence and motivation
- followers and teams
- direction, goals and standards, and
- cooperation and collaboration.

At its most basic, leadership is about how a group of people is influenced (using values and vision) to achieve a common goal.

Leadership is a people-oriented process, role and responsibility where two or more people come together in pursuit of a common goal. It involves the ability to create an environment that values commitment, challenge and growth, in which members of a team are encouraged and supported to realise their potential and give their best.

Leadership resides in the individual who chooses to accept, for whatever reasons, its roles and responsibilities. While social and cultural contexts are important influences on the decisions that leaders make, and sometimes on the style they choose to adopt, how the individual personally embraces, embodies and enacts leadership is the essence of its success. It evolves out of personal capacity of the leader to:

- understand themselves
- accept responsibility
- build and communicate shared values and vision
- inspire interest by living their values and vision
- build trust, relationships and cooperation among colleagues, and
- take action to realise goals of their own and the potential of others.

The priorities of effective leadership are to stimulate connectedness, cooperation, commitment to lifelong learning and change in themselves and others. This requires energy, enjoyment, enthusiasm, motivation and dedication—in other words, effective leaders must believe in their work, develop the trust and respect of others and display personal competence. The most significant contribution effective leadership can make is to help both people and organisations to develop, to improve, to adapt and to change.

Leadership is founded on a desire to make a difference to the lives of others by transforming:

- values into action
- vision into reality
- obstacles into innovations
- challenges into successes
- separateness into collaboration, and
- risks into rewards.

However, effective leadership is not a matter of being a hero, but rather entails acting in ways that support the enablement, empowerment and well-being of others and organisations (Sinclair, 2007).

Opportunities to embrace leadership can present themselves at any time, and anybody who recognises an opportunity, is motivated and chooses to take action displays interest in and a capacity for leadership—that is, they show leadership potential. Every early childhood educator can choose to become a leader by demonstrating increasing competence in their work; by becoming a critical friend to colleagues; by supporting the development of others, including children, families and colleagues; and by acting as an ambassador and advocate for their profession.

Leadership is everyone's business, and everyone can and should share in the leadership process each day. If leadership is confined to positional or formal leadership—that is, official leaders—others who aspire to or display potential for leadership can be excluded. Formal leaders who inhibit or prevent others from aspiring and choosing to embrace leadership are failing in their responsibility to build leadership capacity and plan for succession, thereby abusing their positions of power. Given that all leadership is temporary and transient, wise leaders invest in the future by identifying, developing and supporting leadership aspiration and potential in others.

## An example of how not to lead

Leona holds a designated position of senior leadership in a large integrated service. She is acknowledged for her sharp intellect, but she finds pleasure in manipulating others and using humour to mock and put them down. Sometimes she is actively destructive, pitting staff against one another, subtly deriding individual and team efforts and achievements, and taking her anger and frustration out on others. She only collaborates with or mentors others if she believes she will gain personally. Her lack of people skills means she enjoys little credibility, respect and support from staff, and has yet to achieve the top leadership position she so desires.

Early childhood educators who are not formal or positional leaders may display informal leadership. Here, they recognise the need for action to improve a situation and can be acknowledged by team members as authentic and credible leaders, thereby holding considerable influence and power—sometimes more than ineffective formal leaders.

While leadership resides in the leader—that is, the person who chooses to embrace leadership roles and responsibility—it can also be conceived of as an event, process or relationship between leaders and followers, and therefore may be shared. Some theorists view leadership as a conversation and social process where leadership arises out of social relationships—how people act together to make sense of the situation they face. Shared leadership may be a function of people following and being influenced by social exchanges. This concept will be discussed in Chapter 3, on leadership theory.

Poole (2011) proposes that leadership contributes to organisational and people effectiveness because it:

- addresses values, vision and goals
- inspires people so they remain motivated
- provides direction and focus
- sets a positive working atmosphere and climate
- seeks the resources required to achieve goals and targets
- ensures timely decision-making, and
- recognises and develops a learning community.

Few early childhood educators enter the profession with the ambition to become a leader in the future. Understanding about and recognition of individual potential and capacity for leadership may inspire more educators to see themselves as leaders, which benefits young children and families as well as leading to much-needed advances in community credibility and status.

*Leaders are people who have a public face through professional activities . . . who have been mentored by recognised early childhood leaders to assume these roles . . . [the term 'leader'] does not necessarily mean someone who is a service director, coordinator or manager . . .*
ASSOCIATE PROFESSOR, EARLY CHILDHOOD

Leadership is a dynamic, holistic activity, rather than a set of static attributes, where leaders draw upon personal qualities and abilities that command respect and promote feelings of trust and security in others. Leaders engage in collaborative activities that help write and drive the future.

There are many contemporary definitions and ways of understanding leadership and its enactment. In deconstructing leadership, this book focuses on leadership for early childhood services because, although leadership resides in individuals, it is understood as a shared or distributed social process where effective leaders draw on a range of collaborative strategies to achieve positive, inclusive and ethical outcomes for all who are associated with early childhood services.

*There usually is a defined role of leader—for example, headship—but other roles have an element of leadership which when supported enhances services and allows for effective cooperation between different professionals and services . . .*
HEAD TEACHER, EARLY EXCELLENCE CENTRE

*Leadership can be undertaken for an hour, a day or a year . . .*
TEACHING ASSISTANT

## Reflections on a day in the life of a leader

I'm the director of a large childcare service and I begin my day at 8.00 a.m. where I'm at my desk. An educator has called in sick, so I need to organise the staffing ratios. Children and families arrive at 8.00 a.m. and a couple are waiting to discuss their child's behaviour at home. As I meet with them, the phone rings again. Next, I begin to sort out the mail—for urgent attention, needs attention soon, can be delegated, for the staff room and the rest (meaning I'll get to it some time). It is 9.30 a.m. and I don't have on-the-floor responsibilities this morning, so I visit a room to chat with the children and offer support to the educators; this also allows me to observe teaching, learning and individual needs. By 11.00 a.m. I'm back at my desk, with emails to read and respond to. It's midday; some families arrive to collect children; I've got reports to write—but I want to be visible and accessible, so I go out to reception.

It's lunchtime for some educators, and one has made an appointment to see me to discuss permission and funding to attend equal opportunities training. I agree, subject to available funding and staff cover. I take the opportunity to offer her some well-deserved feedback. I eat lunch at my desk while I read and try to assimilate the latest government publication. I respond to some waiting correspondence.

Afternoon tea is time for one educator's farewell. Many of the children have been collected so anyone who is off the floor attends. It's important to be sociable, to be part of and listen to conversations. I use the opportunity to talk informally about our work. I am interested in passion and creativity in early years' practice, so I introduce these themes and ask whether anyone would explore them in our regular meeting. I meet with two teachers who want to introduce a new initiative. We discuss how to take it forward so that it doesn't increase the workload of others.

It's 4.30 p.m. and I am going to a meeting with other directors in my area. Before I leave, I check that all is under control for Friday, which can be hectic. This meeting finishes at 6.00 p.m. and I go home. In my briefcase, I have a draft of the budget that must be checked tonight because I have a meeting tomorrow with the council's financial administrator. I tackle that at 9.00 p.m. That's a typical day.

Leadership in early childhood becomes the product of the collective endeavour of an interconnected group of educators where:

- shared, collaborative and distributed leadership is evidenced
- diversity is viewed as a strength for responding to constantly changing demands
- authentic and credible authority is conferred on those who are perceived as professional, possessing high levels of expertise, judgement, fairness and wisdom, and
- power, defined as influence and strength, is derived from working collaboratively with others.

## Reflections on a day in the life of a leader

I am an early childhood educator with eight years' experience. Teaching three- and four-year-olds is my main responsibility. Recently, I attended training on the importance of the first three years. The significance of the family as the child's first and foremost teacher was reiterated.

I was extremely interested, and thought I could offer an opportunity to help families of young children under three years in our area. This would be advantageous because it would be a way of prospective families getting to know the service and what we offer, and to have a real choice before enrolling their children. I talked to the director about the idea and she was interested; she suggested that I take the lead in the next meeting to see who might want to be involved. At the meeting, only one educator was interested and willing to take the idea forward. That didn't matter—now there were two of us plus the director when needed.

The two of us spent some time planning and then put forward our plan to the director. She thought that it was a way of our service starting up an outreach initiative and that she could find us some funding from the budget because of the benefits for families, children and the service. We outlined the plan at the next meeting and were supported and encouraged by others—probably because there was no extra work in it for them!

Within three months, we held the first of a six-meeting program with five families and their under-threes. We had six topics to focus on but also listened to the families about what they wanted to discuss. It was a great success and we've run this program twice now. We wrote a report for our newsletter and the local newspaper, and did a talk at our local early childhood forum. It was hard at first to suggest this idea, but working with another educator and the director has been great. I would not have had the courage to take on such an initiative by myself, but working collaboratively gave me so much more confidence. We hope that our success will inspire other educators to feel confident enough to put their own ideas forward.

Today, effective leadership in early childhood is associated with the collective efforts of teams of educators who work together to influence and inspire each other rather than the efforts of one single person who focuses on getting the job done. Therefore, it is imperative that early childhood educators share and discuss their different perspectives on leadership and teamwork, and have access to opportunities for professional preparation and training in leadership roles and responsibilities.

The complexity and diversity of leadership in early childhood have yet to be deconstructed fully. The concept of a 'leader' who influences others in order to administer an efficient, accountable business or service is being assimilated slowly into professional identity. Early childhood educators' perceptions about, comprehension of and confidence in leading staff, families, other professionals and agencies have not yet been developed fully. This partly explains the leadership difficulties encountered in service provision and the ongoing low credibility and status of early childhood compared with other services and professions.

Narrow definitions of professional development and career by many educators have left early childhood with too few specialised advocates who can guide the workforce through the political and economic processes that determine the continuation or otherwise of these services. While early childhood educators continue to define their work and aspirations by an ethos of care and service, they will not meet the need to extend their interest and competence to leadership roles and responsibilities.

## Reflections on a day in the life of a leader

I work in child care and I have never thought of myself as a leader. I always thought that the manager was the leader. In my appraisal, my manager suggested that I attend a course on effective leadership and management in early childhood services. I didn't think that this was relevant to me, but she wanted me to go. I didn't think that I would get anything out of it because I work with children; I don't do much administration like reports and budgets. But after the course, I came away with a different understanding of what leadership in early childhood was, especially the differences between management and leadership. I learned that I could be and probably was already a leader and manager. So I thought about my job and where I could see that I was a leader.

My type of leadership means showing families around the service, talking to them about our approach to learning and the opportunities we offer the children, making displays of children's work for the reception area—I really enjoy that—reading professional magazines like *Practical Preschool* and *Early Educator*—I get lots of ideas from those types of magazines—and I make sure that the two of us in the Under Twos room have a written plan for the week. Apparently, even going on a course shows leadership because it means that you want to improve your skills and that helps raise the quality of early childhood services.

Before the course, I didn't realise that I was a leader simply because I did those things. Now I see that I could learn a lot more about running a childcare service and I could take on more responsibility for other things. If I did that, I would be preparing myself for getting a manager's job one day.

Stimulating interest in and aspirations for taking on leadership is important. Therefore, unravelling the challenge of leadership and identifying key roles and responsibilities within early childhood makes it more accessible at the grass-roots level. This helps early childhood educators to grasp the complexities of and opportunities for leadership that arise in their work. Today, authentic leadership in early childhood stems from focused attention to:

- engaging emotional and intellectual commitment of educators and families
- awakening, stimulating and challenging thinking and reflection
- realising visions of a better future
- enhancing and empowering personal lives and professional careers
- energising and kindling collective activity and responsibility
- transforming workplace cultures and climates, and
- delivering relevant and responsive quality services for children and families.

There are no prescriptions about what to do or how to go about translating such elements into practice. Every early childhood educator who aspires to leadership must discover and learn how best to do this. As educators become more comfortable with and gain confidence in leadership, some will become interested in extending their concerns and abilities to wider arenas outside service provision, such as active contribution in professional bodies, action research, writing and perhaps becoming politically active.

## Differences between leadership and management

Understanding leadership in early childhood has been plagued by its confusion with the concept of management. Early childhood educators and their training still emphasise and value management over leadership (Thornton et al., 2009). It is not clear what differentiates leadership from management and leaders from managers in the early childhood context. In general, leaders lead people in ways that empower and develop others. Managers manage functions, processes and people. They may use efficient strategies but these may not maximise the full potential of people (Poole, 2011). There has been much debate over the differences between leadership and management, with the terms being used interchangeably. Agreement over the definition of leadership in early childhood has not yet been reached, making it an elusive concept and one where not all capacities are necessarily observable and accessible.

It is important to understand leadership and management are different dimensions that are inherently linked and interwoven. Effective leaders in early childhood need to be aware that their leadership role is more than routine management, which focuses on the present and is dominated by issues of continuity and stability.

Managers focus on the smooth running of day-to-day work; they plan, organise, coordinate, monitor and control. Management activities can be undertaken without enacting leadership. On the other hand, leaders focus on the future—what could and should be; they build and communicate shared vision, inspire commitment to shared goals, motivate and build collaborative teams, and model and distribute responsibility. They approach managerial responsibilities as opportunities to engage, enable and empower people. Consequently, they are accorded respect and status as credible and legitimate leaders.

### An example of a manager who is not a leader

Colin is a manager of a family service with ten years' experience. On being offered an opportunity for specialised computer training, he replied, 'I'm too busy managing the service to be away from it for training.' When questioned about the pressing issues he was experiencing, he revealed that he was spending a lot of time comforting reception staff who were upset by contact with angry and aggressive families. Colin's shortsightedness in focusing on a day-to-day issue meant that he lost an opportunity for his personal learning and development. His attitude denied the reception staff an opportunity to grow and develop because he did not recognise their need for training to deal with difficult people and conversations.

Management is related more to maintenance tasks—concerned with carrying on, keeping up, perpetuating and sustaining. An emphasis on maintenance can lead to a preoccupation with staying safe and not advancing.

Leadership emanates out of vision that is grounded in philosophy, values and beliefs, which in turn guides policy, day-to-day operation, procedures and innovation. It is manifested through strategic planning that grows out of reflection. Leadership is associated more with strengthening qualities, behaviours and values through inspirational, politically sensitive public relations, research and dissemination skills, and taking risks to improve quality. Leadership is related to:

- strategic development rather than day-to-day problem-solving
- fostering a culture of trust, developing an openness to learning, encouraging and stimulating learning, communicating aims and vision with clarity, and
- mission, direction and inspiration rather than designing and implementing plans, getting things done and ensuring that other people work efficiently.

Early childhood educators who aspire to leadership are encouraged to constantly scrutinise and challenge traditionally accepted practices because leadership is about learning, and all effective leaders are learners. In fact, if leaders stop learning, they are finished as leaders.

## Reflections on management and leadership in practice

When I think about my management tasks, they generally tend to be around day-to-day issues, such as checking that the rooms and bathrooms have been cleaned properly, that there are no hazardous items in the outdoor area, that the rooms have been set up properly before the children arrive, that the families' newsletter is ready to go out, that the rosters are completed on time and that educators are relaxed and prepared to enjoy the day with the children.

When I think about my leadership responsibilities, I focus on activities such as reading the latest government guidelines and other important literature so that I can raise current issues at staff meetings, matching new educators with a mentor who is more experienced, thinking about different ways to evaluate the curriculum and performance, planning for continuing professional development for all, working with or delegating responsibility to teams for developing specific policies, ways of sharing my expertise and thinking about the best methods of managing some of the changes we have to implement.

HEAD TEACHER, EARLY EXCELLENCE CENTRE

Successful leaders are more than efficient managers. Rather than focusing on the narrow and specific details of getting through the day and keeping everything running smoothly, they allocate time to reflecting on, deliberating about and planning more broadly around values, vision, policies and the need to be responsive to change. They use human resources effectively by delegating responsibility for the fine detail required at the management level.

Effective early childhood leaders are oriented towards the future, where innovation and change are effected through:

- collaborative goal-setting, where the wider the participation, the greater the likelihood of commitment to the goals
- consensus-building, where a productive working environment is created

by shared and distributed responsibility for implementing and adhering to decisions

• personnel development, where educators and families are helped to grow and develop, and

• service development, where initiative is taken to establish, review, evaluate and modify existing services and structures.

In order to be an effective leader, one also needs to be an efficient manager. However, management skills do not equate with and are not the same as leadership skills. Poorly developed management skills will not provide the level of organisation required to free up the time needed to devote to leadership issues. Leaders with highly developed management skills structure their workload to allocate adequate time to key leadership functions.

## Example of leadership enacted with management responsibilities

David is a formal leader of an agency that supports young children and families. He was offered the opportunity to participate in a conference. Appreciating the learning and networking benefits for both himself and the agency, and knowing that some work could not be postponed in his absence, he purposively delegated appropriate responsibilities to suitable team members. He also committed to writing a report for the newsletter and giving a talk at a staff meeting about what he had learned that was relevant to himself and the service. David showed his commitment to lifelong learning and, through the distribution of responsibility to others, his encouragement and support for the service as a community of learners.

Management skills are necessary but not sufficient for effective leadership. The knowledge, abilities and skills of management and leadership overlap but are essentially different. Leadership creates synergy and is a cohesive force that facilitates management.

## Leadership in early childhood

While the study of management is a core unit in the pre-service training of early childhood educators, the same cannot be said of leadership. The lack of agreed definition, limited access to experienced role models and mentors, the reluctance many display towards roles and responsibilities that involve authority and power, and limited opportunities for leadership preparation and training have impeded the development of an understanding about what leadership in early childhood entails and whose responsibility it is. Although demands for professionalism, accountability and credibility are recognised, the concept of leadership as a means of advancing early childhood is not well understood.

First, it is essential to understand that there are many people who can and choose to take up leadership roles and responsibilities in early childhood services, including:

- managers/directors/coordinators
- principals/head teachers
- owners/licensees
- early childhood educators
- team leaders/teams
- volunteers
- committees
- advisers/supervisors
- support staff
- family/non-family members
- children, and
- students.

Everyone can make a contribution to quality early childhood service provision by choosing to recognise and take up leadership opportunities when they arise. When those who are associated with early childhood services—regardless of status and capacity—appreciate that quality is a result of connectedness, cooperation, contribution and commitment, they are embracing a leadership perspective.

Kagan and Bowman's (1997) analysis of the multi-faceted nature of leadership practice is endorsed widely by the vast majority of early childhood educators who accept responsibility for enacting leadership in five distinct areas:

- *administrative*—the day-to-day operation and management of services
- *pedagogical*—children's growth, development and learning, curricula
- *community*—embedding services as an integral part of local context
- *conceptual*—creation of new ideas, innovations and initiatives, change, and
- *advocacy*—promoting and protecting child and family well-being and rights.

However, Heikka and Waniganayake (2011) caution against over-emphasising pedagogical leadership at the expense of other areas. They argue that pedagogical leadership needs to be considered within the full extent of the leadership roles and responsibilities expected today, and that to achieve this early childhood educators need a comprehensive and balanced understanding of leadership theory and concepts.

Different models of leadership are beginning to be discussed—for example, distributed and transformational leadership—and some early childhood educators are thinking about leadership in new ways. However, identifying with the concept of and need for leadership by and of early childhood educators is still problematic for some.

Effective leadership in early childhood also is concerned with working towards creating a community of learners and providing quality services for children and families by:

- inspiring others by sharing values, vision, ideas and thoughts
- setting an example and being a strong role model
- influencing others—particularly educators and families—to contribute to creative early childhood services by articulating a clear sense of purpose, offering direction and finding ways forward
- administering services efficiently by building teamwork, collaboration and inclusion
- supervising educators and guiding families in ways that enhance personal growth, development, progress and empowerment, and
- planning for and implementing change in order to improve effectiveness and quality.

These characteristics are evident in the following definitions of leadership articulated by early childhood educators from a range of backgrounds and experience.

*Leadership means someone who has a vision about their future expectations for self and others ... can articulate what this is to others ... and can garnish the necessary expertise to push forward an agenda that has been jointly constructed.*
SENIOR LECTURER

*Leadership refers to individuals and groups of people who are committed to the provision of high-quality education and care for all children throughout the world ... these people and groups are imbued with a*

*passion that is readily communicated to others ... they are enthusiastic and feel empowered to speak out and work towards change even when the odds are against them.*
DIRECTOR, EARLY LEARNING CENTRE

*Leadership refers to people who instigate and initiate new practices that can stimulate and support others in personal development ... who get commitment from staff and support from them.*
EARLY CHILDHOOD TRAINER

*Leadership means a team that works towards common aims for services by defining ethos and principles, setting aims with achievable targets, valuing every person's contributions and establishing good lines of communication.*
EARLY EDUCATION TEAM LEADER

*Leadership guides, supports and respects members of the team.*
DEPUTY SUPERVISOR

*Leadership sets a good example for everyone to follow.*
PRE-SCHOOL DEVELOPMENT WORKER

Four basic steps are necessary for early childhood leaders to make things happen:

1.   *The definition of organisational and individual goals and/or objectives.* This clarifies the service and its purpose, outlines future directions, describes procedures and identifies resource requirements and agreed roles and responsibilities for each team member.
2.   *The agreeing of individual standards and expectations.* Delegated tasks are agreed in terms of the function for each educator, and include agreed measures or standards of performance.
3.   *The provision of support and feedback.* Assistance is provided for individual team members to develop their expertise with constructive feedback to ensure that performance is maximised.
4.   *The monitoring and evaluation of outcomes.* A process of regular review is essential to ensure that defined objectives are met in relation to professional and ethical standards and within the specified timeframe.

Early childhood leaders have a professional responsibility to attend to child and family well-being, adult morale and goal attainment. These are key concerns of all early childhood services and leaders support them by acting in ways that promote:

- *empowerment*—where authority and obligation are shared and distributed by the leader, resulting in increased responsibility and accountability throughout the team
- *enablement*—where means and opportunities for, and elimination of obstacles to, individual and team growth and development are ensured, and
- *enhancement*—where leader and follower roles are interwoven to produce increased commitment and extraordinary performance.

These factors are important for creating and shaping the right context, tone and psychological climate of early childhood services, which are hallmarks of quality.

## Why does leadership work in some situations and not others?

There are a number of reasons why a leader may operate successfully in one particular context but experience difficulties in another. Sometimes the cultures of the team and the leader do not match or fit. For example, the psychological climate of the team may be focused upon people, their individual needs and relationships, whereas the leader's style might be task oriented and focused on organisational needs.

Sometimes incompatibility exists between the leader and significant members of the team. For example, the leader and the deputy or the president of the management committee might espouse different values or not share the same vision. Consequently, they have conflicting goals for the service.

Sometimes there is a need for task-specific leadership. A mismatch between the nature of the task and leadership style is evident. For example, a task that has to be completed in a specific format and that has a specific timeline—such as fee subsidies or a funding submission—requires task-oriented, goal-specific and goal-directed leadership. Other tasks, such as planning, can be completed in a number of different ways and therefore left to the professional discretion of educators.

To provide effective leadership in early childhood, leaders have to articulate a clear vision of the future and a general plan of action for getting there. They also need to gain the commitment and cooperation of educators and families—perhaps even local communities—to achieve agreed goals. However, a balance has to be maintained between getting the job done and meeting people's needs.

Getting the job done involves providing vision by clarifying goals, aims, objectives, roles and responsibilities; gathering relevant information from educators and families; summarising, integrating and developing ideas as a way of building a vision to guide the team in achieving its goals; and monitoring the team's progress towards the goals through constant evaluation.

Meeting people's needs involves clarifying team goals to help people understand their purpose and to help gain commitment; providing guidelines to help team members know what is expected of them in team interaction; providing a sense of inclusion or belonging and acceptance in order to draw on the team's full resources; keeping channels of communication open; and creating a warm and friendly atmosphere in the service where team members are valued and rewarded through encouragement and recognition.

It is when the leader addresses and balances the needs of task and relationships that motivation, commitment, collaboration and contribution are stimulated in everyone associated with early childhood services.

## Bringing it together

The complexity of the early childhood context makes it difficult to deconstruct, analyse and define leadership in ways that are specific to, and authentic and meaningful for those responsible for service provision. However, the development of open, cooperative, committed relationships between all involved in the early childhood community appears to be of utmost importance in developing and shaping effective leadership. Notions of trust, sharing, inclusion, collaboration and empowerment also seem to be central to successful leadership. The complex and multi-faceted nature of leadership called for in early childhood highlights the need for leadership to be viewed more appropriately as a distributed process and continuum, reflecting the power of communication, relationships, social interaction and cooperation.

# CHAPTER 2

## THE PERSONAL QUALITIES OF LEADERS IN EARLY CHILDHOOD

*Those who feel passionate about early childhood and want to share their beliefs and good practice will become leaders.*
EARLY EDUCATION TEAM LEADER

### THIS CHAPTER EXPLORES

- attributes associated with leaders
- the influence of leaders' personal qualities on followers
- the role of gender stereotypes
- who follows the leader
- who is a leader in early childhood
- who can become a leader in early childhood

Although the literature highlights early childhood educators' limited understanding of and the need for clear definition of leadership, evidence shows that followers themselves hold a separate appreciation of whom they recognise as a legitimate leader. A leader cannot lead without followers, and followers only follow people they believe to display authentic leadership capacity.

*Leaders have a personality that generates respect, they are respected into the position of leader.*
PRE-SCHOOL DEVELOPMENT WORKER

### Attributes associated with leaders

Efforts to explain leadership generally focus on one or other of two theoretical perspectives. The psychological perspective considers that leadership resides in the individual, in personal qualities and attributes, in individual ways of thinking and behaving. Its enactment is a matter of choice about the when, what, how and why, with individual choices influenced by contextual factors. However, the extent to which contextual factors impact on and shape leadership has not been established. The sociological perspective considers leadership to be a product of the societal, cultural and organisational context. It is viewed as a contextual phenomenon:

socially constructed, situational and interpretive. Both perspectives make valuable and valid contributions to understanding leadership.

This book, however, adopts a psychological perspective, and supports the tenet that everyone has the potential to become a leader and everyone can learn and develop the qualities and skills required for effective leadership. Therefore, leadership is considered to reside in individuals. Even though its enactment may be influenced by contextual factors, it is individuals who choose to take up the challenge of leadership, to embody and to enact leadership. It is also individuals who, formally or informally, are accorded the status of leader. However, there is no clear profile of an ideal leader (George et al., 2011), and fortunately there is no stereotype about who or what constitutes a good leader (Koenig et al., 2011).

*Leaders want to make a difference and are able and prepared to take action.*
HEAD TEACHER

How leadership is embodied and enacted depends on a range of factors within an individual (Poole, 2011), including:

- personality
- values and beliefs
- vision and motivation
- skills (strengths and weaknesses)
- level and type of experience
- previous interactions with others within and external to the workplace, and
- specific mood

as well as a variety of factors and circumstances independent of the individual.

Due to their previous experience of both effective and poor leadership, followers hold their own interpretation about the kind of person they think makes a good leader. Overwhelmingly, effective leaders are perceived as credible and believable by followers. Regardless of position or power, followers recognise an individual as an authentic leader when certain qualities, attributes and characteristics are displayed. Credible leaders are perceived as:

- honest
- forward-looking
- inspiring, and
- competent.

In the 25 years of their international research, Kouzes and Posner (2007) found that these were the four most important characteristics consistently identified with effective, authentic leaders.

*Leaders are respectful, fair and motivational ... knowledgeable,*
*forward thinking, decision-makers and problem-solvers, understanding,*
*responsible and reliable.*
NURSERY OFFICER

Character (referring to integrity, courage, honour, moral strength and will-power) is another attribute that is rated highly by followers (Wooden and Jamison, 2009). Displaying sound character means acting in ways that are true to yourself, based on your values, your beliefs and your vision. Warren Bennis's (1989) quotable quote places character as a key attribute for leadership:

*Successful leadership is ... about a set of attributes. First and foremost is*
*character.*

Character, or being true to yourself, helps build trust and better relationships, and engenders follower commitment to and support for goal attainment.

Followers also accord legitimate leadership to those who are perceived as:

- trustworthy
- respectful
- confident, focused and assertive
- perceptive, sensitive and emotionally intelligent
- conscientious and reliable
- enthusiastic and energetic
- inspiring, innovative and imaginative
- consistent and predictable
- inclusive and collaborative
- flexible and adaptable, and
- reflective.

These attributes are recognised by followers as contributing to the development of open communication, productive relationships, enablement and empowerment.

Effective leaders are courageous in their beliefs, conviction, conduct and action. Semann and Waniganayake (2010) argue that many of the difficult challenges faced by early childhood leaders can only be achieved through courage—where they dare to be different, where difficult situations are faced up to, where they take a stand over and fight for what they believe. Courage is associated with risk-taking, goal-attainment and advocacy.

Commitment to lifelong learning is another personal quality associated with effective leadership in early childhood.

*Leaders show a passion for learning, inspiration for those around them and the ability to be humble, caring and build the self-esteem of the community.*
EARLY CHILDHOOD ADVISER

*Leaders have a desire to know more . . . and pass their knowledge widely to others in the early childhood field and/or the public arena.*
ASSOCIATE PROFESSOR, EARLY CHILDHOOD

The characteristics that define lifelong learning and the notion of a learning person include:

- curiosity (interest in learning)
- honesty (speaking the truth, principles and actions open to public scrutiny)
- courtesy (treating others with respect and dignity)
- courage (the willingness to risk and dare, to make mistakes and learn from them)
- compassion (creating trust, empathy, high expectations, hope and inspiration), and
- empowerment (offering opportunities for personal and professional development).

Claxton (2002) regards the development of dispositions for lifelong learning as fundamental to leaders who are responsible for enabling, encouraging and evaluating other people. Because effective leaders need to be better learners so that they can help others to learn more effectively, they must strengthen their own learning power by developing what Claxton (2002: 17) refers to as the 'four Rs of learning power':

- *resilience*—being ready, willing and able to lock on to learning
- *resourcefulness*—being ready, willing and able to learn in different ways
- *reflectivity*—being ready, willing and able to become strategic about learning, and
- *reciprocity*—being ready, willing and able to learn alone and with others.

*Leaders have passion, enthusiasm, compassion … they are flexible in that they are prepared to work across roles—everything from pulling up their sleeves at working bees, scrubbing the floor if necessary, contributing to classroom teaching, counselling parents and staff, advising on policy, etc., all with a sense of humour.*
DIRECTOR, EARLY LEARNING CENTRE

*Leaders are hard workers, dedicated and enthusiastic … they have ideas and opinions, they believe that sharing these helps.*
TEACHING ASSISTANT

Early childhood leaders today operate in challenging socio-political contexts that demand inquiry-based, flexible strategies in collaborative cultures of lifelong learning. Where leadership is associated with lifelong learning, early childhood educators learn from one another when leaders reinforce collaborative learning with and from peers by acting as models, learners, facilitators and mentors.

Part of being a leader in a workplace culture of lifelong learning is accepting that everybody makes mistakes—leaders, educators, families and children. Errors and mistakes can be important signposts to learning and progress. In a learning culture, curiosity, exploration and discovery (which sometimes can lead to errors and mistakes) are more important than always being right and correct (Schulz, 2010). When working with children and families, day-to-day activity and circumstances rarely are predictable and pre-determined, and not everything runs smoothly or according to plan. While learning by adults and children does involve making mistakes, in this context it is essential, where possible, to avoid making mistakes that have harmful consequences.

Followers have identified a range of attributes that they recognise in genuine leaders. These attributes are more important for effective leadership than being popular with and liked by followers. Unfortunately, many people inexperienced in leadership often assume that it is important for them to be liked, to be popular, to know, to be rational, to be right, to be in control and to be invulnerable. However, these assumptions are inaccurate and counter-productive, put leaders under enormous pressure and produce leaders who often feel daunted by and inadequate to the task. The attributes associated with lifelong learning are more likely to produce confident, trustworthy and courageous leaders who are admired, respected and consequently supported by their followers.

Although some personal qualities are enduring and more difficult to change, others are relatively easy to learn and incorporate into a personal repertoire. The majority of attributes and characteristics *can* be learned and developed. It is possible for people to act flexibly and adapt their personality tendencies. In many instances, acting as if you already possess a certain quality helps assimilate it into your personal style. Therefore, it is essential for early childhood educators to reflect upon and aim to develop qualities associated with authentic, credible leadership.

## The influence of personal qualities on followers

The way followers experience a leader's personality—that is, their personal qualities, attributes and characteristics—has a big influence on whether they are motivated, engaged and committed to a leader's vision and goals. In broad terms, leadership determines two critical outcomes: task performance and work relationships. The way these function together governs both goal achievement and workplace morale.

It is the leader's responsibility to ensure that followers are inspired, motivated, engaged and committed to a shared vision and goals, which in early childhood means the provision of quality services. This includes any aspect of productivity, getting the job done and anything related to quality of work or performance. At the same time, the leader needs to ensure that the pursuit of task performance is not at the expense of work relationships—in other words, the perceived and experienced quality of life at work. The leader is responsible for the welfare of others in the workplace and for ensuring that motivation is kept high through building and maintaining constructive interpersonal relationships—that is, morale.

The leader's personal qualities have a significant impact on followers because they affect a leader's general approach to people and goals. Leadership can be understood in terms of the focus leaders put upon achieving the task or results and promoting relationships or morale—for example, the following types:

- *task master*—focused on task/result, not on relationships/morale
- *friend*—focused on relationships/morale, not on task/results
- *motivator*—focused on both task and relationships, and
- *casual, easy-going, 'laid-back'*—focused on neither results nor relationships.

Given that early childhood leaders are responsible for motivating their followers to engage with and commit to a shared vision and goals, they need to develop and display more qualities that are associated with the motivator approach, which means being perceived as:

- warm, flexible and adaptable
- sensitive, creative and encouraging
- supportive and non-judgemental
- communicative and constructive

- engaging, involving and inclusive
- encouraging of learning, self-awareness and self-evaluation
- confident in the abilities and commitment of followers, and
- confident in risk-taking, decision-making and problem-solving.

Leaders who communicate concern for the personal and professional needs of followers as well as confidence in their ability and responsibility are more likely to accomplish the task (quality service) and support cooperative and satisfying relationships (harmonious workplace and high morale).

When leaders focus too heavily on tasks, followers can perceive and experience them as rather cold, distant and process-oriented. When leaders focus inappropriately on relationship, followers may prioritise activities that stoke 'warm fuzzies' and 'feeling good', and neglect to focus on the tasks. Where leaders pay attention to neither task nor relationship, followers may perceive them as uninterested, detached, uncommitted and unengaged, and be influenced to act similarly.

Leaders engage followers' trust and support by personifying and modelling qualities and attributes associated with credible and motivational leadership. Nevertheless, it also is important to 'be yourself', to maximise strengths and minimise weaknesses, not to copy others or change essential aspects of what it means to be genuinely you. Followers quickly discover when leaders deceive them by attempting to be someone they are not, rarely trusting those who they think are putting up a facade or acting (Poole, 2011).

## The role of gender stereotypes

Gender is a factor that, in the past, was thought to affect leadership capacity and behaviour. Goffee and Jones (2011) argue that women are prone to being stereotyped according to differences that tend to be negative rather than positive. Stereotypes about leadership still pose barriers to women aspiring to and taking up leadership roles and responsibilities. These long-standing gender stereotypes have impacted upon women's self-perceptions regarding leadership, and have acted as barriers to women's aspiration and access to positions of leadership.

The representation of women in leadership positions, and the interplay between gender stereotypes and leadership, continue to be of some interest to researchers and the media. In early childhood, which is staffed overwhelmingly by women (typically around 97 per cent), who generally assume the available leadership positions, little research has been undertaken. However, research findings in general no longer support the notion of different leadership styles between men and women (Dunlop, 2008). Interpersonal and communication abilities, rather than gender, underpin effective leadership in early childhood.

Despite such research findings, leadership continues to be viewed predominantly as culturally masculine—that is, assertive and competitive. The traditional masculine models of leadership are characterised by attributes such as control, power, domination and competition. Women prefer more communal qualities, with feminine models of leadership focusing more on relationships, compassion, consensus, collaboration and flexibility.

However, masculine stereotypes of leadership are being weakened with a shift towards more androgynous beliefs, especially in educational institutions (Koenig et al., 2011). Currently, it generally is accepted that both women and men can embody and choose to enact leadership in a facilitating or an authoritarian style. Contemporary theories of leadership focus more on blending both traditionally feminine attributes, such as trust, honesty, communication, diplomacy, insight, cooperation and collaboration, with traditionally male attributes, such as risk-taking, assertion, delegating and making difficult decisions.

More women are expressing interest and are successful in taking up leadership roles, especially in education where a more collaborative, non-hierarchical style is accepted as appropriate and effective. Nevertheless, women are still underrepresented compared with men, with the 'glass ceiling' still a very real barrier to women aspiring to and taking up leadership positions in some businesses and professions.

Debate continues about whether leadership is typically a male preserve, with women displaying little inclination towards, interest in and/or aptitude for it, or whether the reason women have not taken up their rightful role in leadership is due to inappropriate gender stereotypes and fundamental, ongoing sex discrimination in hierarchical organisational structures. Gender stereotypes misrepresent the true capabilities of women as leaders, and work to undermine women's contributions to as well as their advancement in leadership.

Currently, early childhood is in the process of developing its own perspectives, models and language of leadership based on principles of connection, dialogue and community, and enacted through collaborative, consensual, people-oriented and non-hierarchical leadership. Early childhood services are regarded as inclusive learning communities rather than hierarchical organisations. Transformational leadership—the current standard of good leadership embraced by many early childhood educators—is androgynous, thereby liberating both men and women from inappropriate and outdated gender stereotypes.

Leadership in early childhood is exercised in a climate of reciprocal relationships where the leader seeks to act *with* others rather than assert power *over* others. Communication and interpersonal skills are used effectively in interaction with others. The approach is cooperative and affiliative rather than controlling and dividing. Acceptance as a leader is derived from being flexible and adaptable, not based on gender.

Nevertheless, often because of the poor public perception of women in leadership positions and other barriers, many early childhood educators still are reluctant to assume leadership roles. Limited training and access to role models and mentors act as considerable obstacles for those interested in becoming a leader (Thornton et al., 2009). Those who aspire to be, and who already are, leaders have to work harder to prove—both to themselves and to the wider community—that they can undertake leadership roles and positions successfully.

Early childhood educators who are women and who aspire to leadership need to protect themselves from their own unreasonable insecurity and demands for perfectionism. Positive self-esteem is very important for assuming and enacting leadership. Most existing leaders readily admit that they learned to be a leader, and continue to learn, while in the job. Early childhood services need to ensure that mentoring and coaching opportunities are available to assist those with leadership aspirations and those already holding leadership responsibilities.

In conclusion, in a profession dominated by women, it is not helpful to analyse leadership potential, enactment and performance through gender stereotypes. It is important to be aware of gender stereotypes and possible gender-related styles; however, these should be appreciated as valid and valuable differences. Both men and women adopt leadership approaches that are relevant for the nature of team members, goals and context. The effective leader is one who chooses the right approach at the right time for the people, task and context involved.

Aspiring leaders and those who default or are thrust into positions of leadership need to examine the qualities, attributes and behaviours that are associated with effective leadership and to the development of learning communities. Effective leaders create a culture where the values and qualities that underpin leadership are endorsed, be they stereotypically masculine or feminine. Only then will it be possible to develop preparation and training options that optimise understanding of, engagement in and enactment of gender-neutral leadership. What is important in early childhood is the enactment of leading practice, not gender stereotypes.

## Who follows the leader?

Leadership is about motivating others to followship—that is, effective leaders motivate, inspire and persuade others to realise shared goals. Leaders need followers. Inspiring followship in others is based upon an understanding of who the followers are, what their needs might be and what resources they can offer.

The nature of followers for early childhood leaders is complex. Apart from the children and families, early childhood services are made up of heterogeneous groups of adults who range in age, experience, qualifications, who come from diverse social, cultural and religious backgrounds, and who have different agendas and goals. Some are young and inexperienced and may be completing part-time training courses; some are older and possibly more experienced who are able to draw on their own life perspectives but who can be unaware or unaccepting of the value of the professional perspective; some are qualified, both young and mature, with different types and levels of qualifications, expertise and experience; some may be professionals from different disciplines; and some may be family members who may have different assumptions, expectations and goals from those of qualified early childhood educators. In addition, students who are undertaking supervised practical experience and volunteers regularly work alongside team members.

Early childhood educators need to reflect about how to enact effective leadership for such a complex group; the personal and professional attributes required for effective leadership of a diverse group; and the strategies that are appropriate for managing the range of situations that arise from the dynamics of such a group. The development of such expertise requires specialist preparation and training that includes consideration of the nature of the group to be led as well as other features of the early childhood context. In addition, other features of the group point to the need for the development of leadership capacity in every early childhood educator.

Because early childhood educators work with the youngest and most vulnerable of children, they carry enormous responsibility for the quality of the children's daily lives. At the same time, they exercise considerable autonomy over how they fulfil their responsibilities. Given that leadership underpins the quality of practice as well as children's experience, early childhood educators must develop high levels of technical expertise in addition to understanding how to meet leadership challenges and opportunities.

For many, the work context is characterised by physical isolation from peers and colleagues—for example, there may be only two adults working with a group of fifteen children. This means that professional judgement about children, families and pedagogy often must be exercised quickly, confidently and independently. Decision-making and problem-solving skills are essential. In addition, many of the problems encountered in daily practice present ethical or moral dilemmas for educators. Familiarity with standards of practice, such as a code of ethics developed by national early childhood professional bodies, can provide guidelines and direction for many of the difficult decisions that early childhood educators face in their daily work.

Early childhood educators generally have contact with a wide range of children and families. The diversity of the client group means that all educators, including but not only formal leaders, must be motivated to be well informed about current research in child development, pedagogy and government initiatives, and continually upgrade their knowledge and skills in order to make sound professional judgements that will improve service provision. Understanding the role of research is essential for innovative decision-making by everyone, not only formal leaders. Possessing appropriate knowledge and skills enhances the ability to effect change, and allows educators to make services responsive to current family and community needs.

It is possible—even common—for early childhood educators to default or be thrust into positions of leadership early in their career, at a young age, with little experience and while they themselves are still novices (Thornton et al., 2009) and have yet to benefit from learning as followers. Wooden and Jamison (2009) propose that before anyone can be a good leader, they must learn to be a good follower. The stage of personal and professional development at which individuals may choose, default or be given the opportunity to become a leader can vary. Most early childhood educators would benefit from better pre-service preparation, sharing and/or undertaking some distributed leadership responsibility as part of followship and teamwork, thereby preparing them to identity with and incorporate leadership as part of their professional identity before they assume formal leadership responsibility.

## Who is a leader in early childhood services?

Early childhood is perhaps unique in terms of the opportunities it presents for anyone and everyone to access positions of formal leadership, regardless of personal qualities, aptitude or experience, and from the earliest stage of employment in the sector.

*Anyone can become a leader if they possess an interest in the area.*
NURSERY OFFICER

*Who becomes a leader varies hugely ... leaders can be room supervisors or policy-makers but whoever they are they usually are committed to moving practice on.*
DEPUTY SUPERVISOR

*The routes into leadership are not planned.*
EARLY CHILDHOOD ADVISER

*Leadership is not only present in positions of seniority.*
NURSERY OFFICER

Until recently, the formal leaders of a range of early childhood services tended to be qualified early childhood teachers—often called directors, managers or coordinators—despite teacher training offering little information about and skills for working with adults. Teaching qualifications and experience, while valuable, do not offer adequate preparation for the formal, complex leadership and administrative roles and responsibilities required for leading contemporary inclusive, integrated, multi-disciplinary, multi-agency early childhood services. In some countries, owners and licensees of private provision are the formal leaders but may hold no or only basic early childhood or relevant qualifications.

*Leadership in early childhood is generally weak ... leaders are often*
*young, bound by a fairly traditional vision ... we need more leaders in*
*their enchanted years.*
EARLY YEARS ADVISER

As the diversity of services for young children and families expands, and as more multi-disciplinary, multi-agency services are established, formal leadership is being undertaken by individuals from increasingly diverse and non-traditional backgrounds. Such leaders are largely autonomous, but usually are accountable for the quality of policy and practice to bodies, such as management committees, governing bodies, trusts, partnerships auspiced by local authorities, and ultimately to government departments that fund early childhood services.

Because each early childhood service is unique, who becomes a leader will depend on the type of structures that are in place (Ebbeck and Waniganayake, 2003). However, it is evident that in services where there are clearly defined purposes, procedures, roles and responsibilities, and clearly delineated lines of communication and decision-making, leadership can be shared and distributed among educators. In fact, formal leaders can be endorsed as credible and legitimate when they are perceived as delegating and distributing leadership responsibilities appropriately.

Collaborative leadership appears to satisfy the need for a different type of leader in early childhood—one who is guided more by moral, rational and socio-emotional concerns than structures and systems. Opportunities for early childhood educators to become leaders are restricted where formal leaders retain decision-making power. To help more educators to aspire to leadership, formal leaders need to share tasks and distribute more opportunities to lead, thereby smoothing the transition along the continuum from a capable and experienced educator to appointment as a formal and advanced leader.

Appointment or promotion to leadership in early childhood continues to be influenced by three factors: the personal qualities that an individual brings to a position; exemplary practice with children and families; and longevity at a service. While such appointment practices may have been workable in services where there were only a small number of adults working together, the leadership demands of contemporary integrated, multi-disciplinary, multi-agency services now call for more sophisticated knowledge, skills and experience. Quite apart from the demands of providing leadership for diverse families, such large and heterogeneous groups of staff require more informed and skilled approaches to service management. In such circumstances, it is essential that early childhood services avoid the chaos and disruption to communication, decision-making and stability that can result from the appointment or promotion of an inappropriate leader.

There are few professions today that have not recognised the advantages in productivity and relationships from leadership training for suitable personnel. For early childhood, leadership training is associated with improved outcomes for children and families, as well as increased status and credibility in the community (Dunlop, 2008). However, many formal leaders continue to be appointed on the basis of their personal qualities, how well they work with children and families, or how long they have worked in early childhood, rather than on the basis of formal training in or specialised expertise in leadership. Twenty-first century leaders in early childhood need twenty-first century preparation and training to fulfil the role successfully.

Leadership is always transient (Marrin, 2011) because goals are achieved, people and circumstances change and time moves on. Therefore, systematic and comprehensive policies and plans for building leadership capacity and planning for succession should be developed for all services. The consistent provision of quality services through expert leadership will lay the foundation for early childhood educators being acknowledged by the community as having the ability to make executive leadership contributions to the wider society.

## Who becomes a leader in early childhood?

One of the challenges faced by early childhood is identifying those individuals who, given opportunities for personal and professional career development, might emerge as future leaders. Because early childhood education is dominated by women who (compared with men) place different emphases on family and career at different stages in their lives, it is not easy to assess who will exhibit leadership potential and the extent to which this potential can be developed as part of long-term career aspirations.

*Early childhood educators who become leaders are those who find meaning and significance in even the minutiae of their day-to-day work.*
EARLY CHILDHOOD EDUCATOR

*Most staff in early childhood are women. For various reasons historically they have not been good at projecting themselves and taking leadership roles outside their services.*
EARLY YEARS TEAM LEADER

The fact that women who enter the profession are likely to experience training and career interruptions due to time taken to establish and nurture a family means that there are structural obstacles to developing and retaining a professional workforce in early childhood. Many women will require access to flexible preparation and training opportunities, and career structures that can cope with them moving in and out according to personal—including family—commitments.

It is obvious that, for a large proportion of personnel in this sector, a considerable number of years of full- and part-time work is required to accumulate the knowledge, skills and experience that underpin leadership capability.

*To become a leader you need expertise—for example, qualifications, skills and experience plus ideas and forward thinking.*
NURSERY OFFICER

*To become a leader you must have experience, not necessarily as a teacher, qualifications, a personality that gains respect and a proven track record.*
MANAGER, CHILDCARE CENTRE

*Experience counts a lot in terms of who becomes a leader ... there is an expectation that you need to pay your dues in order to maintain your credibility.*
EARLY CHILDHOOD LECTURER

All of those who enter early childhood need to be imbued with the belief that personal potential and aspiration for professional growth and leadership can be nurtured throughout their career, even if it is disrupted.

*It also comes from the individual themself. You may be initially reluctant to take on a position of leadership but you get drawn into the role and it becomes part of how you see yourself.*
EARLY CHILDHOOD LECTURER

Ordinary life experience as an adult, coupled with self-awareness and willingness to learn, bring opportunities to develop and improve the personal qualities and skills that are prerequisites for leadership, and to broaden one's understanding and perspective on life. This can help build a basis from which specific preparation and training in leadership can be undertaken and be of benefit.

*Individuals in more senior positions have a 'feel' for who will make a good leader and foster their leadership development by giving them more responsibility.*
Early childhood lecturer

Leadership preparation and training, while limited in availability and accessibility, can be powerful for improving role perceptions and job performance, increased feelings of self-efficacy and enhanced ability to effect change.

Debate continues about the origins of leadership—that is, can people learn and be trained to be successful leaders, or is leadership dependent upon characteristics that largely are inherited? It is generally accepted that, although certain personal qualities may be associated with leadership, many of these and certain skills can be learned. In addition, it seems that leadership potential can emerge at any time during one's life.

Therefore, all people are considered to be capable of leading at different times and in different situations. A person can be a leader in relation to a specific group or a specific task. The qualities and skills enacted by a leader also are influenced by the demands of the situation—including the task, the people and their relationships. Consequently, there is no exclusive list of personal qualities associated with effective leadership. However, a thorough understanding of the needs of the situation—which includes the task and the people—will enable effective leaders in early childhood to develop a repertoire of qualities and skills that is essential for meeting their service's goals. Awareness of the needs, capabilities and interests of the followers will help the leader to act in ways to which they will be receptive.

Distributive leadership, which focuses on growing knowledge and expertise through openly or subtly dispersed responsibility, offers certain advantages. Knowledge provides the foundation for early childhood educators' capacity for leadership. Knowledge refers to both pedagogical and practical understanding, which can be dispersed within early childhood services and can fit with other specialisations, such as visionary, advocacy, community, cultural, conceptual and career development leadership.

Such perspectives support the notion that leadership is a complex, multifaceted, collaborative endeavour undertaken by effective teams of leaders and followers that operate in an inclusive culture of learning and shared knowledge.

Many of the personal qualities and skills that early childhood educators bring to leadership are indeed strengths to be valued and pursued. While such qualities may be difficult to observe, assess and evaluate, early childhood educators may wish to reflect about and assess the extent to which they possess, need to develop and/or improve the following qualities and skills that are associated with effective leadership.

On a scale of 10 (Very much like me) to 0 (Not at all like me), to what extent are you:

- friendly, confident, amenable, open and accepting
- positive and realistic with high expectations
- caring, nurturing, calm, sensitive and tolerant
- energetic, enthusiastic, with a sense of humour
- perceptive, empathetic, intuitive and responsive
- articulate with good communication skills
- open-minded, adaptable and flexible
- self-motivated and able to motivate others
- imaginative, creative, visionary and innovative
- organised, using common sense and initiative
- fair, consistent and able to set clear boundaries
- reliable and emotionally intelligent
- independent and collaborative
- reflective, questioning and analytical, and
- committed to learning and professional development?

The above list is daunting, and if it were included in a job specification few would apply! However, the list offers guidance about the types of qualities that aspiring leaders could pursue as goals for professional development.

## Bringing it together

Effective leaders in early childhood embody and enact a range of personal qualities that are recognised as strengths in their work, including honesty, enthusiasm, vision, inspiration, trust, respect, collaboration, inclusion and lifelong learning. The increasing complexity of early childhood services has broadened leadership roles and responsibilities for early childhood educators, many of whom may have had limited experience, formal education and training. The expanded roles and responsibilities, together with the opportunity to aspire to, default or be thrust into leadership positions from the earliest stage of one's career in early childhood, means that everyone—both educators and students—should be encouraged to acquire an early and thorough understanding of the essentials of leadership. The factors outlined above point to the need for leadership skills, including the personal qualities of leaders, to be considered just as essential to the early childhood educator as the fundamental skills of child observation, pedagogy and administration.

# CHAPTER 3

# THEORIES, MODELS AND STYLES OF LEADERSHIP

*A leader is a caring and respecting human being who is emotionally intelligent.*

EARLY YEARS ADVISER

## THIS CHAPTER EXPLORES

- selected theories of leadership
- selected models and styles of leadership

As interest in leadership has grown, numerous theories and models have been devised and put forward to explain and predict the 'hows and whys' of successful leadership. The purpose of a theory is to provide a framework for understanding human behaviour, thought and development. A broad understanding about the nature of human behaviour, in this case, leadership, helps us to understand ourselves and others better, and use that understanding to develop attributes and skills associated with effective enactment.

A theory is a cognitive model of perceived reality. It is a set of coherent statements, propositions or principles created from observation, experimentation and reasoning to explain a group of facts or phenomena, especially one that has been tested or is widely accepted and is used to explain or predict phenomena in the natural world.

Some early childhood researchers have adopted a post-structuralist perspective for understanding leadership, remaining sceptical about the idea that theory and research can arrive at any 'truths' with certainty (Mukherji and Albon, 2010). Post-structuralists argue that there are no 'truths', only multiple ways of viewing reality, because people's positions in and perceptions of the world are constantly changing. In addition, some early childhood researchers employ interpretivist sociological theory to analyse leadership. Here, the world (and leadership) is understood or 'interpreted' by different people in different situations in different ways. They argue that culture impacts on the way we see the world, and within this cultural framework we develop an understanding of the world *with* other people. Reality (in this case, leadership) is perceived and experienced subjectively. It is context-bound and focuses on the meanings that people attribute to it. Everything is relative to everything else, and the best researchers can do is describe reality from the perspective of those who define it—the people involved.

Theories may be good, bad or indifferent. They may be well established by factual evidence or they may lack credibility. Usually, no single theory is able to explain all aspects of any phenomenon. Theories are always changing and evolving because, as new information becomes available, they are modified and adapted to take new information and thinking into account.

It is beyond the scope of this book to describe and evaluate all of the available theories, models and styles of leadership. Suffice to say that they are based on different philosophies, values and understandings about the world. Theories, models and styles do not teach how to lead, but attempt to explain some of the concerns and dynamics that leaders typically encounter and how they respond to them (Yaverbaum and Sherman, 2008). Aspiring leaders should become familiar with the range of theories, models and styles—especially those currently in vogue—and, on the basis of their own values, personality, strengths and context, adopt and adapt those that suit and work best for their circumstances.

The next section briefly summarises some of the theories that have contributed to contemporary understanding of leadership in early childhood.

## Theories of leadership

Theories are useful tools for building an understanding of leadership appropriate for early childhood contexts. Both psychological (focusing on the individual) and sociological (focusing on the influence context) theories have developed their own analytical frameworks to explain leadership.

Many different leadership theories have been proposed, including the traditional, trait, behavioural and contingency perspectives, the more recent transactional and transformational perspectives and—although less familiar in the context of leadership—the socio-cultural perspective. Many different terms are currently applied to leadership—for example, heroic, charismatic, open, authentic, strategic, ethical, learning-centred, constructivist, emotionally intelligent, distributed and sustainable. It is important to understand the theoretical basis of these terms in order to assess their relevance to early childhood as explained below:

- *Trait* theory explores what type of person make as a good leader and focuses on the personal traits, characteristics, attributes and qualities associated with effective leadership. Its major limitation is that it cannot explain people who possess these qualities but are not leaders.
- *Behavioural* theory explores what a good leader does, and focuses on how leaders behave and act. Three general approaches to leadership are based

on behaviour: autocratic (task-oriented), democratic (people-oriented) and laissez-faire (an easy-going, 'do your own thing' orientation). An advantage of this theory is that it proposes that people can learn the skills to become leaders but, at the same time, it does not explain people who display the skills and are not leaders.

- *Contingency* theory explores how the situation influences leadership and suggests that leadership is contingent upon, depends on and is related to the nature of and interplay between the followers, task, situation and context. Each situation is regarded, and consequently treated, as unique. Different leadership styles are appropriate for different situations. It is a skilled leader who recognises, matches and enacts the most appropriate style of leadership for the circumstances. A major limitation of this theory is that it does not provide for any generalisation or transfer of leadership style and skill to similar situations: what works in one situation may not work in a similar one. It also fails to explain why some leadership styles are more effective in some situations than in others. Nor does it offer any guidelines when a mismatch occurs between leader and workplace situations. Because no single approach to leadership is best in any specific situation, and because success depends on a range of contextual factors, it is difficult to for leaders to match and apply what they previously have learned about effective leadership to comparable conditions or circumstances.

- *Transactional* theory explores the use of power, influence and transactions to motivate people and achieve goals. Power may be positional (legitimate, reward and coercive) or personal (expert and referent). Goals are achieved mainly through reward, so leaders focus on manipulating task and reward structures to motivate people. Managers often adopt the transactional approach to ensure that routine work is done reliably. Research indicates that vision and intrinsic motivation are more powerful influences on how people behave than extrinsic rewards.

- *Transformational* theory focuses on how leaders inspire people with shared values and vision to want to make the world a better place for all. There is a strong moral element to this theory of leadership. Leaders use their personal enthusiasm, energy, drive, ethics and commitment to generate trust and willingness to follow. They employ a flexible range of thinking strategies to look for new ideas, innovations and initiatives that add value. This approach is considered to be the most effective for contemporary organisations.

While theoretical perspectives offer insight into aspects of contemporary leadership, there is no right way. None of the leadership theories fits all people, situations or structures. The early childhood sector is becoming increasingly complex. Therefore, effective leadership requires capacity for flexibility, agility and diverse types of expertise. The leader's ability to adapt their approach to the skill level and experience of the team, the nature of the work and the work environment, demands for change and new challenges is critical.

- *Distributed leadership* theory falls broadly under the category of transformational leadership and currently is popular for explaining leadership in early childhood. It focuses on leadership as practice (Harris and Spillane, 2008) and proposes that, because many people hold knowledge and expertise, it is sensible to purposively disperse or distribute leadership responsibilities. A collective identity, which grows out of common and shared values, vision and goals, motivates commitment, cooperation and collective responsibility in teams. Leadership is a product of interaction between multiple leaders who contribute by specialising in what they do best. Distributed leadership permits, encourages and acknowledges contribution from those in both formal and informal roles.

  Although distributed leadership is an attractive concept and strategy to many early childhood educators, how it is implemented in a service is problematic. Distributed leadership is not the same as shared leadership. Its distribution, diffusion and dispersal are not 'managed' by a leader who 'decides' to share leadership: that is delegation. Distributed leadership evolves out of a culture of collective responsibility, where individuals spontaneously and voluntarily choose to act when they perceive something that needs to be done—that is, they understand and act to meet the needs of the situation or context. Leadership becomes distributed only when leaders create spaces for others to rise to its challenges and when it is infused through, subtly pervades and permeates every aspect of workplace culture.

- *Socio-cultural* theory—originally a framework for understanding young children's cognitive processes and learning—can be useful for analysing leadership. This theory conceptualises leadership as a process of social construction through which certain understandings evolve and are validated. The role of language and interaction is emphasised in the development of potential (Vygotsky, 1978). Leadership is viewed as a higher order function that develops out of social interaction—particularly cognitive and communicative experience—and is a process of social influence through which values, attitudes, ideas and behaviours are constructed and produced, coordinated and changed in both the leaders and others.

Leadership is constituted, defined and constructed in an interactive web of followers, culture, language, tools and symbol, and context. How leaders frame situations and challenges (through their individual cognitive and communicative styles), and how they scaffold leadership activity in others (the processes employed), are very important. Kouzes and Posner (2007) argue that leadership is a conversation, a dialogue and a relationship with followers. A leader's words, actions, decisions, interactions and styles are thought to affect the beliefs, values, feelings and behaviour of the people they work with and are seen as critical in determining how others respond in a team.

This theoretical perspective has much to offer those interested in understanding and developing leadership in early childhood because of the key roles played by communication and interpersonal skills. The ways in which early childhood leaders communicate and interact with followers, inspiring, encouraging, imparting information, reporting, explaining, questioning, scaffolding and advocating, affects followers' awareness, insight, comprehension, mastery and commitment to their work.

*I do create opportunities for us to talk about our values, vision, mission and ideology in meetings but I wouldn't use those words because they would frighten some of the team and they wouldn't participate. I introduce the discussion using language that they are more receptive to, that they relate to so everyone can be involved.*
EARLY CHILDHOOD COORDINATOR

Where early childhood leaders are able to make issues and challenges explicit and transparent for followers, it is more likely that followers will be stimulated to employ higher order thinking skills to grasp the essence and complexity of what the leader hopes to achieve and commit support and energy to the endeavour.

This theoretical approach also informs distributed leadership because it points to the importance of distributed cognitive activity (Hartley, 2009). Distributed cognitive activity provides a considerable advantage for multi-professional and multi-agency teams where previously discrete roles and structures overlap and merge by allowing people to contribute through their specialised thinking strategies. Socio-cultural understanding of leadership is relevant for early childhood because it defines leadership as a process and pathway that involves complex webs of relationships, interaction and influence for and by all concerned.

Research into leadership has been criticised as being too focused on exploring what leaders do, the attributes they possess and the styles they enact rather than what is actually involved in leadership practice. The leadership theories that focus on the trait, behavioural and situational aspects are examples of such approaches. However, while useful in deconstructing some key components, they do not offer insight into the intricacies of leadership, which is complex, subtle, multi-faceted and grounded in relationships and social interaction.

Early childhood educators prefer distributed and collaborative rather than single and lone leadership styles to conduct their day-to-day activities. They acknowledge the multi-faceted nature of leadership by identifying the need to explore the relationship and interaction between the various leadership styles. Socio-cultural theory conceptualises leadership not only as a trait or behaviour that resides in the leader or as contingent upon situations but as an event, process or relationship between leader and followers. Leadership therefore may reside in a leader or in an action or idea, but it is the social exchanges, conversations and contributions that focus, reframe or restructure the thinking about the situation and the way others respond to it.

Theories offer different perspectives on leadership, and should be explored as a means for improving understanding about and practice in leadership. Theoretical approaches that are relevant for early childhood view leadership as a process, grounded in the ability to interact with others in ways that:

- offer inspirational and credible values and vision
- encourage open communication
- develop a collaborative team culture
- set realistic and achievable goals and objectives
- monitor and celebrate achievements, and
- foster the development of individuals.

Such theories do not constrain leadership to positional status but open leadership opportunities to those who recognise the need for, and choose to take up, purposeful activities aimed at improving quality and moving early childhood forward.

## Models of leadership

Leadership is essentially a synergistic and holistic concept in which the whole is more than the sum of its parts. Given that leadership is a complex construct and sometimes difficult to identify in early childhood, a review of some models of leadership may help early childhood educators appreciate some of the factors that underpin effective leadership.

A model is a means of, or framework for, classifying selected factors or features. It can be used as a summary or protocol for understanding the structure of a phenomenon. While it can be argued that a model over-simplifies what may be a very complex concept, models can be helpful for understanding essential components, especially where it is believed that certain features may be acquired through training.

All aspiring leaders—like early childhood educators—proceed along a continuum of development of professional knowledge, skill and understanding from novice and beginner to capable and confident, and some advance through to specialist, expert and executive. A range of inventories, profiles or models offers frameworks to analyse and describe the progress of leadership development. They focus on different conceptions of leadership, although few have attempted to relate such profiles to specific context—an important factor in effective leadership, especially in early childhood.

One advantage of looking at models of leadership is that aspiring and formal leaders are alerted to significant features of effective leadership, thus avoiding a trial-and-error approach to preparing for and learning how to be an effective leader. Given that many early childhood educators comment on the limited availability and accessibility of specific preparation and training before taking up leadership responsibilities or while in the position, models may be effective in helping to pinpoint important features and for developing an understanding of what constitutes leadership in early childhood, as well as for enhancing self-perception as a leader.

Leadership is considered by some to be related to a particular stage of career development—that is, people with more experience are more likely to have acquired the expertise required to undertake leadership roles and responsibilities. While this may be true in many professions, early childhood is different in that educators may choose to take up, default or be thrust into, or enact informal yet legitimate leadership. However, it is useful to understand that, for most educators, being acknowledged as a credible and legitimate leader is a pathway by which people move from being capable individuals to being senior executives.

Collins (2001) proposes a model that describes different levels of leadership, with 'level 5 leadership', the pinnacle of the hierarchy, being what most leaders aim to achieve. Because most early childhood educators enter the field as novices, the stages are summarised below from basic to advanced levels:

- *Level 1: Capable individual.* At this beginning level, the individual is more an apprentice and makes standard or superior contributions to day-to-day work with children and families. Here, early childhood educators possess basic and useful knowledge and skills. Early childhood leaders need to ensure that all educators are offered opportunities to develop the self-awareness, qualities and skills needed to be effective in their work.
- *Level 2: Contributing team member.* Capable individuals become contributing team members when they have acquired skills and understanding that

enable them to help the team to work together. Early childhood educators may have developed some specialised skills or interests that they are able to contribute, and they understand that greater satisfaction and better results are achieved through collaboration with others and teamwork. Early childhood leaders can build educators' confidence and skills by purposively delegating, sharing and subtly distributing responsibility.

• *Level 3: Competent manager.* At this level, an educator is usually a senior professional with expanded knowledge and skill base. Early childhood educators who are competent managers often assume greater responsibility for organising others in the team, and for achieving specific goals and targets. The focus tends to be on the present and smooth running of the service. At this stage, some will show the potential to develop into credible leaders, and this potential needs to be nurtured and mentored by current leaders to support the transition to the next stage.

• *Level 4: Effective leader.* Those who are recognised as credible and legitimate leaders in early childhood have moved into this stage. Here, the focus is on the future—the early childhood leader possesses the ability and skills to galvanise individual and integrated services, and multi-disciplinary and multi-agency teams, to meet high-level expectations and performance standards, and realise shared vision.

• *Level 5: Executive leader.* To advance to and be acknowledged as an executive leader, an early childhood leader needs to possess all of the qualities and skills required for the other levels but also demonstrate advanced insight, expertise and power that can shape the future direction of early childhood. Executive leaders in early childhood exemplify sound character; they are not arrogant or self-promoting but genuinely respectful and unassuming. At this level, early childhood leaders request help when needed, take responsibility for their own and the teams' actions and mistakes but attribute success to collaborative teamwork. Executive leaders in early childhood are passionate, find meaning in even the most mundane and routine aspects of their work and inspire others to a shared vision.

Not everyone progresses through the stages in the same order or at the same time. Moving to a higher stage requires passion, energy and determined effort to acquire the skills essential to achieve level 5 leadership.

In early childhood, the majority of educators enter services as capable individuals and over time, with increasing insight and experience, most become contributing team members. Some aspire to become competent managers of services. These individuals may or may not undertake professional development activities to help acquire the higher order skills necessary to be effective at this level. Those who are truly competent managers will recognise the need for further training and skills development.

The majority of early childhood educators can be observed in levels 1 to 3. Far fewer educators aspire and choose to become effective leaders, and it is rare to find educators who see themselves in, and possess the required qualities and skills for, advanced and executive leadership. The challenge for those who are level 4 and 5 leaders is to help more early childhood educators to make the transition to higher levels by stimulating closer identification with the need for and benefits of leadership and through meaningful supervision, mentoring and other professional development and learning experiences.

Maxwell (2011a) suggests that aspiring leaders sometimes do not know where or how to start to develop as leaders. His model outlines five levels of leadership, each of which has different follower motivations and implications for those who aspire to credible, legitimate leadership. While Maxwell's model has some similarities to Collins' model, it is not a career-stage hierarchy. It places positional leadership as the basic level of leadership, whereas the role of position does not feature in Collins' model:

- *Level 1: Position.* People follow you because they have to. The leader occupies a position where people feel that they have no choice but to comply and follow, even if they do not want to. This is leadership at its most basic. It is not about empowering people, but rather about compliance and control.
- *Level 2: Permission.* People follow because they want to. Good working relationships are established between leader and followers, and followers enjoy being with and working with the leader.
- *Level 3: Production.* People follow because of the results the leader achieved. The leader is perceived as someone who is competent, gets on with the job, is serious and can deliver outcomes.
- *Level 4: People development.* People follow because of what the leader has done for them. The leader moves forward towards goal achievement by investing in and helping people to develop. Followers need to feel that they have been empowered, as opposed to rewarded or gratified in some way.
- *Level 5: Pinnacle.* Leadership is accorded out of followers' respect for and commitment to the leader's identity, values and vision. The leader engages and empowers others to achieve optimum results without compromising relationships. This is the pinnacle of achievement as a credible, legitimate leader.

This model is not a career-stage hierarchy of leadership because people who are not formal, positional leaders can enact leadership in the relationships they develop, the results they achieve, how they empower others and how they inspire others to commit to their values and vision. For aspiring leaders in early childhood, the important point is that it is not necessary to hold a formal position or title to be a leader. In fact, position, title or power hold little sway with followers today, and do not guarantee that others will recognise you as a legitimate leader. Your people skills, personal qualities, leadership skills, competence and vision are more important for recognition as a genuine leader in early childhood than a title or position.

Several models of leadership have been devised specifically for early childhood, with some including the aspect of career-stage development.

Vander Ven's (1991) model proposes three stages of career development in early childhood that focus upon levels of cognitive understanding regarding the complexity of roles and the types of responsibilities associated with these roles. The basic level, *direct care: novice*, identifies the non-professional, affective and professionally immature orientation of young and inexperienced educators. The next level, *direct care: advanced*, identifies those who are more able to demonstrate logical and rational behaviour, to make choices, and to predict and explain the outcomes of their actions. The higher stage of *indirect care* identifies those who have moved beyond working directly with children and families, and now possess the understanding and expertise to take up leadership roles and responsibilities. Vander Ven argues that those who have moved to the stage of indirect care could demonstrate leadership capacity and expertise.

Katz's (1995) four developmental stages for early childhood educators identify *survival* at entry level, where the educator's concern is surviving and getting through the day. With experience, these educators move to *consolidation*, where they build on the experience gained earlier. The *renewal* stage is achieved when the educator becomes very competent in working with children and begins to look for new challenges and ways of extending expertise. Finally, in the advanced stage of *maturity*, the educator's activities and interests are directed towards and guided by meaningful, professional insight, perspective and realism. Katz argues that interest and expertise in leadership are displayed in the renewal and maturity stages.

In acknowledgement of the possibility of being appointed, defaulted or thrust into leadership from the earliest stage of one's career in early childhood, Rodd (2006) outlines a research-based model profiling the effect of early childhood leaders' experience on their understanding of the qualities, skills and responsibilities associated with leadership. At the entry level, Rodd found that leaders with less than three years' experience associated leadership with nurturing qualities—that is, someone who supports, cares and helps. For those with longer experience and in leadership positions such characteristics were perceived as 'givens'—that is, all people working with young children and families would be expected to display them. Being nurturing is a necessary but not sufficient leadership quality, but it could also be a style.

Leaders with between three and ten years' experience considered leadership to require skill in the rational, logical and analytical use of a professional knowledge base and expertise. A leader was considered to possess experience and expertise to understand the job, work well with others and deliver results. Most formal and designated leaders are at this level.

Leaders with ten years-plus experience considered professional confidence and empowerment essential for effective leadership, reflecting their knowledge, experience (and possibly leadership training) that enabled broader perspectives on leadership. Such leaders usually display vision and see beyond the present to imagine what the future might look like for children, families, educators and services. Rodd found that early childhood leaders at this advanced stage displayed an understanding of the complexity of leadership roles and responsibilities, both in services and the wider community.

Leadership potential is likely to emerge in those with more experience, but that experience must be cumulative—that is, growing in quality, complexity and robustness—and not merely the same type of experience repeated over numerous years. The critical question is: 'What preparation opportunities, strategies and training help early childhood leaders and educators transition to more advanced stages?' Appropriate professional support—for example, through training, shadowing, mentoring and coaching—needs to be available to encourage those who display leadership aspirations and capacity in different stages of leadership and career progression.

Ebbeck and Waniganayake (2003: 32) propose a model that integrates the dispositions, skills, roles and responsibilities of administration, management and leadership. This model helps early childhood educators to appreciate the range of roles, responsibilities, skills and dispositions that they may need to develop in order to work towards becoming an effective administrator, manager and leader. Leaders develop a long-term perspective and possess skills at a macro-level. They are visionary, passionate, empowering, articulate and adaptable, actively involved in delegation, collaboration, networking, advocacy, lobbying, policy formulation and analysis, critical thinking and research.

Moyles (2006) devised the Effective Leadership and Management Evaluation Scheme in recognition of the increasingly complex roles faced by leaders and managers in early childhood services. This model aims to provide guidance and support for educators in a managerial role, and to enable them to evaluate their own skills and knowledge. The skills and attributes identified are those that are essential and desirable in four broad areas: leadership qualities;

management skills; professional skills; and personal characteristics. The model also offers four levels of operation, similar to stages of professional development: intuitive and pragmatic; reasoned and articulate; involved and collaborative; and reflective and philosophic.

In order to be effective, leaders are required to be visionary, responsible, accountable, charismatic, trustworthy, respectful, collaborative, motivating, flexible, knowledgeable and innovative. Each of these qualities and skills is defined very specifically so that managers and leaders can evaluate themselves in order to work out where problems and weaknesses lie, which professional areas need developing and which areas are easy and enjoyable. This model attempts to deconstruct the complexity of leadership in early childhood, allowing aspiring and evolving leaders to set their own goals for personal and professional development. It must be remembered that effective leadership is subtle and holistic, with specific combinations of qualities and skills for particular situations, contexts and times key to its success.

Some models of leadership for early childhood illuminate the types of experience gained over time and how that affects understanding of leadership, especially where early childhood educators are appointed to positions of formal leadership before they are, in professional terms, developmentally ready and capable. Up until now, many have reported that they were not prepared—or only somewhat prepared—to take up a formal leadership role. Yet strong leadership is necessary to ensure quality services. It is therefore essential that, in a profession where early childhood educators can step into a leadership role at any stage in their career—including the very beginning—appropriate professional support related to different stages of career progression is available.

Regardless of stage of career development, leaders personify qualities that enable them to:

- build trust and rapport, establish solid relationships and influence culture through inclusive, respectful relationships
- support colleagues and promote growth among colleagues
- communicate and especially listen effectively
- address conflict, negotiate and mediate
- work collaboratively and support teamwork
- assess, interpret and prioritise needs and concerns, and
- understand the big picture and envision the impact of decisions.

The research into the qualities and skills of effective leaders in early childhood, although packaged differently in the various models, reveals many similarities and much common ground in terms of the qualities, skills, knowledge and capabilities considered to be associated with leadership. It is important not to interpret the lists as prescriptive. Their usefulness lies in the fact that they act as markers and points for reflection about current circumstances and what changes may be needed to enhance or improve leadership.

## Styles of leadership

Basically, a style is a way in which something—in this case, leadership—is said, done, expressed or performed. It is a combination of distinctive features of expression, execution or performance, and may characterise a particular person, group or approach.

*Style* is a term that refers to how leaders relate to followers. Leadership style is the manner and approach of providing direction, motivating people and achieving outcomes. A style is a behavioural model that is adopted relatively consistently by leaders when working with others. Understanding leadership styles can help early childhood educators to be flexible, and to customise their style to the needs of the followers and situation.

Numerous leadership styles have been developed from an interest in the effect of differences along a continuum of autocracy, power or coercion, and democratic consultation, participation and freedom. However, research consistently indicates that authoritative or participative styles (where leaders involve followers in the decision-making needed to arrive at a clear vision, expectations, boundaries and standards) achieve better results for both goals and morale than autocratic, authoritarian or laissez-faire styles.

Goleman, Boyatzis and McKee (2002, 2004) include the authoritative style in their model of primal leadership. They propose that successful leaders build resonance with followers by meeting the needs of different situations in a particular way. Good leaders are emotionally intelligent, communicating sensitivity and interpersonal awareness in the way that they choose to respond to the needs of people and situations.

Goleman, Boyatzis and McKee describe six styles of leading, each of which is associated with the various elements of emotional intelligence in different combinations and with different effects on the emotions of followers. Effective leaders should master all the styles, and use each of the following appropriately as circumstances demand:

- *Visionary*—an authoritative style used when vision, clear direction or radical change is needed. The leader inspires with vision and moves people towards shared aspirations and goals.

- *Coaching*—a nurturing style used to improve individuals' strengths and team performance. Through encouragement, counselling and delegation, the leader helps individuals to improve their skills and performance.
- *Affiliative*—a people-oriented style used to bond, build relationships and teams through friendliness and empathy, heal rifts, motivate in stressful situations and address problems.
- *Democratic*—an authoritative and participative style that uses listening to support and build consensus and collaboration; it involves people and values their input.
- *Pacesetting*—a 'superperson' style used to set challenges to get high-quality results and performance. This style can motivate a competent team, but also can leave less competent people behind, dissatisfied and resentful.
- *Commanding*—a coercive style used in a crisis, with problem staff or when an urgent change is needed. The leader gives direction when problems arise or calms things down in a crisis, but this style may disempower or disillusion people.

All the styles are useful at times, but skill is required in matching the right style to the right situation. The first four styles are associated with positive workplace climate, with the visionary style consistently having the most positive effect.

In summary, theories, models and styles reveal that effective leaders demonstrate a capacity for:

- *Emotional intelligence*—the ability to identify and respond sensitively to the feelings of oneself and others.
- *Critical thinking*—the ability to influence others through logical and analytical reasoning.
- *Directional clarity*—the ability to set, articulate and motivate people to commit to clear goals.
- *Creative intelligence*—the ability to solve problems by integrating and applying knowledge, understanding and skills.
- *People enablement*—the ability to empower people by offering support and mentoring.
- *Reciprocal communication*—the ability to listen empathetically and to network with others.
- *Change orchestration*—the ability to lead change proactively and constructively.
- *Perseverance*—the capacity to behave assertively, confidently and professionally.

The various theories, models and styles build a picture of leadership comprising qualities, skills, roles and responsibilities that are generic for early childhood leaders. However, it must be remembered that theories, models and styles tend to simplify what is a very subtle, complex and holistic responsibility. It is important for early childhood leaders and educators to decide whether these are indeed requisite and/or desirable features for leadership in their own context.

When assessing one's own leadership potential or that of others, it may be helpful to check which of these features are either emerging or developed and whether or not specific features can be learned:

- shared goals ('We know where we're going.')
- mutual respect ('Everyone has something to offer.')
- lifelong learning ('Learning is for everyone.')
- collegiality ('We're in this together.')
- continuous improvement ('We can get better.')
- responsibility for success ('Together we can succeed.')
- risk-taking ('We learn by trying something new.')
- support ('There is always someone there to support me.')
- openness ('We can discuss our differences.'), and
- celebration and humour ('We feel good about ourselves and our achievements.').

Effective leaders in early childhood generally display and are acknowledged for their:

- recognised experience and expertise
- extensive knowledge about pedagogy
- clearly developed personal philosophy of education
- individual responsibility for their actions
- respect from colleagues
- sensitivity and receptivity to the thoughts and feelings of others
- cognitive and affective flexibility, and
- administrative skills that help accomplish workloads.

## Bringing it together

While theories, models and styles offer a range of interpretations about effective leadership practice, no single theory captivates its subtle and intricate nature. Where identified and recognised features can be learned or developed, it is important for early childhood leaders and educators to gain access to professional preparation, training and development opportunities to practise, refine and extend them. In many ways, leadership is similar to the concept of quality. Definitions of and understandings about leadership evolve as leaders and educators learn more about the needs of those associated with early childhood services. All early childhood educators—not only those in leadership positions— should become familiar with contemporary understanding of the theoretical underpinnings and current research findings related to the personal qualities, skills, types and stages that underpin effective leadership in early childhood.

# PART II

## LEADERSHIP IN PRACTICE

The practice of leadership, rather than leadership as a role, is a current focus of interest and activity for theoreticians, researchers, employers and employees, particularly where quality, improvement and change are of concern. According to Harris and Spillane (2008: 33): 'It is the nature and quality of leadership practice that matters.'

Effective leadership in early childhood is grounded in a thorough understanding of the sector's contemporary, common and accepted conceptions about it, the personal qualities associated with it and contemporary leadership theories, models and styles. In order to put leadership into practice, early childhood educators and aspiring as well as existing leaders need to devote significant time and effort to acquiring and refining the core competencies and skills that underpin its authentic enactment.

Research indicates that effective leaders possess and employ specific abilities and, in order to be recognised as authentic and credible, those who aspire to lead early childhood services need to identify, develop and sharpen relevant practical competencies and skills in:

- communication and relationships
- conflict resolution
- decision-making
- problem-solving
- collaborative leadership and teamwork
- supervision
- mentoring and coaching, and
- change management.

Although these are not the only competencies and skills required, they are the ones most agree are basic and essential to enact effective leadership. Remember that leadership is holistic, and it takes a lot more than proficiency in particular abilities to be recognised as an authentic, credible and therefore legitimate leader.

# CHAPTER 4

---

# LEADING THROUGH COMMUNICATION: MEETING OTHERS' NEEDS

*People skills especially in communication are required to be an effective leader ...*
DEPUTY HEAD, EARLY CHILDHOOD CENTRE

## THIS CHAPTER EXPLORES

- emotional intelligence and leadership
- skills for meeting others' needs
- sending accurate and unambiguous messages
- overcoming physical and psychological barriers
- listening for understanding
- appropriate responding
- managing feelings
- communication in diverse contexts

Human beings are social beings, and as such have a need to belong and to find a place in the group (Adler, 1958). People—both adults and children—are motivated to behave in ways that help them to achieve a sense of significance in the groups in which they live. When people believe that they belong, they also feel connected, capable and competent, willing to contribute to meet the group's needs.

Leadership plays an important role when it comes to determining and understanding human behaviour in groups. It is the leader who determines the psychological climate of the group and motivates individual members' level of performance in the achievement of the group's goals. Goleman (1996: 148) argues that leading and 'managing with heart'—that is, the use of emotional intelligence— is essential for organisational survival and efficiency. For Goleman, leadership is the ability to use people skills in order to motivate colleagues to collaborate so that they can achieve a common goal.

Successful leadership in early childhood is a matter of communication more than anything else. Communication is the critical skill that underpins all others (Kouzes and Posner, 2007). Early childhood services are specifically 'people' services, where communication and interpersonal relationships are the building blocks on which pedagogical activity is based. Positive human relationships between adults and children, and between adults themselves, are both the basis and outcome of early childhood services. Better relationships develop out of feelings of safety, security and trust, and are characterised by openness and sharing between people. These qualities are created and maintained by the type of interaction that takes place between people (Johnson, 2008).

Leadership in early childhood is more than the style adopted, the personal attributes and psychological make-up of the individual, and the conditions, circumstances and contexts in which leadership is enacted. It is about how communication skills—the early childhood educator's tools of trade—are used as a means to build more satisfying relationships. Such relationships contribute to enhanced development and learning by the children, families and educators who are associated with early childhood services. Given that it is the responsibility of the leader to ensure that early childhood services meet a diversity of needs and expectations for a range of clients and consumers, it is essential that leaders understand the importance of communication and its relationship to leadership.

Because every leader plays a unique part in determining the psychological climate of early childhood services, leaders need to demonstrate a certain level of self-awareness and understanding in order to be able to influence others—both children and adults—through interpersonal communication. To gain the basic trust and confidence of others—something that is fundamental for the operation of quality early childhood services—leaders need to convey a specific set of attitudes and beliefs to others. In other words, leaders must transmit an image or profile that is authentic, attractive and inspirational to the people with whom they work. The following attributes are essential for leaders in early childhood.

*First, leaders must convey confidence in self and the profession.* The personal styles of early childhood leaders influence how they are perceived by children, adults, educators and other professionals, and can influence the status of early childhood in the wider community. Early childhood leaders who do not believe in their own ability to do the job well—perhaps as a result of limited self-understanding of values, attitudes, strengths, weaknesses, roles, responsibilities and goals, or under-valuing the importance of their occupation—may convey these attitudes and beliefs both in subtle, non-verbal ways and in more overt ways to people with whom they interact. On the other hand, confident and enthusiastic leaders who communicate through beliefs, actions and words that they have a strong sense of self, enjoy and value their work and are committed to making an impact on the lives of the children and adults with whom they interact, will attract followers who are willing to be guided in the direction taken by the leader.

*We believe in our leader because she believes in herself.*
CHILDCARE WORKER

For families in particular, it is important that early childhood leaders convey confidence, enthusiasm and a genuine acknowledgement of the importance of the job. Families place their most important extensions of self—that is, their children—in the guardianship of early childhood educators. The anxiety and mixed feelings reported by many families can be exacerbated or diminished by the personal presentation of early childhood leaders. Confident leaders have the potential to reassure families that they have the welfare of their children in mind, and will ensure that they spend a safe, happy and productive day at the service.

A confident leader can support early childhood educators through displays of positive attitudes about their contribution to children's and families' growth and development, and by modelling positive ways of coping with the daily demands of working with young children, relating to families who may be vulnerable, stressed or have unrealistic expectations, and simply getting through the demands and stresses of the day in this people-intensive working environment.

A reality of working in early childhood is that there is a lot of routine drudgery involved in assisting young children to cope with the demands of daily living and learning. Early childhood leaders find meaning and value in even the mundane and repetitive tasks that take up a lot of time.

*The leader keeps things running smoothly by setting a good example for everyone to follow.*
CHILDCARE WORKER

*Second, leaders who inspire the confidence and support of children, families and staff are self-aware.* They have devoted time to understanding and knowing themselves. Successful leaders possess high levels of proficiency in a range of practical skills—for example, motivation, delegation, financial management, planning and curriculum implementation—but also accept that personal and professional growth takes time and is partly a result of experience. Such leaders are able to make a realistic self-assessment about their strengths and assets, and limitations and vulnerabilities, and do not under- or over-state what they bring to early childhood. Nor will they be harshly or overly critical of any shortcomings in others, accepting that it takes time to acquire and refine the sophisticated and complex skills and understandings that are needed for working with and leading other people.

*Third, effective leaders have positive attitudes to new experiences.* The history of early childhood is a history of change with a tradition of action, requiring some daring and risk-taking, and considerable persistence; it is also the result of a combination of societal, cultural, political and economic forces. These forces necessitate leadership activities in the macro contexts of social development and change, the meso contexts of groups and organisations, and the micro context of individual relationships. Given that change has been part of the fabric of early childhood, leaders need to develop positive attitudes to new experiences and the skills required for responding to change.

Individuals who perceive change as a challenge and therefore possess the power to create change are by definition lifelong learners. Learning is a process of active engagement with experience that brings about increased skills, knowledge, understanding, a deepening of values and capacity to reflect. Some of the core features of lifelong learners are robust self-esteem, openness of communication and a wide skill repertoire that promote confidence rather than crisis in the face of challenge, as well as a flexible problem-solving approach in response to new experiences.

At the other end of the scale are those who are not open to new experiences and who resist change. These people may exhibit low or inflated self-esteem, defensive communication, a routinised, inflexible behavioural repertoire that fosters an unwillingness to risk new experiences, and a perception of change as threatening. A positive attitude to new experiences is an integral part of the process of the development and transformation of early childhood educators into leaders.

*Fourth, effective leaders have a positive attitude to relationships with others.* They think that the quality of relationships in the workplace is as important as the task-related aspect of goal achievement. They value activities that assist with really getting to know children, families and educators. They are interested in the effects of their own behaviour on others, use feedback to modify it and are willing to try different ways of relating to other people. They can see the benefits of building and maintaining satisfying and harmonious relationships as a way of meeting children's and adults' need to belong and feel significant in the group, and as a way of providing mutual support between the providers, clients and consumers of early childhood services.

## Reflections on leadership in practice

In our day-to-day work, the way we treat other people shows our leadership qualities and skills. Leadership is shown through respect, understanding, caring and communication—especially listening.

DEPUTY HEAD, EARLY CHILDHOOD CENTRE

Developing positive attitudes to relationships with others is essential for leaders in early childhood because children's optimum development and learning are dependent upon quality interpersonal relationships, as is the quality of engagement and partnership that will develop between educators and families. In addition, morale, commitment and performance levels are affected by attitudes to and expectations about relationships in the workplace. Positive attitudes to relationships can influence early childhood educators to interact with each other (and the leader) in a caring, respectful and constructive manner. The extent to which children, families and educators feel trusted, accepted and respected by early childhood leaders determines the quality of communication and interaction.

*Finally, effective leaders maintain positive interactions with others.* Even though employees may have the best of intentions about interacting with colleagues positively in the workplace, disagreement, dispute and conflict are inevitable. This is more likely in work contexts where individual and personal value systems can influence and determine professional policy and practice. In early childhood, individuals (families and educators, trained and untrained, mature and young, experienced and inexperienced) bring their own subjective, highly personalised, socially and culturally determined beliefs and values about child-rearing, early learning and education. Effective early childhood leaders understand the destructive impact of inappropriate, negative interaction styles on levels of trust, feelings of security and safety, and performance. They actively model and promote mutually respectful, cooperative and collaborative interactions with others as a means of enhancing the general self-esteem and goal achievement of all.

## Emotional intelligence and leadership

While 'academically' intelligent and clever individuals often are appointed to positions of leadership, they do not necessarily become successful leaders if they have not developed considerable emotional intelligence. Emotional intelligence is similar to Gardner's (1983) earlier notions of intrapersonal intelligence (that is, self-awareness, self-control, persistence, self-motivation and energy) and interpersonal intelligence (social understanding and the ability to get things done with and through others), which constitute two of his original seven multiple intelligence definitions.

According to Goleman (1996), emotional intelligence is the master aptitude that deeply affects all other abilities, either enhancing or interfering with them. Emotional intelligence, as opposed to traditional notions of intelligence, is considered to account for outstanding performance in top leaders.

Emotionally intelligent leaders have the power to raise standards, encourage personal and professional growth, and foster organisational sustainability. They appreciate the need to support colleagues in developing emotional competence and, through them, contribute to the building of emotionally competent organisations. In very simple terms, emotional intelligence (Goleman, 1996) involves:

- knowing your own feelings
- the ability to manage your own emotions
- having a sense of empathy
- the ability to repair emotional damage in yourself and others, and
- being emotionally interactive—that is, tuning into people so that you can interact with them effectively.

Effective communication skills are the tools that underpin the ability to act in an emotionally intelligent and competent manner. Emotionally intelligent leaders are able to identify and talk about their own feelings, are good listeners, ask appropriate questions and engage in meaningful dialogue. They are able to approach and hold courageous and courteous conversations about difficult issues.

In addition, emotional intelligence underpins enhanced job performance and satisfaction. When people feel emotionally competent, they feel more positive about their jobs and how they perform them. Consequently, the workplace can be a source of personal and professional satisfaction, enhancement and empowerment for all.

Gardner's (1983) concept of multiple intelligences has been applied to organisations, including educational workplaces, where nine different intelligences—one being emotional intelligence—have been identified. Intelligent leaders in early childhood services employ the full range of intelligences to address quality of provision, including teaching, learning, effectiveness and improvement. The collective capacity of early childhood services to achieve shared goals successfully depends on having emotionally intelligent leaders who in turn nurture and value the emotional intelligence of educators, thereby enhancing the capacity of the service to work in emotionally intelligent ways.

## Communication skills for effective leadership

Communication is a basic human function; it is the means by which we represent our thoughts and feelings to others, transmit knowledge, solve problems and build relationships. Effective communication has many functions and purposes. It can include 'speaking, listening, encouraging, reflection, translating, interpreting, consulting, debating, summarising, understanding, acknowledging and verifying' (Siraj-Blatchford and Manni, 2006: 17). Early childhood leaders gain personal power from the proficient use of communication skills because, regardless of the situation, they help others to feel encouraged, rewarded and optimistic rather than diminished, punished and pessimistic.

For early childhood leaders and educators, two major areas need to be balanced in order to survive at a personal level and effectively achieve the goals of the service. First, they must meet the needs of other people. Specific communication skills are helpful for meeting this responsibility. Second, it is essential that skills be developed for meeting personal needs in the work context. While there is some overlap between the two sets of skills, they can essentially be divided into two groups, as set out in Table 4.1.

**Table 4.1:** Communication skills

| Skills for meeting others' needs | Skills for meeting personal needs |
| --- | --- |
| Sending accurate and unambiguous messages | Appropriate self-assertion<br>'I' messages for 'owning' statements |
| Overcoming physical and psychological barriers | Conflict resolution |
| Listening for understanding | Delegation |
| Appropriate responding | Time management |
| Managing feelings | Stress management |

Many early childhood educators claim that they have few problems with communication—no difficulties in understanding others and being understood themselves. While this may be true, there is always room to improve, refine and sharpen skills. This is part of being a lifelong learner. It is not sufficient for early childhood leaders to communicate at the basic 'get-the-message-across' level. Effective communication is a dialogue, not a monologue. More sophisticated and complex skills are required to deal with the diversity, complexity and difficulty of situations that present themselves when the job involves working with people. It would not be acceptable for a cabinetmaker to build a fine piece of furniture with a second-rate, blunt and rusty saw. In the same way, it is not acceptable for early childhood leaders and educators to consider fulfilling their roles and responsibilities with second-rate, unrefined, insensitive communication skills.

Because the early childhood leader's primary responsibility is to meet the needs of others—such as children, families and educators—the skills for meeting others' needs are described first. Chapter 5 examines the skills needed to meet personal needs.

## Skills for meeting others' needs

In many ways, effective communication in early childhood is dependent on the leader's sensitivity to other people's need to feel understood. Imagine what it would be like to work in an early childhood service where everyone was skilled in emotional competencies—where they were attuned to the feelings of others, able to handle disagreements constructively and able to go with the flow when necessary! Early childhood leaders who are accomplished communicators set the example and encourage others to respond to the challenges and difficulties they encounter in the workplace in emotionally intelligent ways.

It is the early childhood leader's responsibility to create an emotional climate from which self-disclosure, empathy and honesty will emerge, and to foster the perception of 'being understood'. The skills that leaders employ to communicate with others on a day-to-day basis contribute to that process.

### Sending accurate and unambiguous messages

Early childhood services are 'people' services where the business of the day is providing quality learning opportunities and education for young children, understanding families' needs and expectations, supporting them in child-rearing and employing available human resources effectively. Communication plays an important role in all of this. While early childhood educators who are trained in child development possess a good understanding of young children's language and communication abilities and limitations, and attempt to match the style and complexity of messages to children's developmental capabilities, this sensitivity may not extend to communication with adults. Given that it is the leader's responsibility to disseminate large amounts of information at different levels within early childhood services, it is important to consider the extent to which clear, accurate, unambiguous and non-toxic messages are constructed for the intended receiver. Clear and accurate messages are constructed from a consideration of the characteristics of the intended receiver, the need to have the message understood in the way that it was originally intended and an awareness of points of potential breakdown.

Because verbal messages usually are sent only once, and have to compete with all sorts of distractions, it is essential that care be taken with the construction of these messages. Never assume that the message received was understood as it was intended. The communication styles used by sensitive early childhood leaders and educators are different for babies, toddlers and four-year-olds. Similarly, when constructing a message for adults, a range of factors need to be taken into account—for example, the needs of families versus educators, the needs of those from diverse cultures, languages and dialects, trained and untrained educators, experienced and inexperienced educators, as well as the relative importance of the message. Because people tend to hear what they want and expect to hear, it is important to check the recipient's understanding of the message. Early childhood leaders and educators do this with children, and need to ensure that they also use this skill in their communication with adults—particularly for those from diverse heritages.

Subtle power plays can be identified in some of the messages communicated in some work environments. In early childhood services, it is not uncommon to come across hurtful gossip, unkind humour, subtle insults, 'tiny lies' or omission of truth and covert pecking orders. These toxic exchanges signify emotional immaturity and insensitivity, and contribute to the development of uncooperative and even hostile work environments. Remember the example of Leona in Chapter 1? It is important that leaders recognise such emotionally incompetent messages for what they are, understand their ultimately destructive outcome for all, and act to stop and/or prevent them from occurring.

## Overcoming barriers to communication

Since anything that competes for our attention can be a barrier to effective communication, clearly early childhood services are not conducive to effective communication. The physical arrangement with educators isolated in separate rooms, the staff roster system, the noise that young children make, the constant ringing of the telephone, the interruptions by families who want immediate attention and the primary child supervisory responsibility of the staff are obstacles to effective communication, and increase the possibility of communication breakdown.

Although not all communication exchanges require high levels of skill, certain situations—such as dealing with a complaint, providing feedback to educators and obtaining information about the progress of a certain child—require discreet and tactful handling. Effective early childhood leaders are aware of the range of barriers to communication within services, and consider ways in which their impact can be eliminated or at least minimised.

Barriers to communication that exist in physical surroundings can be manipulated and used by those who wish to sabotage communication efforts. For example, some adults may manipulate barriers to prevent effective communication taking place when they, for example, deliver an important message to a listener who is occupied with a group of children in a noisy toddler room, when they call a message out as the listener passes by the office or at the same time that they are involved in a telephone call, or when they give unnecessary attention to distractors and interruptions.

The physical barriers in early childhood services can be handled relatively easily when compared with the psychological barriers to effective communication that may occur. These include the subjective attitudes, values, beliefs, stereotypes and prejudices that all of us bring to a communication exchange. It is interesting to note that many of the subjective and enduring attitudes used to interpret messages we receive are formed by the age of five. This is why it is important for early childhood leaders and educators to be aware of the sub-context, as well as the content, of their communication with children and adults. While on the surface it may appear that a particular message is being conveyed, an underlying value-laden or emotionally unintelligent communication can influence how the receiver interprets and understands the conversation.

Leaders in early childhood services need to be aware of their own and educators' values, attitudes, prejudices and stereotypes, and be conscious that they may influence how they understand and meet others' needs. What we hear other people saying can be influenced by our own preconceived judgements. Take the example of a teenage mother who comes to discuss behaviour problems that she is experiencing with her three-year-old son. Certain value judgements may spring to mind immediately—such as poor, uneducated, inexperienced, neglectful, incompetent, irresponsible, immoral and so on. In fact, none of these may apply.

Human beings have a tendency to associate or interpret difference negatively before fully thinking through the reality of difference or variation. If negative value judgements about difference dominate the way in which early childhood leaders or educators perceive this mother (or indeed anyone else who may be different), they will act as barriers to communication and influence how well the other's need to be understood and supported is met. Sensitive early childhood leaders do not underestimate the power of psychological barriers to interpersonal interactions.

### Listening for understanding

Listening is the critical ability all leaders need to strengthen—the skill to hear and understand what is important to others (Kouzes and Posner, 2007). The biggest criticism of early childhood leaders and educators about those in positions of formal leadership is that they do not listen. This is possibly the greatest barrier to effective communication because poor listening communicates a lack of interest and preoccupation with other matters to the speaker. Early childhood educators consistently rate the ability to listen effectively as one of the key leadership attributes.

The most effective communicators are those who are able to put aside their own egocentric preoccupation with speaking and instead direct their attention and energy to listening for the meaning behind what the speaker is saying. This type of listening is different from simply hearing the words. While there are often many distracting noises in the background—such as cars passing by, doors banging or the radio next door—we do not specifically listen to them unless they are meaningful in some way. Goleman (1996) suggests that non-defensive listening (as well as speaking)—that is, listening to the *feelings* behind what is being said—is essential for helping receivers to be receptive to a message. When we listen—especially in a professional capacity—we are trying to meet others' need to be understood. Therefore, an effort needs to be made to comprehend and use all the available information—including underlying feelings—to understand the meaning of the message as it was intended. This kind of listening is referred to as 'active listening' or 'reflective listening'.

What is involved in listening for understanding? First, the listener ensures that appropriate time and space are available and can be devoted to the speaker. If time is likely to be insufficient to meet the speaker's needs, the listener needs to convey interest in the speaker's issue and negotiate a more appropriate time to devote to the speaker. If the time is suitable, the listener needs to eliminate or minimise potential barriers to communication, such as redirecting telephone calls, preventing interruptions and sitting in positions that communicate positions of equality rather than power.

Second, the listener deliberately focuses attention on the speaker by using appropriate eye contact, body posture and non-verbal communication to indicate interest in the issue and that they are following the speaker. Third, the listener gathers information from three speaker-related sources: the content, or the actual words heard; the speaker's body language, or non-verbal communication (a more reliable guide to the accuracy and importance of the verbal content); and the para-linguistics—*how* the speaker says the words (tone of voice, emphases, breathiness, fast or slow delivery).

Fourth, the listener uses all of these sources of information to interpret the speaker's message, and reflects and clarifies understanding about the essence of the speaker's message in a short recapitulation.

Finally, the listener modifies understanding of the speaker's intended message in the light of the speaker's response to the listener's clarification. This process communicates interest, empathy and respect in meeting the speaker's need to be understood, and encourages further communication and interaction.

## Appropriate responding

In the communication process, listening is the most important skill that needs to be developed and sharpened in most people—both children and adults. However, communication is a two-way process, and the way in which early childhood leaders respond to children, families and educators affects the quality of the interaction.

Five response styles (Rogers, 1961) typically account for approximately 80 per cent of the verbal communication in which professionals engage within human service occupations. The other 20 per cent consists of the unintelligible grunts, groans and acquiescent noises that people scatter throughout their conversations. People tend to develop preferred response styles, which are produced automatically in the short space in which a timely response is expected to ensure the flow of human communication. The use of one response style for 25 per cent or more of most communication results in the speaker being stereotyped by the listener as 'always' responding in that way, thereby diminishing the speaker's perception of being understood. This blocks further communication and decreases the possibility of the listener meeting the other person's needs. The five typical response types are:

- *Advising and evaluating*—typical responses being 'What you should do now is . . .' or 'If I were in your shoes, I'd . . .'
- *Interpreting and analysing*—responses such as 'The problem you really have here is . . .' or 'You've missed the point! The real issue is . . .'
- *Supporting and placating*—the aim is to diminish emotions in responses such as 'Don't worry, they all go through that stage!' or 'Forget it! He'll get over it.'
- *Questioning and probing*—the intent is to gain additional information, but this may turn into an interrogation, such as 'Did she have a disturbed night? Did anything unusual happen this morning? Is everything all right at home?'
- *Understanding or reflecting*—the listener's response focuses on the under-lying feelings as well as the content and indicates their understanding of the message to the speaker in a short paraphrase such as 'You're concerned about Sam's adjustment to pre-school' or 'You seem very pleased with the new music curriculum!'

Of the five typical response types, the understanding or reflecting response is the most under-developed and under-used, with early childhood leaders and educators frequently and indiscriminately employing the remaining four. The other four response types, while appropriate at times, can have detrimental effects upon communication if they are adopted insensitively. That is, they can be received as emotionally unintelligent responses.

They also contain inherent disadvantages as an initial response in a communication exchange because they do not acknowledge the speaker's feelings, allow for the possibility of clarification of meaning or communicate that the intended full meaning of the message has been understood.

The understanding or reflecting response, in addition to overcoming these limitations, enables the speaker to explore the issue in greater depth and can be used to empower individuals to solve their own problems without having to rely on an expert professional. This is an important consideration for early childhood leaders and educators, whose role and responsibilities include supporting the personal development of families and the professional development of colleagues.

Effective leaders in early childhood are aware of the advantages and limitations of the different response types, and use their experience and expertise to determine which would be the most productive for meeting others' needs in the circumstances. The appropriateness of response type is the hallmark of a highly sophisticated and competent professional communicator.

## Managing feelings

It is commonly acknowledged that 'people professions' inherently contain work-related pressures that often result in work-induced stress. Early childhood leaders spend their working day immersed among people, their expectations, needs, problems and demands; consequently, they are required to respond to and deal with situations that can elicit emotional reactions on their part. While it is important to recognise and articulate personal reactions and emotional responses to events in our professional lives, it is essential that these be managed in a professional and emotionally intelligent manner that neither impedes early childhood leaders' and educators' ability to meet the needs of others nor diminishes others' sense of self-esteem.

Early childhood services around the world are staffed predominately by women. Despite advances in rights and roles, women generally are socialised to smooth over or placate others in emotionally arousing situations. Typically, women have difficulty acknowledging the legitimacy of their emotions and expressing them in a constructive manner. The usual strategy is to deny and bury feelings until they build up to explosion point. Instances where early childhood educators avoid issues by storming out, slamming doors, crying, name-calling, blaming and absenting themselves from work until 'things calm down' continue to be common.

It still is more the exception than the rule for women in early childhood to confront emotionally arousing incidents in an assertive manner. To add to this difficulty, early childhood leaders interact with a diverse group of people such as babies, toddlers and pre-schoolers; younger, mature and older families and educators; and professionals from other disciplines and agencies who have their own agendas, who differ in their ability to manage their own emotions and who are experiencing various levels of stress and vulnerability in their own personal lives. It is therefore even more important that early childhood leaders and educators become emotionally competent and model emotionally intelligent ways of managing feelings.

## Communication in culturally diverse contexts

With increasing global migration, there is growing and significant contact between people from different countries, cultures and heritages. An advantage of this diversity is that early childhood educators connect, share and work with people from new, unfamiliar and different backgrounds, customs and traditions. However, people from different backgrounds have different experiences, understandings and expectations. In the workplace, this means that they have different assumptions and views about group dynamics, leadership and management styles, social customs and communication norms. Goleman (2011) comments that, because cross-cultural conversations can easily be misinterpreted and misunderstood, leaders to have a deep understanding of the existence and importance of cultural differences.

Culture and language are critical to learning and play a key role not only in the way people communicate but also in how they think about and understand the world. Different cultures have different ways of knowing, solving problems, communicating non-verbally and dealing with conflict (Pratt-Johnson, 2006). By becoming culturally competent, early childhood leaders and educators can avoid some of the problems that may arise when living and working with children and families from diverse backgrounds.

The skill with which early childhood leaders and educators communicate is most important because it is through communication that information is shared, trust established and relationships developed and maintained. Therefore, it is essential that any obstacles and/or barriers to effective communication in culturally diverse contexts be identified and addressed so that children and families are not disadvantaged by language, customs and cultures that are different. The only way to offer equitable access to children and families who use early childhood services is to acknowledge, respond to, respect and value diversity.

Early childhood leaders and educators need to develop knowledge, understanding and skills that enhance their cultural competence. Cultural competence is the ability to understand, communicate and effectively interact with people across cultures and heritages. It involves:

- being aware of your own understanding of the world
- displaying positive attitudes towards cultural differences, variations and diversity
- acquiring appreciation of and knowledge about different cultural practices and perspectives, and
- developing appropriate skills for meaningful communication and interaction.

Communication is always a complex and challenging process, but there are some strategies that can help clarify understanding across different cultures and backgrounds. Culturally competent communicators learn about the various cultures, perhaps even gaining basic proficiency in the community languages that are represented in early childhood services. In their personal communication efforts, they:

- are patient, courteous and tolerant
- focus on being clear, simple, unambiguous and explicit
- allow sufficient time for processing what has been said
- avoid humour (which is notoriously culture-specific)
- are aware of their own part in communication problems
- are flexible, adaptable and open to new ways of communicating
- avoid idioms, culture-specific terms, abbreviations and acronyms
- use a variety of communication channels, clarify, review and follow-up
- avoid stereotypes about different cultures, customs and traditions, and
- access training in cross-cultural communication, inclusion and diversity.

Communicating in culturally diverse, inclusive contexts is now the norm, and early childhood leaders and educators should develop in-depth understanding of the different cultures, backgrounds and heritages represented in services to ensure that all aspects of curriculum, pedagogy and policies are implemented in a climate that is respectful, inclusive and empowering for children and families.

## Bringing it together

Effective leaders in early childhood are aware of the potential for emotional arousal in the interaction between children, families and educators, and understand the need to listen to and accept the emotional responses of others. Emotionally intelligent leaders respond to these on a genuine and professional level, and are aware of personal biases. They possess resources and skills for flexible responses, managing personal feelings and overcoming barriers to communication in the workplace. They possess awareness about and skill in culturally competent communication. This is the tipping point where the connection between meeting others' needs and meeting one's own personal needs is balanced. In order to manage their personal feelings in the professional situation, early childhood leaders and educators must also develop skills to meet their own needs.

# CHAPTER 5

## LEADING THROUGH COMMUNICATION: MEETING PERSONAL NEEDS

*Most workers in early childhood are women, and we are not good at projecting ourselves and taking leadership roles both in and outside our services ... we need to gain more confidence, speak out and be heard in the community ... I had to learn to stand up for myself and my beliefs.*
MANAGER, DAY NURSERY

### THIS CHAPTER EXPLORES
- skills for meeting personal needs
- appropriate self-assertion
- 'I' messages
- conflict resolution
- delegation
- time management
- stress management
- information technology and electronic communication

The development of the early childhood sector has been shaped by the position of women in society (Ebbeck and Waniganayake, 2003) and is rooted in the tradition of philanthropy. The profession's pioneer women wanted to improve the lives of young children, and were guided by an interest in child development and its promotion in order to rescue children from what they thought of as moral, spiritual and economic slums—that is, they were interested in meeting the needs of others. Their motivation to act as advocates for child-rearing, mothers and motherhood also stemmed from their desire to enhance the development and quality of their own moral, spiritual and intellectual lives—in other words, to meet their own personal needs.

Early childhood has been slow to achieve professional credibility in the community commensurate with its history and achievements. The focus on nurture, care, unselfishness and improving the quality of children's environments has been used to avoid taking responsibility for meeting professional needs for economic and political improvement. In other words, some early childhood educators still perceive themselves as powerless to meet their own professional needs because they have sublimated their personal needs into an almost evangelical crusade to meet the needs of others, such as children, families and staff. The dual goals held by the pioneer women should be reclaimed so that early childhood educators can redress any imbalance between personal needs as professionals and the needs of the consumers of their services.

*The sector needs stronger representation at government decision- and policy-making levels and within union movements to ensure the continuation of funding for early childhood services and parity of wages and conditions for early childhood personnel that are commensurate with other educators.*
MANAGER, CHILDREN'S CENTRE

In caring professions such as early childhood, it is often easier to put others first at the expense of personal needs. However, neglecting personal needs over a period of time incurs costs, for the individual, for the workplace climate and eventually for the quality of service provision.

The ability to meet personal needs lies in the concepts of self and self-esteem. Early childhood leaders need to value their occupation and its contribution to society, and have a realistic assessment of their own assets, strengths, limitations and vulnerabilities in order to meet their own and others' personal needs. If early childhood leaders and educators perceive themselves or their job as inferior, inadequate or less worthy than other professions or occupations, they may lose confidence about perceived and actual requirements necessary for discharging professional roles and responsibilities.

Leadership in changing times entails many, possibly overwhelming, responsibilities that can give rise to feelings of frustration for both leaders and followers. Ongoing frustration can contribute to work-related stress, which in turn can bring about diminished coping strategies. The potential for burnout is significant.

The early childhood sector today is characterised by a multiplicity of demands, many pressing responsibilities, courageous decision-making about highly complex issues that may involve ethical choices and dilemmas, in a context of potentially conflicting needs from a range of parties. In order to meet the needs of others, it is essential that leaders simultaneously respond and work in ways that meet their own personal needs. This is not being selfish: it is being realistic. Observation and experience reveal that, in life and at work, many people are unpredictable, some are needy and many have self-esteem issues. In addition, people will treat you the way you let them treat you—which is not necessarily the way you expect or want to be treated. If leaders' professional and personal needs are not balanced or well managed, ultimately they may suffer burnout, which usually contributes to deterioration in work productivity and workplace relationships. Burnout can lead to:

- loss of enthusiasm and dedication
- a growing sense of frustration and anger
- a sense of triviality regarding work
- withdrawal of commitment to work and relationships
- a growing sense of personal vulnerability, and
- a sense of depletion and loss of caring.

Burnout leads to reduced performance, absenteeism and turnover—all of which diminish the stability and quality of early childhood services.

One way to avoid this outcome is to ensure that a balance is created between meeting the needs of others and meeting one's own personal needs. Early childhood leaders and educators can work on meeting their personal needs and overcome some of these issues by cultivating supportive, reciprocal, give-and-take relationships with colleagues, families and other professionals. They can also employ specific communication skills, in particular:

- assertion, including the use of 'I' messages
- negotiation
- delegation, and
- conflict resolution

and work towards infusing a pervasive culture of distributed leadership throughout the workplace.

A starting point for early childhood leaders and educators who wish to give their own needs higher priority is to examine:

- *How work is assigned*—what competing demands are there? Are tasks assigned thoughtfully and in a realistic timeframe or at the last minute?
- *How work is monitored*—does micro-management cause stress? Are there too many interruptions? How is feedback provided—is it appropriate, sufficient and frequent?
- *How information and direction are given*—verbal messages are open to misinterpretation and are easily forgotten. The tone and style of written messages can appear formal and heavy-handed. Text messages can appear rude.

- *How others interact with you*—do colleagues express their emotions through outbursts of anger or by crying? Are colleagues rude to one another? Do some educators appear stressed, agitated or disinterested and detached?

Early childhood leaders and educators also can meet their personal needs by:

- undertaking a needs inventory (identify where you mostly operate on Maslow's hierarchy of needs, see pp. 87–8)
- prioritising tasks (starting with what is important and urgent, postponing non-urgent and non-essential work)
- asking for help (using the resources of the team, delegating)
- learning to say 'no' (being assertive), and
- choosing challenges (negotiating tasks, declining work that you don't have the time, interest or expertise to undertake or complete).

Ultimately, when early childhood leaders and educators work in ways that as far as possible balance their personal needs with the needs of others, they feel and are more enabled, enhanced and empowered, and the general atmosphere at work is improved.

## Appropriate self-assertion

One of the most important skills early childhood leaders and educators can acquire, both for themselves and for the clients and consumers of their services, is appropriate self-assertion. This skill is useful in situations such as setting limits with children, communicating a request to a family, expressing an opinion to a colleague, setting parameters with a committee, meeting personal needs to express positive and negative feelings appropriately, being honest in their responses to others and asking not to be interrupted. It is an appropriate skill for responding to feedback from families, colleagues, other professionals and external evaluators such as quality assessors and inspectors. It is important for other people with whom early childhood leaders interact because it is a skill that enables effective communication in ways that preserve others' sense of self-esteem.

### What is assertion?

Assertion is a matter-of-fact statement that conveys rights, opinions, beliefs, desires and positive or negative feelings in ways that do not impact on the self-esteem of other people. It is a professional strategy for interpersonal communication because it is a direct, honest and courageous expression that conveys personal confidence and respect for self and others. Being assertive does not guarantee that you get what you want; rather, it supports and enhances professional relationships through the use of emotional honesty, confrontation of issues and problems and respect for others' responsibility for managing their own feelings and responses. It is an emotionally intelligent ability.

Assertion (or using fair play) is the point of balance between two other familiar behaviours: non-assertion (avoiding conflict) and aggression (winning at all costs). These three communication styles can be seen as a continuum from the passive, indirect, self-denying, non-assertive style to the confronting, inappropriately emotionally honest and self-enhancing at others' expense aggressive style. Both non-assertion and aggression have negative and destructive effects on further communication, and ultimately on future relationships, whereas assertion is considered to act as a facilitator to further communication and helps to build and maintain relationships as well as personal confidence and self-esteem.

Most people have some difficulty in communicating assertively, either in certain situations or with certain individuals. Few of us possess the level of self-confidence, skill and courage necessary for consistent, appropriate self-assertion. Inability to act assertively usually is related to lack of self-esteem, where our own needs are undervalued in relation to others' needs, and consequently suppressed or denied. On the other hand, aggressive behaviour can occur if our own needs are perceived as dominant and superior to those of others, and self-righteously, coldly, angrily or aggressively pursued.

These differences explain why individuals can be seen to fluctuate between the three communication styles described above. For example, an educator may feel sufficiently confident to be able to be assertive with young children when being interrupted by saying something like: 'Excuse me, Gianni, I'd like to finish talking to Susan.' The same person might have difficulty being assertive in a similar situation with Gianni's family, and may respond non-assertively by passively accepting being interrupted. Often, negative feelings of hurt, anxiety and guilt for not taking responsibility for one's personal needs will be experienced later. Early childhood educators who persistently engage in non-assertive behaviour can experience high levels of frustration, which ultimately erupt in an aggressive outburst—that is, the mouse turns into a lion and intimidates the surprised recipient of the emotional explosion.

On the other hand, the same educator may only be able to confront an issue that is of concern to them by fuelling action with anger. For example, the educator may confront the issue of being interrupted by a colleague with an aggressive response such as: 'Well, that's just typical of you! You never let anyone finish what they are saying. I'm just not going to bother anymore!' The colleague on the receiving end of this outburst is likely to feel attacked, angry and vengeful, which will affect the relationship at a later time.

Early childhood leaders and educators should be aware of their own obstacles to appropriate self-assertion. Continued non-assertion and disregard for personal needs might be a symptom of poor self-concept and low self-esteem, and generally leads to anxiety and frustration. A tendency towards aggressive responses that infringe upon the rights of others also reflects problems with an unrealistically inflated or poor self-concept and self-esteem. This eventually results in unmanageable relationships in the workplace. Those who are uncertain about their ability to be assertive in specific situations or with certain people usually do not believe that they are entitled to basic personal rights. In order to increase one's confidence in such situations, an examination of one's belief system in relation to personal rights is useful. All human beings have the right to make decisions about their body, property and time, and to be treated with respect by others. Moreover, everyone has the right to express personal opinions, feelings and wishes in an appropriate way.

Another obstacle to appropriate self-assertion is fear of the consequences of assertive behaviour. Non-assertive individuals usually believe that other people will not like them or will reject them if they express their feelings. In fact, the opposite is true. People generally respond well to appropriately assertive individuals and feel irritation with, pity and eventually disgust for chronically non-assertive individuals. Aggressive individuals often believe that the use of power achieves their desired goals in relationships. This may appear so in the short term, where others may defer to the demands of the aggressive person. However, the long-term consequences of aggression are that the support, cooperation and goodwill of the recipients of aggressive displays are lost and a desire to take revenge, get even and retaliate can emerge. This negative reaction can escalate into situations where the aim is to sabotage.

Assertive responses usually are appropriate for incidents or situations that occur frequently and with people with whom one wishes to continue a positive relationship. Therefore, there are usually many opportunities to practise assertive responses and to learn from the results. Learning any new skill takes time and practice, and learning to act assertively is no different. The following steps are helpful to develop appropriate self-assertive behaviours in early childhood services:

- *Identify what you actually want to accomplish—that is, the goal of the assertive situation.* For example, you may wish to have a particular family pay their fees on time each week.
- *Clarify how being assertive will help you to achieve this.* In this instance, being assertive will permit you to explain your needs in the situation, such as the budget requirements.

- *Analyse what you would usually do to avoid being assertive in this situation or with this person.* In the past, you may have sent a note home with the child, left messages on the family's answering machine or dropped subtle hints.
- *Clarify what the likely advantages would be of being assertive instead.* The direct expression of your needs and wishes will minimise misinterpretation and misunderstanding of your requirements, and maximise the probability of the family responding to your request to pay the fees on time.
- *Identify what might be preventing you from being assertive here.* Do you lack the courage to address the issue directly? Are you holding unrealistic and unlikely notions about the consequences of being assertive? Could it be that your non-assertion is related to mistaken beliefs about the need for politeness in interactions about money? Do you fear an aggressive or tearful response?
- *Identify any other sources of anxiety and think about how you will cope with and reduce them.* Are you anxious about what might be said about you to colleagues or other families? Think about and reaffirm your own rights in the situation.
- *Construct a model response that you would feel comfortable saying in the situation or to the person, and practise it aloud several times.* Refine the statement if necessary until you find one that feels genuine. You could say something like: 'I need to speak to you about the payment of fees. When the fees are not paid on time I become concerned that the service will not have sufficient funds to meet its operational demands. I'd prefer it if you could let me know if your fees cannot be paid on time. That will give me time to assess my budget and give us an opportunity to negotiate some alternatives.'
- *When the situation arises, have the courage to put your assertive response into practice, knowing that you will probably have another opportunity to try again.* Rarely is success achieved with the first assertive response.
- *Reflect upon the results of your assertive statement in terms of what you liked about what you did, the outcome and what you would change in the next opportunity to be assertive.* You may have liked that you were direct, that you explained your needs and responsibilities, that you stayed calm and weren't aggressive, or that you opened up a chance for further discussion.

These steps help early childhood leaders and educators to become more assertive and self-confident in managing communication exchanges. The way in which assertive statements are phrased is the next important skill in meeting your own needs.

## 'I' messages

The aim of communicating assertively is to express honestly and directly personal opinions, feelings and wishes. Unfortunately—particularly when emotions are aroused—personal opinions can be turned into statements of blame. These are not conducive to productive relationships and can act as barriers to further communication. The use of the word 'you' to begin statements may arouse defensive tendencies and provoke a retaliatory attack.

Consider the effects of the following two statements on an educator when you want to discuss the issue of punctual return from breaks. The first statement is: 'You're late back again, Kerry. You've got us all behind in the lunch routine! This had better not happen again!' An alternative is: 'I'm concerned about the effect of our breaks on the lunchtime routines, Kerry. I'd like us to discuss the issue when you've got some time.'

The first statement puts the blame for the problem squarely on Kerry in a fairly threatening way, and does not lay any groundwork for problem-solving. Kerry is likely to react in a defensive manner, become angry at the attack and find reasons why the problem is nothing to do with her. She may try to deflect the concern to other, possibly unrelated issues. In the second statement, the speaker is able to employ a matter-of-fact tone of voice to define the issue at point of discussion and provide a non-threatening framework to explore with Kerry what factors could be contributing to the issue. Kerry is less likely to perceive herself as the focus of blame and attack, and therefore more likely to discuss the issue openly and constructively.

In terms of owning personal statements, it is important to commence sentences and statements with the 'I' pronoun rather than generalised terms such as 'we', 'they' or 'some families'. This subtle change in emphasis eliminates emotional overtones that can impede clear communication and reduces the likelihood of petty disputes about the source and intent of the message. The 'I' message allows the appropriate expression of feelings in a professional context, such as: 'I was annoyed to find that the kitchen was not cleaned after the meeting last night. I'd prefer it if we could come up with a satisfactory arrangement for the next meeting.' Using this framework, early childhood leaders and educators can address issues and express opinions in a constructive manner, thus providing a model for professional communication exchanges.

## Conflict resolution

Disputes, disagreements, differences of opinion, bickering, friction, clashes, confrontations, dissention, in-fighting, quarrels and antagonism are examples of the types of conflict that can be observed in any early childhood context. Conflict is an inevitable part of living and working with other people and, because the early childhood profession is essentially about working with people, the potential for conflict is high.

The possession of sound conflict-resolution skills is crucial for effective leadership. The many requests from early childhood services for assistance in dealing with and managing conflict indicate that this is an area of concern for personal survival and job satisfaction. Many early childhood educators report having few skills in this area, and acknowledge the need for assistance to strengthen their confidence and competence in handling conflict in a professional manner. Conflict resolution is discussed in detail in Chapter 6.

## Delegation

One of the biggest problems identified by early childhood educators is the amount and diversity of the work that is required in order to fulfil their roles and responsibilities. In terms of completing the workload, the effective leader will know when and how to delegate work to others so that the goals of the service are achieved. Effective delegation of authority and tasks can help to reduce administrative pressure and workload and free up time that can be devoted to other professional demands.

Delegation is a skill. It is not simply asking or directing a colleague to complete a task. Delegation requires a match between the task to be undertaken and the skills, interests and characteristics of the colleague seen as an appropriate delegatee. In order to delegate successfully, early childhood leaders have to be willing to relinquish and share some of the duties and responsibilities that previously have been associated with their roles. It is important that the tasks considered appropriate to assign to others include some of the pleasant, rewarding jobs as well as some of the more mundane, tiresome and unpleasant jobs. Delegation is not simply getting rid of all the tasks that are unpleasant, unpopular or boring!

Nor is delegation a feature of distributed leadership. Delegation is part of the rational, considered process of decision-making about tasks, duties, responsibilities, authority and power. Leadership is not distributed through delegation but subtly infused into the attitudes, expectations, norms and actions of workplace culture concerning communal and collective responsibility for achieving shared goals.

Delegation involves having confidence in individuals and team members, and their ability to act as responsible and accountable professionals. However, there are various barriers to delegation. These are illustrated in some typical comments overheard in early childhood services:

*I don't want the staff to think that I can't do my job.*
*I've done this job for years. Nobody can do it as well as I can.*
*I'll only get the blame if someone else makes mistakes.*

*It will take less time if I do it myself.*
*The staff won't see me as part of the team if I don't do the job myself.*

Delegation is the thoughtful, purposeful process of empowerment. First, the delegator needs a clear understanding of the relative importance of the various tasks that are considered suitable for delegation. It is essential to distinguish between key leadership functions that should always be retained by the leader (such as evaluation, policy development and key reports) and other duties that could be undertaken by suitable others (such as fee subsidies, petty cash and organising professional development events).

Second, the delegator needs to consider the staff member or members to which it may be appropriate to delegate responsibility for the task, and select the most suitable. Third, the delegator needs to think about the way in which the nature of the task is communicated to the selected individual. When selecting the appropriate person to undertake a specific task, the early childhood leader needs to know the potential of the staff member by being familiar with their strengths, weaknesses, personal characteristics and learning styles as well as their work aspirations. Maslow's (1970) hierarchy of needs is useful in understanding why individual staff members come to work, their predominant motivation and their potential to undertake special delegated tasks.

This framework for understanding people's motivation describes lower level needs that, if fulfilled, permit the individual to progress to higher order needs. At the lowest level are physiological needs, such as the need for food, water and sleep. The financial remuneration gained through employment enables these needs to be met, and is a fundamental motivation for all workers, regardless of how much they earn. When these basic needs are met, the individual is able to pursue fulfilment at the next level of need—safety needs. At this level, the worker is motivated by needs for security, stability, structure, law and order, protection and freedom from fear and anxiety. Casual employment and casual relief work are unlikely to assist in meeting these needs. The employee will be interested in undertaking tasks that are perceived to contribute to their personal safety and security, such as meeting minimum work expectations and competency, detailing rosters of who is responsible for what tasks and any other activities that ensure predictability in the work environment and the continuation of employment.

Maslow's third level is characterised by belonging and love needs, where individuals are motivated to work in order to be part of a group, to extend their social network and to meet needs for affectionate relationships with others. Such individuals will be interested in tasks that build and maintain relationships and in working as a member of a team. These are the people who will arrange the Christmas party, suggest staff dinners and organise staff farewells. Their need for harmonious relationships means that they may also take on the role of mediator when conflict between colleagues occurs or relationships are strained.

The fourth and fifth levels of Maslow's hierarchy of needs describe motivation typologies that are relevant to efficient delegation of important responsibilities. The need for esteem is the dominant motivator in relation to work at the fourth level. There appear to be two sub-levels of this need. First, individuals are motivated by the need to demonstrate mastery, competence, autonomy and self-confidence; and second, they have a need to feel appreciated and important and to gain a sense of respect from others. Status, prestige and perhaps even fame become dominant motivators. Individuals who wish to demonstrate their competence and gain public recognition for a job well done generally respond well to delegation, particularly if the task is introduced with the phrase: 'I think you are the best person to undertake this important task.' However, if the task is perceived to be beyond the personal capability of the staff member and there is a chance of failure, it is unlikely that the individual will accept the delegation. In such a situation, assurance from the leader about access to support and assistance if required may help to convince a staff member to accept the task.

The highest level of Maslow's hierarchy of needs is described as the need for self-actualisation. This is the level where the individual is motivated by the need for personal growth and development. Level 5 leaders usually operate on the basis of self-actualisation. Individuals at this level work because they want to develop their potential and become the best that they can be. This is the level where the greatest differences between individuals are evident. In terms of delegation, individuals at this level will be interested in challenging tasks that may demand the acquisition of new skills or knowledge. They truly are lifelong learners. The main difference between this level and the previous level is the role of demonstrated competence and public recognition versus personal standards of achievement, success and growth. A staff member's contribution is a result of intrinsic motivation rather than factors external to the self.

The effective early childhood leader will consider individual educators' motivation in relation to their employment, and match this with the kind and level of task deemed suitable for delegation. Having decided that a particular task is suitable for delegation, and having selected a potential delegatee on the basis of characteristics, skills, interests and motivation type, the early childhood leader needs to *invite* the chosen educator to undertake the task. It is important that the leader explains:

- the nature of the task to be undertaken
- the timeline for completion of the task

- the level of authority and accountability that will be assigned to the person who undertakes the task, and
- the reasons why they are considered to be the best person for the job.

The leader also should ask for some input from the educator concerning any aspect relating to standards of performance and completion of the task. In effective delegation, leaders need to define their role explicitly as one of support and facilitation for independent work, and avoid engaging in unnecessary control, supervision and micro-management. An agreed timeline and procedures for reporting back should be decided upon, as well as a means for evaluating the work.

In delegating tasks and duties to colleagues, it is important for early childhood leaders to keep in mind that others are likely to approach and complete the job differently from the way that the delegatee would have done. Therefore, reasonable expectations of others and the final outcome are essential if early childhood educators are to perceive delegation as a means of professional preparation and development and a pathway to job satisfaction.

## Reflections on leadership in practice

The best leaders in services always delegate duties to people who will be able to perform them the best. This is because they know the team, the service and the children. Good leaders always give others the opportunity to share their ideas too, and that helps them know what you are interested in and good at.
NURSERY NURSE

Inappropriate delegation can lead to early childhood educators feeling exploited, misunderstood and frustrated in their work. It can also result in early childhood leaders losing confidence in the team and themselves, and retreating to the unproductive position of: 'If you want a job done well, then you have to do it yourself.' Delegation should result in an improvement of the morale and performance of the entire work community as well as ensuring that there is sufficient time for early childhood leaders to devote to their own work. If time is still a problem, then time-management strategies need to be investigated.

### Time management

One of the most pressing problems facing early childhood leaders and educators is insufficient time to complete the range of responsibilities that are associated with delivering services to young children and families. Yet the notion of time management is often greeted with scepticism. The work demands of formal and positional leaders of early childhood services have increased dramatically recently, and with ongoing and accelerating change this is likely to continue. Time management is about how early childhood leaders and educators develop short-, medium- and long-term coping strategies to meet the demands of professional roles and responsibilities.

The concept of 'time in the working day' in early childhood services is difficult to define because working with young children and families involves 'duty of care'—that is, children's needs must be met regardless of whether or not educators are officially on duty—and because, for many, there are no or very liberally interpreted rules about overtime. No early childhood educator would leave a child abandoned outside a service if a family or previously nominated person were not on time to collect them. Because of split shifts, many educators have to attend staff and other meetings outside their allocated hours. Therefore, for many the job takes as long as it does to get done, regardless of statutory working hours. This can place pressure on work–life balance. Many early childhood leaders and educators report that the long and often unpredictable hours required to do their work properly put a strain on their personal relationships and leisure pursuits.

Although many tasks—especially those involving paperwork—can be taken home and completed outside work time, the impact of such a practice conducted on a regular basis is likely to be destructive in terms of increased personal stress levels and less time for personal pursuits and family life. While the work may get done, it is often at a personal cost. The effects of poor time management will be taken up in the next section on stress management.

Time management is simply a strategy that helps early childhood leaders and educators to meet all of the demands that are placed upon them during a typical day. There are also various activities that take place during the evening and on weekends, such as mentoring, meetings, further study, workshops and conferences, fundraising functions and maintenance working parties. A 40-hour working week is not the norm for those who work in early childhood. In addition, because early childhood educators are 'public figures' in that their performance is observable by the clients and consumers of their service, it is essential that they are able to handle the variety of demands on their time in a manner that reflects competence and efficiency.

At this point, a distinction needs to be made between 'being busy' and 'being efficient'. A 'busy' leader might well examine their willingness to delegate some duties and responsibilities to other appropriate colleagues. It may be that a leader's difficulties with delegation interfere with and hinder efficient task accomplishment, and, consequently, effective leadership.

Time management is a means of getting things done as efficiently and quickly and with as little stress as possible. It essentially involves clarifying and prioritising goals in one's personal and professional life, and establishing action plans and timeframes for the tasks to be undertaken in order to achieve these goals. The major obstacle to time management in early childhood services is interruption. Therefore, skill in dealing with this problem must be developed. Appropriate self-assertion, discussed earlier in this chapter, is useful here. If an early childhood leader manages time efficiently, the result should be more time available to work towards achieving distinct goals without feelings of stress or pressure.

Time management involves:

- *determining goals* (long- and short-term goals for personal growth, work, professional development and career progression)
- *analysing the task or steps that will help reach a particular goal*
- *breaking down the task or project into small, achievable steps* (evidence of progress towards a goal is motivating), and
- *establishing a priority rating* (which task needs to be completed first to progress towards the goal?).

Although this seems an obvious strategy, it is important to remember that lists are useful to help you plan each day, week and month. To avoid asking 'Where did the time go?' some people find making a list of general headings useful in establishing effective time management—for example, things to do, people to see, phone calls to make, meetings to attend, deadlines to meet. Other headings can be based on priority (Hunsaker and Hunsaker, 2009):

- urgent and important—do it now
- important but not urgent—do it some time today or tomorrow
- this week—attend to it in the next few days
- this month—record deadlines in a diary to prompt attention, and
- term break/non-contact time—make time to respond to non-urgent tasks.

Such headings help to focus attention on the demands on your time, and can assist with establishing priorities for tasks. As each task is completed, cross it off the list. If a task remains unfinished, examine why it was not completed. Was there enough time? Were there too many interruptions? Weren't you interested in it? Was it too difficult? Did you have all the information necessary? Is the morning better than the afternoon for complex report-writing? Was this a task that could have been delegated?

The way office space is arranged physically is associated with how efficiently time is managed. The early childhood leader's office usually is a multi-purpose space that often doubles as a storeroom, staff room, resource library, family room and interview room. It may not be easy to keep it in perfect order. However, the more chaos and clutter in the office, the less accessible it is for efficient use of time.

The creation of a workable filing system is essential to handle the amount of information that comes through to leaders of early childhood services. A modern computer and software are essential items of equipment that can ease the administrative load. The time initially spent mastering specialised software can produce considerable savings later. The impact of information and computer technology is examined at the end of this chapter.

Telephone calls continue to be reported as a major source of stress for early childhood leaders and educators. The telephone is an important link between the service and the outside world, especially in the current security-conscious environment. Families have the right to contact staff about their child at any time. It is not the telephone itself that is the problem; it is people's poor telephone skills. The most important strategies are keeping incoming and outgoing telephone calls short; ensuring you have communicated the purpose of your call accurately; making all necessary calls in one session; and considering whether some calls can be delegated to others. Finding a way of freeing yourself from answering the telephone and creating an uninterrupted period of time to complete an important task is essential.

Meetings can be another source of inefficient usage of time. Meetings abound in early childhood services, and because services can be physically remote from the administrative offices in which many meetings are conducted, the time needed to attend a one-hour meeting can easily amount to two hours with associated travelling time. Early childhood leaders who manage time efficiently will assess the need to hold or attend meetings in terms of their services' goals. Only those people who are relevant to the purpose of the meeting should attend, and the person who chairs the meeting should ensure that discussion is focused on the topic. Learning some techniques for chairing group meetings can be valuable if meetings are substantial elements of duties and responsibilities, and can assist with the effective management of time.

The increasing roles and responsibilities undertaken by early childhood leaders and educators necessitate a change of mindset. Efficient and effective leaders in early childhood now work smarter, not harder or longer.

## Stress management

Pressure of time is only one of a number of stressful factors associated with employment in early childhood. Working with young children is physically, emotionally and intellectually demanding. Families appear to face considerable pressures associated with the demands of contemporary living, so the scope of the early childhood educator's job has broadened to include a wide range of responsibilities that include supporting families in their child-rearing roles, mentoring and training, working collaboratively with professionals from a range of disciplines and agencies, and acting as advocates for children, families and the profession.

Many of the recent changes in the roles and responsibilities of early childhood leaders and educators have not been supported by access to relevant preparation and training, with many having to 'learn on the job'. Given the statutory staff-to-child ratios mandated by government regulations for early childhood services, it can be difficult for early childhood leaders and educators to gain time off or be relieved from duty in order to attend professional development opportunities, many of which are offered during the hours in which early childhood services operate. It is therefore common for those who do engage in further study and training to have to undertake pre-service, in-service and post-initial training in their own time. This demand can affect the quality of personal lives and result in increased stress levels.

Stress in itself is neither good nor bad; whether a situation is deemed stressful by anyone depends on how it is perceived and experienced, and on individual coping abilities and resilience. Human beings need a certain amount of stress to get going each day. When perceived as a challenge, stress is a good motivator and activator. Stress is part of modern life and work, and as such it is unrealistic to expect that stress can or should be eliminated.

However, by the nature of their personalities or experiences, some individuals are more prone to stress than others. It is important that such people examine their tendencies to perceive situations as stressful rather than in more optimistic terms. They need to work towards reframing their perceptions, and subsequently their reactions to such situations. Work should enhance our feelings of well-being or self-esteem and generate a 'feel good' factor. For example, looking for the positives in our situation can help alleviate stress. Emotionally intelligent early childhood educators understand the links between thoughts, feelings and reactions. They appreciate that usually there are choices regarding how one perceives a situation, and that different consequences arise from different choices. They use such insights in deciding how best to respond. Consequently, they see that stress can be managed by either changing the situation or changing themselves.

Stress is self-induced to some degree, in that it is a product of the balance between the number of demands in our lives and our individual perceptions regarding our capacity or resources to meet these demands. In the case of many early childhood leaders and educators, the demands often outweigh personal resources, with stress being the result of this imbalance. While time management and delegation can assist with the reduction of stress levels in the workplace, a broader strategy for approaching stress in all aspects of life is more useful.

Stress levels determine effectiveness in both our personal and professional lives. Too much stress or over-stimulation brings about ineffective problem-solving, low self-esteem, physical exhaustion and illness, all of which result in low-quality performance in the workplace. Burnout, as discussed previously, develops from an imbalance between too many demands or high levels of tension and one's personal resources to respond appropriately. Lack of stress or under-stimulation can have an equally negative impact on coping strategies with boredom, fatigue, frustration and dissatisfaction reducing professional effectiveness, resulting in 'rustout'.

Neither of these extremes meets the needs of others or personal needs. With an optimum level of stimulation or challenge, early childhood leaders and educators can demonstrate the capacity for rational problem-solving and creativity, which creates positive attitudes to progress and change and enhances self-esteem and job satisfaction. With such a balance, it is possible to meet personal needs as well as be responsive to the needs of others. However, achieving this balance requires self-awareness, an understanding of work demands and continued effort to keep both of these in perspective.

The first step in managing stress in personal and professional arenas is to determine who and what is causing the stress. In other words, a stress inventory needs to be compiled that lists all the people, incidents, situations and circumstances that are associated with feeling stressed. Such an inventory also permits reflection upon typical coping strategies and an evaluation of their effectiveness. The following steps are helpful in exploring the main causes of stress:

- *Briefly describe the stressful situation.* For example, a conference with a family concerning their child's unacceptable behaviour can be perceived as stressful.
- *Identify who is involved in the situation.*
- *Establish how frequently this situation occurs.* Conferences with families can occur frequently—on a weekly basis with some.
- *Determine the degree of control you have over the situation and/or people involved.* In such a case, you consider that you have some ability to influence families' attitudes and behaviour.
- *Identify typical ways of responding to or dealing with the situation.* For example, when you encounter stressful situations, you tend to ignore them, hope the problem will resolve itself without your intervention or avoid direct confrontation by dropping hints.

- *Evaluate how effective these strategies are for accomplishing your work and maintaining positive relationships.* In your past experience, you have found such non-assertive strategies to be ineffective but you are too anxious to try anything new.
- *Brainstorm possible alternative ways of dealing with the situation in a more constructive manner for your own needs.* Assertiveness training to help you express your needs and practice in mutual problem-solving could be beneficial.

In meeting the need for a relatively stress-free working environment, two important aspects must be considered: how frequently the situation occurs and the degree of control over the situation. If a situation occurs frequently, it would seem that current coping strategies are not adequate and require reviewing. Where situations cannot be changed because of the lack of personal control, exploring strategies for changing personal perceptions and thinking can be more productive than trying to change the situation. In the above example, rather than thinking that your ability to deal with family conferences is weak, try changing your thinking to, 'I don't like family conferences but I can cope with them. I can learn skills to help me feel more confident.'

Stress-management strategies focus on changing the situation or changing yourself. Most people are reluctant to engage in personal change if another option is available. Therefore, strategies for changing the situation will be discussed first.

In early childhood, analysing and making minor or more substantial changes to duties can reduce work-related stress. If stress is related to the demands of the job, then the workload can be reorganised by using the following techniques:

- *Reduce the workload.* Delegate appropriate tasks to others. Other colleagues will benefit from—and may even appreciate—the opportunity to learn new skills. This provides another advantage in that additional backup is available if the leader is unavailable for any reason.
- *Establish priorities for the demands placed upon you.* Learn to be assertive, deal with only essential demands and avoid becoming involved in tasks that are peripheral to your role.
- *Use and improve time-management techniques* to ensure that you use time as efficiently as possible.
- *Assume control.* There are always options in any situation. Avoiding situations will not resolve any difficulties but can exacerbate them. Make choices and decisions rather than being at the mercy of events.
- *Complete any unfinished tasks* before starting new ones. The sense of completion can quickly neutralise anxiety about the amount of work that has to be done and promote the 'feel good' factor.

- If possible, *minimise change* and *keep to a routine.* Stress is often associated with uncertainty about change. If stress is a result of chronic change, such as has been occurring in early childhood for many years, then routine, predictability and stability can build up self-esteem and nurture feelings of security.
- *Access or establish a support group or network.* Avoid withdrawing from and possibly alienating colleagues, peers and friends. Stress is a common experience for early childhood leaders and educators, who therefore can empathise with one another when they feel overwhelmed by pedagogical, social, economic, political and organisational demands and changes.

When early childhood leaders and educators have little personal control over a stressful situation and cannot change the situation to ameliorate stress levels, it is possible to manage stress by *changing the way the situation is perceived or viewed.* The following personal stress antidotes can help change the way we think about stressful situations:

- *Change your perception about stress in general.* Rather than seeing stressful situations as things to be avoided in life, view these situations as challenges and opportunities for growth and personal development. Accept that it is not the situation but how the situation is perceived that produces stress.
- *Change your thinking to less catastrophic, less extreme, less polarised, less stressed and therefore more positive and rational thinking.* Emotionally intelligent educators use self-talk to define situations. Self-talk is simply the ability to listen to the internal messages we give ourselves about any particular event. Instead of thinking, 'Isn't this dreadful! I just can't stand anymore!' try something like, 'Well, I don't like this very much but I can deal with it! I could . . .' In this way, the tendency to irrational, over-emotional thinking is limited without denying the basic emotional response. An opportunity to perceive the situation more realistically and to adopt a rational, problem-solving approach is provided.
- *Keep your sense of humour.* Sometimes it is necessary to take a step back, get things into perspective and see the funny side of work. Laughter and humour produce good moods and enhance the ability to think flexibly and creatively, helping you to notice different aspects of a situation and find solutions to problems. According to Goleman (1996), bad moods 'foul' or undermine thinking. Having a laugh at yourself or the situation helps stimulate positive and pleasant feelings that move us in more positive directions.
- *Learn to tolerate uncertainty in life.* Not everything can be controlled, directed, planned or predicted. Don't try to swim against the tide but learn

to 'go with the flow' sometimes—particularly when you don't have the power to control events. Worrying will not improve or change the situation. It will only increase your sense of uncertainty and your stress level.

- *Don't dwell on past mistakes because it's too late to change them now.* Mistakes are opportunities for learning. Focus instead on what you can learn and how to approach such situations more effectively in the future.

- *Learn to anticipate change.* Working in a 'people profession' means that constant change is inevitable, but there are usually numerous signs to alert you to the need for change or an imminent change. Perceptive early childhood leaders and educators are attuned to signs of impending change, plan for change and facilitate the implementation of change in order to minimise stress in those affected by the change. Skills for managing change are discussed in Chapter 10.

- *Develop the skills necessary to perform your job efficiently.* Attend preparation and professional development opportunities and perhaps upgrade your qualifications to ensure that you possess high levels of professional and technical expertise.

- *Improve the communication skills that are related to stress management, in particular assertion and conflict-resolution skills.* Express your feelings appropriately and deal with incidents as they occur.

Effective early childhood leaders appreciate that it is important to create a positive emotional environment by communicating that they value each individual. Valuing helps those who are stressed to be more open about how they feel. While it does not eliminate stress, feeling valued by significant others in the workplace— for example, formal leaders, colleagues and families—may help to compensate for perceived imbalance between the demands of the job and personal resources. Valuing also helps to promote motivation, collaboration and teamwork.

In addition to the techniques described above, there are two basic strategies for stress management in both personal and professional life. The first one relates to personal health and the second relates to relaxation. Stress has an underlying physiological component. Consequently, maintaining good health can reduce susceptibility to stress. Anyone who wishes to function effectively needs to have a balanced diet, avoid or minimise the use of drugs (including caffeine, nicotine and alcohol), take regular exercise and have adequate sleep. This is especially important in professions such as early childhood that require physical, emotional and intellectual stamina. Learning to relax and developing recreational interests are also means of ensuring psychological health and stamina.

Enacting effective leadership is high-stress work (Ancona et al., 2011), and insightful leaders appreciate that they need a strong support team around them to help them lead integrated and balanced lives (George et al., 2011).

## Information technology and electronic communication

Information and communication technology, commonly referred to as ICT (including the internet, email, mobile and smart telephones, texting and video conferencing) has brought many benefits to the workplace. This technology has freed many employees from the grind of repetitive and time-consuming administrative tasks, and has given them access to different forms of communication, learning and social engagement. In fact, some governments now use the internet and virtual environment to engage the public, and to publicise and offer services (Krotoski, 2010). It is increasingly obvious that anyone who does not have access to or chooses not to use ICT will be left behind. However, the growth of such technology is not without its problems. Effective relationships in life and at work cannot be built purely from electronic communication, with misunderstandings caused by lack of face-to-face contact, inappropriate emails and texting highlighted as common problems.

Many early childhood leaders and educators still report that they simply do not have access to the latest equipment in the workplace, that the equipment they do have is slow—especially when accessing the intranet or internet—and that they do not have the time to read and respond to ever-increasing downloads and email communications. Unfortunately, some in the sector still hold negative attitudes about new technologies.

Given that accelerating development in electronic communication impacts significantly on the working lives of early childhood leaders and educators, it is important that they become confident and motivated to use it appropriately. Access to better equipment, training and support is essential, as is employee understanding of the personal and professional benefits to be gained by appropriate engagement with the technology. Technology should empower people, not act as a barrier to communication, relationships and learning.

Email has become an important means of communication in the workplace, but it must be used in an appropriate and responsible manner. Information can be shared easily by email. However, firing an email to someone giving them work to do will not get the best out of them. Senders need to think about the impact of receiving information in the form of an email because certain barriers exist in this form of communication. The following factors should be considered:

- *Is email the most appropriate form of communication? Would this message be delivered more appropriately in person?* For example, it is always entirely inappropriate to criticise staff performance or terminate someone's employment via an email. This type of communication needs to be delivered in person. Any sensitive issue, such as appraisal, mentoring and any unpleasant message, needs a face-to-face approach. Recognition for best practice is more powerful when delivered in person.

- *Is the language used open to different interpretation and meaning by different people?* We all tend to hear and read what we want to hear and read. In an email, the message's intention is not clarified or highlighted by access to non-verbal communication. It is essential that the message's intention and meaning are clear, unambiguous, acceptable and understandable. For example, explaining a policy decision in an email may result in different understanding about what was meant by some educators. Very abbreviated messages and the use of acronyms may not be understood, or could be misunderstood as well as perceived as curt and arrogant.

- *If a response or action is required, can you be sure that the person actually received the email?* Many emails still seem to vanish into the ether. Conflict can arise if the sender believes that the recipient did not respond to the message or if intended recipients argue that they did not receive the communication. Just because you sent someone an email does not mean that you have communicated with them.

- *Is the distribution list of recipients inclusive?* It is important to think about who needs to receive the message. Support and ancillary staff need to be included in some messages. Networking and teamwork can be enhanced, diminished or sabotaged by who is included in email communication.

- *If an email is forwarded to a third party, it is essential to examine the chain of emails contained within the communication.* There may be compromising or hurtful statements in earlier emails that are part of the chain.

As with face-to-face verbal communication, good electronic communication is about sending messages in the most appropriate manner at the most appropriate time. Email is a valuable tool for improving communication, but it also can be used as a weapon if the message shows lack of concern for the recipient. Inappropriate use of email can cause pressure on people that produces stress, overload and resentment.

Some early childhood educators, especially those in formal leadership positions, have identified the time needed to respond to emails as a source of stress. Many report being 'bombarded' with emails, a good proportion of which are irrelevant and redundant. To minimise this difficulty, some people chose an hour—usually later in the day—to read and respond to emails, thereby preventing important time being swallowed by email correspondence. Others report that, if possible, they dealt with email correspondence at home rather than at work. One disadvantage of this strategy is the invasion on personal time. Dealing with email is a time-management issue that requires strategies suited to individuals and their professional circumstances.

The intranet (within the organisation) and internet (beyond the organisation) are useful tools for accessing information, sharing information, learning and professional development. However, as with email, these need to be used legitimately for professional concerns. There have been instances where employees have used the technology for personal rather than professional agendas. In early childhood services, where access to equipment and time are both limited, the technology needs to be used to meet professional needs and goals aimed at improving standards and quality. Social networking, looking up holidays, mortgage or energy rates and new jobs at work are not appropriate or professional uses of the technology.

Mobile telephones and texting offer instantaneous communication with others anywhere and at any time. However, personal mobile phones need to be used appropriately and responsibly at work—that is, in your own time and never when on duty, where there is responsibility for the supervision of children. When used inappropriately, mobile phones are intrusive and impact negatively on quality of work and relationships.

Texting has become a popular form of communication because it is quick, easy and convenient in that it does not rely on the recipient being available to receive a message at the time it is sent. However, it does rely on recipients turning on their phone and accessing messages at regular intervals. Texting is subject to the same issues and limitations as emails. Some early childhood leaders do not regard text messages as respectful and appropriate communications. For example, some find it disrespectful to receive a text late at night to inform them that an educator will not be coming into work the next day. Others find it helpful to know about such situations early so that suitable arrangements can be made. The appropriate use of texting should be discussed in meetings so that everyone is clear about what and when it is acceptable to use texts as the main form of communication.

Social networking via the internet has transformed the ways in which human beings connect and communicate with others, but online interaction does not necessarily generate responsible and genuine real-life interpersonal engagement (Krotoski, 2010). The growth of social networking has posed problems and created ethical issues for both employers and employees. Employers can scrutinise sites such as Facebook, Flickr, YouTube and Twitter to access information about potential and current employees. They may use such personal information in employment decisions—for example, to appoint, promote or terminate. Many employees, to their cost, have left very intimate information and photographs as well as derogatory and unprofessional comments about their workplace on such sites without thinking that their employer or colleagues might read them. Employers are entitled to monitor and penalise those who use work and/or personal equipment inappropriately in the workplace. Employees may regard this as 'snooping' and a breach of their privacy. However, both parties need to treat social networking with care, respect and common sense.

Early childhood services should develop policies regarding the use of social media in the workplace in order to avoid possible abuse and confusion about what is and isn't allowed. Such policies can be grounded on the principle of acceptable, unacceptable and forbidden usage. Sensibly, many organisations allow employees limited and reasonable use of work ICT if usage is not excessive and time-wasting, doesn't interfere with their own and others' work, involves minimal time and expense and does not bring the organisation into disrepute or expose it to risk or legal action. It is always forbidden to use work ICT to run a private business or to access and/or distribute pornography or other inappropriate content.

Employers may appropriately monitor employee usage of workplace ICT to ensure compliance with social media policies and to provide evidence of transgressions, as part of training and quality assurance systems, to prevent or detect crime and to maintain the security of the ICT system.

The benefits of information and communication technology are many. However, there are pitfalls that need to be avoided. Services are encouraged to develop policies to cover the use of information and communication technology in the workplace. Early childhood educators need to assume that everything they download from or upload onto the internet could be made public and should think about who they would want to (or may) access it. Early childhood leaders must strive to ensure that information and communication technology is well managed so that it saves time, frees educators from laborious tasks and improves inclusive communication.

## Bringing it together

Effective early childhood leaders and educators need to create balanced personal and professional lives that enable them to meet others' needs while ensuring that their own personal needs are met. This balance is a result of effective communication skills, the ability to delegate and to respond to conflict constructively, as well as the capacity to manage time and personal stress effectively. Early childhood leaders and educators must take a responsible approach to the use of workplace and personal forms of information technology and electronic communication.

# CHAPTER 6

## LEADING CONFLICT RESOLUTION: FROM DISCORD TO ACCORD

*We have our differences about what to do but just because she is the leader does not mean she is always right ...*
CHILDCARE WORKER

### THIS CHAPTER EXPLORES

- sources of discord and conflict within early childhood services
- common responses to discord, disharmony and conflict
- constructive approaches to addressing conflict

Discord, disharmony and conflict appear in many forms in early childhood services—as petty or major disputes, small or significant disagreements, minor to major differences and clashes of opinion—and are exhibited as friction, irritation, bickering, in-fighting, aggressive confrontations, passive or active dissension, quarrels and mild to severe antagonism. Discord, disharmony and conflict in various forms are features of many psychological climates in early childhood services, given the frequency and intensity of disagreements, arguments, quarrels and disputes that are reported.

People can become uncooperative, difficult, hostile and conflict-prone at work for many reasons. They may have reached the limits of their current ability, they may have become disengaged or distracted or they may have lost motivation (Osborne, 2008). What eruptions of discord, disharmony and conflict signify is the breakdown of communication and interpersonal relationships in the team.

Where a workplace depends on harmonious social interaction, conflict is inevitable. This is a serious problem for early childhood services because the basis of quality provision is social interaction and harmonious, reciprocal relationships. In any service where team relationships are related to the achievement of goals, or where relationships need to be maintained in order to ensure stability and quality, skill in addressing and transforming discord, disharmony and conflict into accord, harmony and cooperation is essential. Early childhood leaders and educators need to learn to approach conflict in a positive manner and deal with it in ways that strengthen team relationships and productivity.

Quality early childhood services depend on the commitment of and ability of all involved to work collectively towards achieving agreed goals. Early childhood leaders need to develop skills to assist educators in confronting issues that arise as teams work towards these goals. Unfortunately, many early childhood educators still think that discord, disharmony and conflict would and should not occur if people could just get on reasonably well with one another. 'Why is she so hostile to me when I try something new?', 'Why are we having all of these problems?', 'What is wrong with our service?', 'Why can't we stop fighting and get on with the job?' are questions typically asked by early childhood educators who also erroneously believe that theirs is the only service having problems. These types of questions are inappropriate for the work situation, and illustrate that discord, disharmony and conflict are misunderstood phenomena.

Rather, conflict needs to be considered as a natural part of life and work. The situation would be of more concern if it did *not* occur. In fact, discord, disharmony and conflict can be positive and functional in that they can stimulate new ideas, growth and change. The real issue is not that conflict exists, but how it is approached and addressed. The question early childhood educators should ask is, 'Given that discord, disharmony and conflict are normal parts of the work experience, how are we going to address them?'

Discord, disharmony and conflict in early childhood are expressions of interpersonal interaction in which two or more people struggle or compete over claims, beliefs, values, preferences, resources, power, status or any other desire. Evidently, the early childhood sector provides a ripe arena within which conflict is likely to emerge, given that individual philosophy about the early learning and education of young children can be grounded in subjective beliefs, values and preferences supported by personal experience. In fact, many early childhood educators regularly report that dealing with conflict is a major source of tension in the workplace. All educators and families will have their unique perspective on what is the best—and therefore, in their view, the only—way to stimulate young children's development and learning. The right to relate to children on the basis of one's subjective philosophy, regardless of the extent to which it complies with the service's philosophy, can be defended by families and educators with emotional, irrational and contradictory arguments.

Unaddressed and chronic discord and conflict at work are harmful to both the quality of work and productivity, as well as to the quality of life and relationships. People spend their energy in dysfunctional ways, such as fighting, arguing, ridiculing each other, competing and using resources inappropriately when they need to be cooperating and collaborating to provide quality services for children and families, and a pleasant and harmonious working environment for themselves. However, it must be remembered that it is not conflict itself that is the problem. Conflict only becomes unhealthy and unproductive when it is not handled effectively.

In addition, conflicts that are not addressed adequately may appear to be resolved but can re-emerge at the next point of tension in a team or in other forms. The fact that many early childhood leaders report continuous bickering, quarrels, minor conflicts and ongoing tension suggests that their attempts to deal with the difficulties do not address the source of the issue, but rather deal with symptoms of other underlying, unacknowledged work-related problems.

Conflict in the workplace used to be regarded by employees and theorists alike as negative, counter-productive and to be avoided if possible. Only pessimistic and harmful outcomes were associated with conflict, with statements such as 'It will take some time for us to get back on our feet!' signifying the destructive outcome on work performance and 'Give her some time. She'll get over it!' illustrating the detrimental impact on team relationships. Discord and disharmony engendered by feelings of anger and competition were considered to stunt personal and professional development, weaken relationships, decrease flexibility and result in lowered levels of performance; consequently, conflict was regarded as unhealthy. Yet discord and disharmony, if handled sensitively and creatively, do not necessarily produce adverse outcomes for teams.

Fortunately, the role of conflict in the workplace is better understood now and, given the right situation and timing, discord, disharmony and conflict are viewed as having functional—even positive—aspects for teams. Because they provide an impetus for learning, growth, development and change, they are seen as inevitable and necessary aspects of team-building. Conflict signifies that there is life, energy and activity in a team and offers an opportunity for healthy learning. It can stimulate increased interest and curiosity, expose underlying tensions and unsatisfied needs, create new channels of communication and, if appropriately addressed, result in the resolution of issues, increased flexibility in performance and strengthened relationships. The ways in which discord, disharmony and conflict are addressed can turn perceived setbacks into positive learning experiences for everyone.

## Sources of conflict within early childhood services

In order to approach and address conflict positively and effectively, early childhood leaders need an understanding of the origin of the conflict—where and how it arose. The source of a conflict can provide guidelines for dealing with it appropriately. Most conflict stems from interpersonal differences, and usually signifies that one party feels threatened or specific needs are not being met—for example, the need to feel safe and secure, respected and valued or close and intimate. Communication skills form the basis of addressing conflict, but it is important to acknowledge that some conflicts in early childhood are a result of structural elements, and therefore will be difficult to resolve.

## Structural features

Certain structural features inherent in the physical environment of early childhood services can increase the likelihood of conflict occurring in comparison with other workplaces. First, early childhood educators work in small teams in separate rooms, making communication difficult. If educators form allegiances to their sub-groupings—for example, the babies' room, the toddlers' room or the pre-schoolers' room, team spirit can decrease. The fact that two or three educators work closely together in relative isolation from others can lead to misperceptions of favouritism by the leader, resentment about imagined benefits or privileges that educators in other sub-teams might receive and rumours about the leader's attitude to performance in the various teams.

Given that many early childhood services operate for almost twelve hours every weekday and that consumer demand requires even more flexible hours of operation, early childhood educators are required to undertake shiftwork. This also affects the ease of communication between them because there will be very few times when everybody is together (off the floor and free of responsibility) to discuss issues. Where information is passed on at second hand, there is a possibility of communication breakdown and misunderstanding, which can lead to conflict.

Staff breaks need to be rostered to meet the minimum supervisory requirements for young children. Consequently, there is not even a common lunchtime in which to communicate as a team. Add rostered days off and holidays to these constraints and it becomes obvious that many factors work against effective communication within the team and increase the likelihood of communication breakdown and conflict.

Time is an important issue in all early childhood services, and there is usually insufficient funding to employ relief workers to free individual educators to attend meetings or to communicate in their small teams outside allocated planning time. This means that anything additional such as staff meetings, professional development and training events or special planning meetings must be held in the evenings or at the weekend—that is, in educators' own time. Not everyone holds a concept of professionalism where it is an accepted expectation that some personal time will need to be devoted to work. Also, many educators have other responsibilities, such as their own family commitments or study. Consequently, not all are able to meet outside the opening hours of the service in order to share information. Those who can are usually on a tight time schedule and want meetings to be held as quickly as possible, which influences the depth of information-sharing and discussion that can be achieved.

Even within normal working hours, the potential for conflict due to communication failure is high. Early childhood educators have a responsibility for the safety and welfare of young children that entails constant and alert supervision at all times. Therefore, it is difficult to discuss an issue that arises during the day between two or three educators because they are not able to give it their full attention. Lack of attention to one educator's comment may be interpreted as lack of interest, selfishness or some other negative explanation about why the comment was not taken up and acted upon. The need to focus attention on the children means that sometimes educators will not have their own needs met and, instead of being appropriately assertive, they may become angry and initiate disharmony in the team.

The contact between families and educators in the dropping-off and picking-up routines can also be conducive to conflict where neither families nor educators stop to consider the needs of the other adult in the situation. Usually dropping off and picking up are hurried processes because all of the adults have other responsibilities to meet. Educators may feel disregarded, unappreciated and exploited by families who do not respond to their request to discuss a particular aspect of a child's progress, and later respond to the family in an off-hand or deprecatory manner. Educators may evaluate and label the family in stereotyped terms, and in future relate to them in terms of this stereotype. It may only take a few such experiences before an educator may generalise this prejudice to all families, which will produce very unsatisfactory relationships with families who use the service. Similarly, if an educator does not immediately respond to a family's request for attention, the family may evaluate them as insensitive, uncaring and unprofessional. These concerns may be discussed with other families or the leader, which may leave the educator feeling vulnerable, exposed and angry. The fact that neither families nor educators have appropriate time or physical surroundings to discuss concerns at dropping-off and picking-up times can lead to misunderstanding and conflict. The problems with finding alternative times outside normal supervisory duties and working hours have been highlighted already.

Early childhood educators need to be aware that the inherent structural features of services can create communication difficulties that can very easily flare into situations of conflict if they are not dealt with immediately and effectively. There may be very little that can be done about the team structure and the physical environment, but educators and families can be alerted to and aware of the potential difficulties that these factors can foster.

### Goals and policies

Successful teams are characterised by a set of achievable goals that are understood and accepted by all. The same can be said of roles and responsibilities that need to be undertaken within a service for its successful operation. For a range of reasons, some early childhood teams do not have the opportunity to be involved in the development of goals, policies and job descriptions, and many early childhood educators do not consider this area to be part of their responsibility. However, all services have some form of philosophy, statement of mission, aims and objectives, and policies that guide their operation. If generated by an individual leader and/or management committee, not every early childhood educator will agree with and accept such goals and policies.

Discord and conflict regarding goals and policies can be overt (where an educator or family openly disputes the validity of a certain policy) or covert (where the policy is superficially or tacitly accepted but is not supported or complied with in terms of action). Overt verbal or behavioural disagreement with goals or policies is easier to deal with because the conflict is obvious and there is a possibility of problem-solving. Covert disagreement can sabotage the implementation of goals and policies because people may deny verbally that there is a conflict and refuse to engage in discussion. The leader needs to be assertive about their concerns regarding the issue and encourage open problem-solving to help resolve it.

Unwritten laws that develop as part of the history of certain early childhood services can also provide grounds for conflict. Given the high turnover of staff in the sector, it is likely that some early childhood educators will have had experience with different ways of dealing with issues and of meeting staff needs. Confusion about the acceptability of certain practices—such as 'mental health' days and unwritten laws that are so-called 'common knowledge'—can provide a rich source of inequality, discrimination and conflict between leaders, educators and families. The potential for conflict arising in such situations can be minimised if as many aspects of policy as possible are explained to educators and perhaps families, and made accessible to public scrutiny.

The reason that conflict can spring from goals and policies is that they have a value basis. Part of the ethics of leadership requires that, in relation to conflict, early childhood leaders make decisions about and act on the basis of a clear personal and professional value system. Individual beliefs, values and perspectives that often have a strong emotional component can be very influential in early childhood service provision. Understanding that not everyone is likely to accept or agree with services, goals and policies is important. Providing opportunities for discussion, the sharing of perspectives and regular review can help avoid conflict in this area.

## Values

Many of the goals, policies and practices in early childhood services are based on ideologies and values. Value systems are individual and, although certain values may be held in common with other people, each of us develops a unique set of values that are used as guidelines or standards for decision-making and behaviour.

Particularly when it comes to young children and families, each of us holds strong personal, emotionally laden values that are used to make decisions about what we believe to be in the best interests of children.

The personal ideas, values and beliefs of early childhood educators can be as influential on practice as professional value systems, particularly for those new to the sector. It is not uncommon to find conflict between early childhood educators that is based on differing values systems and their relationship to practice in areas such as goals for children's behaviour, children's needs, group management, planning and organisation, resources, development and learning, children's characteristics, educational processes, educational play, evaluation and assessment and home and family background. Early childhood leaders should facilitate the clarification of value beliefs on practice and articulate the relevance of professional values while acknowledging the role of personal values in making decisions about children and families.

### Reflections on leadership in practice

When I was a coordinator of an inner-city childcare service, I had two educators in the toddler room who just would not cooperate in their work. Their fighting and disagreements over work practices and values were affecting the children and the other staff. I had talked to them together and separately several times but could not get them to resolve their differences. So I decided to invite a mediator, someone outside the service with skills in conflict resolution, to meet with them to see whether she could help them cooperate to work together. I was willing to invest funding in the mediation process because I didn't want to lose either of the educators but I couldn't allow the fighting to go on. They met with the mediator a number of times and, while I don't think there was complete resolution of their differences, they at least agreed to work more cooperatively together. I exercised leadership by recognising that I needed to get an expert in to help resolve this situation.

EARLY CHILDHOOD LECTURER

The values of the multicultural pluralist societies found in many countries today demand as much respect as dominant community values. The early childhood sector has long endorsed the right of children to have their culture of origin, its value system and customs affirmed, and has supported families' desires to have their children interact with adults from their own heritage while attending early childhood services. However, this is another area where the potential for conflict is high. The values of specific cultures and backgrounds sometimes are quite different from those of the general community and of the early childhood sector—for example, the status and privileges that are given to young male children compared with young female children in some cultures, and the lack of respect accorded to female educators by men from various backgrounds. Such differences can lead to conflict between educators from different cultural groups, and to conflict between educators and families. Appreciation of the ethics of leadership is important in guiding responses to conflicts that arise from different value systems.

### Leadership style

Although leadership style should not contribute to or exacerbate conflict, the level of conflict experienced in an early childhood service may be related to how leadership is enacted.

Leadership style is sometimes related to levels of maturity and experience of employees where, for example, younger and less experienced educators may be responsive to a more directive style that, if used with mature and experienced educators, could produce antagonism and conflict.

Early childhood leaders who have a tendency to be authoritarian may generate higher levels of conflict than leaders who are more democratic and encourage staff participation in decision-making about appropriate matters. This is because most adults, particularly mature and experienced adults, resent being told what to do and think by someone else who does not recognise their expertise. Immature and inexperienced educators who are looking for direction and guidance in the workplace initially may accept authoritarian leadership. However, as they develop in confidence, they usually want more involvement in matters that affect their work. Early childhood leaders who do not vary their style to match educators' needs for involvement may inadvertently stimulate resentment and potential rebellion.

Authoritarian early childhood leaders may assume responsibility for acting as a mediator in conflicts between various educators, and between educators and families, rather than facilitating the management of the conflict between the relevant parties. When the power hierarchy is invoked by either educators or families to resolve disputes, one or both parties may be left feeling dissatisfied that their claims to justice were not given appropriate consideration and that resolution was imposed from outside. While the immediate issue may appear to be resolved, any remaining underlying tension will re-emerge in another form or at another time. Early childhood educators need to understand that conflict has to be worked through by those parties immediately affected, with the leader demonstrating confidence that the parties themselves can cooperate to reach a mutually acceptable solution. Support can be offered by modelling appropriate communication skills and discussion of alternatives in problem-solving sessions.

Permissive, casual, 'anything goes' leadership does not avoid the issue of conflict. Early childhood leaders who do not provide direction and guidance, who accept poor-quality performance from educators, who do not provide constructive feedback and who do not communicate high expectations of educators and families can also generate tension, resentment and disagreement in the service. 'Anything goes' leadership communicates a lack of respect and regard for children, families, educators and early childhood services. Such disregard for the rights and needs of individuals, lack of tolerance and subjective prejudices cause conflict because there are few standards to act as guidelines for educators and families.

A democratic leader appreciates that conflict is a symptom of a breakdown in communication and interpersonal relationships, and will involve relevant people in a cooperative and egalitarian process of problem-solving. This collaborative style of leadership is likely to result in issues being addressed by those involved before they develop into larger problems. In this way, fewer problems are likely to develop into full-blown conflicts because they are dealt with as they arise. It is not the case that early childhood services which have leaders with democratic or collaborative styles of leadership are less conflict prone; rather, the conflicts are approached and addressed differently. Techniques for effective management of conflict are discussed later in this chapter.

### Job expectations and demands

One important aspect of leadership style is the degree of definition provided by early childhood leaders concerning job expectations and demands. Over-definition and leader domination of job expectations and demands can diminish educators' motivation and initiative. On the other hand, where roles and responsibilities have not clearly been defined and accepted as part of the team-building process, uncertainty and ambiguity about where responsibility lies can lead to disputes. Job expectations can be formed on the basis of previous experience, or can be derived from personal preference and presumptions. Expectations derived from such sources may not be appropriate for or relevant to the current situation. Therefore, it is essential that early childhood leaders provide opportunities for educators to clarify and negotiate who is responsible for what task or job.

Failure to articulate performance expectations can also lead to tension and eventually conflict, where educators can argue that 'I didn't know that you wanted it done that way!' or 'We didn't have to do it at the last place I worked! The coordinator always did it!' People often experience stress in situations where expectations and demands are not clear. Educators may deal with stress by becoming defensive and blaming the leader for not adequately informing them of what was required. Therefore, in order to avoid this source of conflict, perceptive early childhood leaders will ensure that all educators (and families if necessary) clearly understand what is expected from them.

### Employee distrust of authority

The ways in which leadership in early childhood is enacted and displayed or perceived and experienced—for example, the autocratic style—can suggest to educators that the leader does not have the best interest or the welfare of the team at heart. Uncertainty regarding the motivation of early childhood leaders for certain actions can arouse negative attitudes towards them, and result in a lack of cooperation from educators. For example, the introduction of appraisal by a leader who is not trusted may be perceived in negative terms, such as the leader wanting to terminate the employment of one or more educators, whereas the leader actually may want to introduce a professional development and training program based upon mutually agreed goals.

Where educators distrust early childhood leaders and their motivation, they are unlikely to support and participate in any initiatives they suggest. If conflict appears to stem from this source, early childhood leaders need to work on building the level of trust, ensuring that feedback is welcome and respected, and that educators have access to as much information as possible where policy and practical decision-making are involved. In addition, educators' participation in decision-making and problem-solving can help overcome any distrust of the leader.

### Inability to accept feedback

One of the characteristics of effective communicators, and therefore of effective early childhood leaders, is skill in delivering constructive feedback on employee performance. While many people understand feedback in terms of the negative aspect of criticism, the term 'feedback' also encompasses the positive aspect—that is, compliments and encouraging statements. The mistake many leaders make is to focus on the critical aspect and communicate personal blame to the individual for not accomplishing a desired or expected outcome.

The purpose of feedback is to improve, correct and change, never to embarrass, demean, humiliate or personally attack (Wooden and Jamison, 2009). Early childhood leaders cannot influence educators positively if their feedback annoys, irritates or alienates them.

Probably due to the many demands on their time and attention, few early childhood leaders consistently encourage educators by commenting on the aspects of the day that have gone well, their strengths and assets, their contribution to the service or the areas in which they have improved. For example, instead of saying 'You haven't included adequate information in your outdoor plans', the leader could say 'I can see that you've put a lot of effort into your planning this week. I'm a little concerned about the lack of detail for the outdoor experiences. Could we find a time to discuss the outdoor aspect?' Alternatively, the leader might make encouraging comments such as 'I notice that you've improved considerably in writing objectives for individual children', 'I really appreciated your contribution to the discussion on next week's plans at the meeting this morning' or 'Since you've been writing fuller plans, I've noticed that the day seems to be running more smoothly with your children'.

If early childhood leaders focus on the critical rather than the encouraging aspect of feedback, educators can learn only to expect a negative appraisal by leaders when the word 'feedback' is mentioned, and consequently may adopt defensive attitudes to any feedback. They may think that they need to defend themselves from the leader's expected and supposed attack on their competence with a justification about why they did what they did. In some ways, early childhood educators' inability to receive feedback is often a function of their previous negative experience with feedback and criticism from other leaders.

However, if early childhood leaders can phrase feedback in ways that do not arouse defensiveness in educators and that open channels for further communication, feedback can become a means of facilitating learning and professional development rather than a point of contention. Most early childhood educators would consider the following type of comment as helpful and acceptable: 'I noticed that you had set up a music experience which the children found very enjoyable. Can we get together to explore ways that you might extend Luca's participation? He seemed to be only peripherally involved.' Assisting early childhood educators to become familiar with constructive feedback by phrasing it in an understanding and supportive style can avoid arguments, especially where educators believe that the leader has little understanding of and empathy for their position.

The introduction of regular appraisal for both leaders and educators in early childhood services, where aspects of professional growth, learning and development are acknowledged and goals established for future improvement, is one way of assisting everyone to learn the role of feedback and how to accept and use it constructively.

### Sharing information

The importance of accurate and unambiguous communication (because of the potential for communication breakdown) is the foundation of the effective operation of early childhood services. The basis upon which information is shared—that is, who has access to what information—is another issue in this area. Information is power. Those who possess information relevant to a particular situation are in a better position to protect and provide for themselves, to make better decisions and to demonstrate competent performance. In other words, information empowers people, while a lack of information has the opposite effect.

The growth of multi-disciplinary teams and multi-agency services has drawn attention to the ethics of sharing information—that is, what information is shared with whom. Early childhood leaders and educators encounter many situations where ethical choices arise in terms of whether and to whom information is made available or withheld—for example, requests for information from social workers, psychologists, physical and speech therapists or Family Court counsellors, and access parents, as well as requests for information from other families about children who bite or hit. Some early childhood educators have reported feeling forced to make ethical choices about sharing information in the mandated reporting of suspected child abuse. Early childhood leaders and educators are required to bring sensitivity, discretion, professional expertise, judgement, values and ethics to such decisions. In human relationships, very few decisions are clear-cut, and many decisions can result in conflict and unintended harm if they have not been thought out fully. The use of a code of ethics for guiding decision-making in ambiguous situations is an important professional strategy, and is discussed in Chapter 13.

Effective and respected early childhood leaders collaborate with others. They are willing to share information openly and do not use the sharing and withholding of information as a means to wield power over others. This is important because much information comes directly to the formal leader, who then has sole responsibility for making decisions about to whom and how that information will be disseminated. Early childhood educators who believe that they are being kept uninformed or denied access to information essential for them to perform their roles and responsibilities may lose confidence in the leader, and perhaps ascribe negative motivation to such action.

Families believe that they have the right to available information concerning their child, and will quickly lose trust in those who do not provide them with what they regard as essential information. Sensitive early childhood leaders use discretion about the information provided to families simply because the majority of parents and carers are not trained to interpret accurately the kind of detailed observation that early childhood educators make. For example, a family might comment on how other children's drawings look more sophisticated than those of their child. Rather than going into details of possible developmental delay, the sensitive educator might respond in terms of the factors that influence children's art and focus on the strengths of their child's drawing skills. Another common situation is meeting a family's demand to know who bit their child. Biting is a very difficult behaviour to prevent, and educators may or may not know who the perpetrator was. However, it may be in the best interests of all concerned to withhold that information so that children are not labelled and ostracised by other families and to protect the biter's family from the possible emotional backlash of the victim's and other children's families. Reference to a professional code of ethics or standards of practice may provide guidelines for the responsible management of information.

Confidentiality is a key and sensitive issue in information-sharing. In meetings, early childhood educators might discuss a child's progress or problems that a family has shared about their child. One educator might seek assistance from the team to improve the learning opportunities designed for the child. Such professional discussions are beneficial for all—early childhood educators and children. However, the information and opinions shared in meetings must remain confidential and not be passed on to anyone else, particularly other families. It is imperative that children and their families are not discussed with anyone outside the service or in inappropriate venues, such as a corridor, supermarket, gym or shopping mall. Experience shows that families usually hear about such discussions 'on the grapevine', and justifiably can be most upset at this breach of trust. Early childhood leaders have the responsibility to ensure confidentiality to families and, by the same token, to educators if for any reason their performance needs to be discussed. Conflict about inappropriate information management can destroy basic trust between the leader, educators and families, and diminish the quality of service.

### Personality clashes

Conflict between early childhood educators has been explained and often dismissed by the use of the term 'personality clash', the implication being that the conflict was inevitable and could not be resolved because of the fixed nature of the different personalities involved. However, presumed personality differences are not sufficient to explain why conflict occurs in the first place, or why those involved continue it. The more logical explanation is that these educators have chosen not to co-operate and not to meet the needs of the workplace by negotiating a mutually acceptable solution to their differences. In addition, the fact that the conflict is public in nature and is able to continue in the workplace suggests that the service's psychological climate accepts, and perhaps even subtly encourages, interpersonal friction as a way of responding to incidents that arise when working with and for others.

Conflict that is continued by educators in the workplace can be very destructive to morale and family confidence in services, as well as displaying a poor model of human interaction and problem-solving for young children. The stereotype of 'personality clash' sometimes is used by those who have no intention of working to resolve their differences or who wish to absolve individuals of responsibility for the conflict. The final outcome of the disruption caused to early childhood services by educators who choose not to cooperate and get on with the job is that inevitably one of the protagonists becomes unemployed. This outcome may occur either because one educator chooses to resign (or both do so) or because the leader or employer decides that the adverse effects of continued conflict are affecting the quality of the service and terminates either one or both educators' employment.

### Prejudices and stereotypes

Some people—perhaps because of general personality tendencies—maintain their prejudices and stereotypes even when confronted with contrary evidence. In early childhood, where knowledge and understanding about young children and families is increasing in complexity, educators need to be adaptable and flexible, willing to embrace new ideas and practice as they become available. Professional relationships are grounded in communication and cannot function properly if some educators are psychologically bound by outdated assumptions and stereotypes. Prejudices and stereotypes rarely enhance interpersonal communication and relationships. Rather, they act to constrain, limit and diminish them, and sometimes can lead to unlawful action—for example, unlawful discrimination on the basis of gender, race or age.

Attitudes to children and understanding of appropriate early childhood practice have changed dramatically over time, and some attitudes and practices that were once accepted have become outdated, irrelevant, unlawful and inappropriate in today's society. For example, until the 1960s, physical punishment was believed to enhance obedience. Research now indicates that this is not true and it is illegal in some countries. In the same way, it used to be thought that tight authoritarian control over employees was necessary to ensure that they met their work commitments. However, it now is accepted that this attitude has a negative effect on many employees' commitment to, motivation for and initiative at work. Children of single-parent families once were considered to be inherently disadvantaged. It is now accepted that the quality of children's experience depends on a range of factors.

Insensitivity to the need to consider new developments in early childhood can promote conflict between educators who want to maintain policy and practice derived from theories and ideas that are now outmoded and those who wish to incorporate current and new knowledge, understandings and skills into their work. In the contemporary early childhood sector, keeping up to date with current theory and research is considered to be an ongoing professional obligation.

## Resistance to change

Change and its management is a core leadership responsibility, and will be discussed in detail in Chapter 10. However, it is important to recognise that employer and employee attitudes to change and subsequent resistance to change can be sources of conflict. Quality early childhood services are responsive to social, cultural, economic and political changes, among others. If either leaders or educators perceive change as a threat rather than an opportunity for growth, they may misdirect energy into resisting rather than anticipating and easing the implementation of change. This can produce tension and frustration on the part of those who understand the need to be responsive to change and can be a source of conflict.

Effective early childhood leaders understand that many people find change threatening, and that resistance to change is a normal human response. Nevertheless, leaders have to work to engender positive attitudes, in themselves and/or educators, and towards overcoming areas of resistance in constructive ways rather than permitting any uncertainty about change to escalate into a situation of conflict.

## Bullying and horizontal violence

Sadly, many early childhood services have witnessed the emergence of workplace cultures where bullying and horizontal violence are evident, and in some cases go unchecked (Hand, 2009). Given that early childhood has a reputation for an ethic of care and nurture, this is surprising. However, early childhood leaders need to be aware of the potential for bullying, harassment and oppressive behaviour because of the psychological harm it will inflict on individual educators, teams and the service itself. Leaders have a duty of care to employees and must ensure that psychological and physical safety is maintained in the workplace at all times by naming, confronting and addressing instances of such behaviour immediately.

Bullying usually is perpetrated by individuals who hold a degree of power, whereas horizontal violence more often is perpetrated by peers or co-workers. Both forms of intimidation involve displays of aggressive or hostile verbal or physical behaviour towards another member of staff or a small team within the larger staff group. Such forms of active and passive interpersonal and inter-group conflict were identified by Frière (1972) and later observed in nursing, another female-dominated profession (Duffy, 1995). Unfortunately, they have also been observed within the early childhood workforce.

Bullying and horizontal violence in early childhood services are associated with unequal power relationships, where certain educators think that they are more powerful than others. Early childhood services are characterised by staffing diversity, which means that some educators are bullied because they are different in some way—for example, inexperienced, older, disabled, male, culturally or socially different. The bullying or intimidation can take different forms, all of which aim to belittle or demean another person (Duffy, 1995). They can include:

- discouraging body language (rolling eyes, folding arms, staring into space, ignoring, indifference)
- demoralising verbal comments (sarcasm, humorous put-downs, gossiping, jokes, slurs and veiled insults based on difference, any form of humiliation), and
- unkind acts (rudeness, sabotage, unfair or hurtful criticism, scapegoating, marginalisation, exclusion from social activity).

Bullying, harassment and belittling behaviour have a devastating effect by crushing self-confidence and self-esteem, and increasing self-doubt, work-related stress and absenteeism. If unchecked, ultimately such behaviours will destroy the delivery of quality early childhood services.

The source of bullying and horizontal violence usually lies in a workplace culture where respect, trust, equality, inclusion, communication and conflict-resolution skills are absent, under-valued or not cultivated by the leader. In fact, they can occur only when leadership is weak, ineffectual and lacks courage. Early childhood is grounded in professional values where such behaviour can never be condoned or tolerated, and early childhood leaders must show courage to name, confront, discuss and address the sources of intimidating behaviour. Creating opportunities for the team to discuss the ways in which early childhood educators engage and interact with one another, and examining the motivation behind bullying and belittling behaviour, can help early childhood leaders to begin to tackle the problem (Hand, 2006). It is important for leaders not to let what initially could be a small problem grow into a large one before taking action. Constructive conflict-resolution skills such as assertion and problem-solving are helpful approaches to responding to bullying, harassment and horizontal violence.

There are many potential sources of conflict in early childhood services, and the preceding discussion has highlighted just a few. Other potential sources of conflict include differing salary scales, high staff turnover levels, staff appraisal, emergencies, the care/education dichotomy, an inability to implement policies and career progression (Ebbeck and Waniganayake, 2003). Effective early childhood leaders identify the likely sources of potential conflict in their service and assess whether any structural modifications could be made to reduce the potential for conflict. However, because conflict is inevitable and necessary for organisational growth, the next step is to address it constructively.

## Common responses to discord

There are a number of commonly used approaches to dealing with discord, disharmony and conflict that vary in their outcomes and degree of effectiveness. Unfortunately, the family appears to have been the training ground for many people; here, through observation and personal experience, ineffective and even destructive ways of addressing discord and conflict have been the norm. Unless people are particularly skilled in techniques for conflict management, the methods used by individuals in their personal relationships usually are inappropriate for professional relationships and situations. Effective leaders are aware of their own tendencies for addressing discord, disharmony and conflict, and evaluate their outcomes in terms of the service's goals, relationships and morale.

The following typical ways of dealing with discord, disharmony and conflict can be observed in early childhood services, but tend to have unproductive or negative outcomes for leaders and educators.

### Denial and withdrawal

A frequently observed response to conflict is to deny its existence. For example, the leader announces the new roster. Jana notices that she has another week of early shifts. Her tense body language and tone of voice communicate that she is unhappy with the new roster as she mutters to herself, 'How typical! I'm always given the worst shifts. She [the leader] must really dislike me!' Overhearing this complaint, the leader asks Jana whether she has a problem with the new roster. Jana is non-assertive about her problem and replies, 'No, nothing's wrong. Everything is just fine.' Then she walks away. This form of denial means that, even when an opportunity is presented to bring a potential problem up for discussion, there will be no movement towards acknowledging that there is a difference of opinion, defining what the difference is about or discussing possible alternatives. By denying that a problem exists, Jana has locked herself into a situation with which she is unhappy, and she will experience the problems associated with being non-assertive that were discussed in Chapter 5.

In this example, Jana has also walked away. She has withdrawn from the situation and her behaviour indicates that she is not willing to participate in any discussion that may arise out of the posting of the new roster. It is almost impossible to resolve a conflict if one of the parties withdraws by turning silent or by physically leaving the situation. Unless the other person is willing to be assertive and follow up the person who has withdrawn, it is unlikely that the issue will be resolved. The 'silent treatment' is manipulative and destructive to relationships as well as to productivity, and the unresolved tension that is sure to build up probably will be released in an explosive outburst where the problem may be exaggerated and other past issues brought up to illustrate the injustice that has been suffered.

Denial and withdrawal do not resolve discord, disharmony and conflict, but keep the dysfunctional tension buried just beneath the surface. The problem—which initially was small—is likely to re-emerge later in a different form or as a larger problem for the leader to deal with.

## Suppression and placating

In this approach to conflict management, the parties acknowledge that a conflict exists but devalue its importance or significance to them. Using the above example of the new roster, Jana could acknowledge that she was not happy with the shift arrangement but would proceed to suppress or deny her real feelings about the matter, saying something like, 'Well, I don't really want to do those early shifts again but it doesn't matter. I guess I'm used to them by now.' The leader could attempt to placate and smooth over the problem by commenting, 'It all works out in the long run, Jana. We all have to do our share of early shifts. I'll probably be on next time.'

Another way of suppressing and placating discord, disharmony and conflict is to minimise the degree of difference between the two parties. Educators who disagree about a discipline practice might comment, 'I know it's pretty much the same thing but I would have done it differently' or 'Basically we're coming from the same point of view. It's just that I would not have done it that way.'

The aim of suppression or placating is to smooth over and to move away from the problem as quickly as possible, thereby avoiding any potential for real exploration of the different perspectives. The outcome is that the two parties are no closer to understanding one another's perspective or to negotiating a mutually acceptable practice; however, both are likely to feel that their position is really the right position and they will continue with the practice that initiated the feelings of tension. The problem is likely to re-emerge at a later time or in a different form, and be more difficult to deal with because people have become entrenched in their positions. An opportunity to gain a different perspective, as well as for learning and professional growth, is lost when suppression and placating are used.

## Power and dominance

The use of power in conflict situations demonstrates a basic lack of respect for the other parties. Power can be wielded from one's position in the hierarchy—for example, by the leader as the legitimate authority; by the deputy with delegated authority; through team unity with the room staff standing against administration from the perspectives of longevity, seniority or possession of qualifications; or by essential ancillary staff such as the cook or cleaner, without whom it is impossible to meet minimum standards and requirements. Power also can be exerted by dominating conversations with a loud voice, by interrupting others and not letting them finish what they want to say, by crying and by using intimidating non-verbal communication. When power is asserted inappropriately in a conflict between professionals, it can turn into bullying or horizontal violence.

Taking the example of Jana and the new roster, Jana could exert power and dominance over the other educators by behaving in an angry and aggressive way, by confronting the leader and demanding that the roster be changed, by pressuring non-assertive educators to change shifts with her, by interrupting others and refusing to leave the leader's office until she got what she wanted, or by threatening to take the issue to a higher authority, such as the management committee, chair of governors or the union. While Jana's behaviour might achieve a change in the roster, it will be at the expense of respect from and relationships with others, and will also lower the quality of the service while educators deal with the other disruptions that accompany such aggressive outbursts.

The use of power to force others to submit or give way for the sake of peace and harmony can appear to result in the resolution of the problem, but also can create resentment, anger, bitterness and eventually rebellion or subtler forms of sabotage from team members. Power is an aggressive means of responding to conflict and, rather than resolving conflict, power and dominance are more likely to escalate discord, disharmony and conflict in the long term. While other educators might accept that one person can achieve their own ends in such a way, eventually they will feel exploited, perceive the leader as weak, and possibly interpret the organisational climate as one where power and dominance are accepted as the norm for moving towards one's goals. Instead of resolving one problem by permitting a display of power to be used to achieve certain ends, early childhood leaders may find that they have to deal with others who perceive this to be an effective form of conflict resolution.

## Constructive approaches to addressing conflict

There are a number of ways in which conflict can be addressed in early childhood services that are more likely to produce harmonious, positive and cooperative outcomes for all involved. The basic premise of conflict resolution is to open and maintain channels of effective communication so that both parties perceive themselves to be acknowledged and understood. Such courageous conversations require a balance between empathy and assertiveness.

Successful conflict resolution depends on the emotional awareness and intelligence of all parties—that is, the ability to recognise and control emotions and behaviour. However, if early childhood educators had developed strong emotional intelligence, many of the petty disputes would not have arisen in the first place. Encouraging everyone to develop and strengthen their emotional intelligence is a worthy preventive measure.

Given that conflict inevitably will arise, the following three-step framework of assertion, negotiation and problem-solving is simple and easy to implement for leaders of early childhood services.

## Assertion

When an incident is perceived as having the potential to develop into a conflict, the first important step is to recognise it as a problem that needs to be addressed. If the leader or any party involved in the incident can make an appropriately assertive statement that describes the behaviour, problem, performance, issue or action and associated feelings, this signals that one party has a different perception of the incident from that of other people. For example, when Jana read the new roster, she could have made an assertive statement to the leader, such as 'When I saw that I had been rostered on for another week of early shifts, I was upset because I have just finished doing a week of early shifts. I'd prefer to have a week of late shifts next week.'

The advantages of being assertive in this situation are that Jana has described the specific issue to which her concern is related, has vented her emotional reaction in an appropriate way, and has indicated a preference for addressing the situation in a way that will meet her needs. Other advantages are that Jana has directed her statement to the appropriate person—the leader who is responsible for the roster— and responded to the situation when it occurred, therefore avoiding a build-up of emotional tension and associated apprehension about confronting the leader. She has focused on the issue and not blamed or focused on the personality. The use of the 'I' statement indicates that she has taken responsibility for owning the problem. While being assertive cannot guarantee that Jana will be allocated the shifts that she wants, she has the satisfaction of having expressed her views and has attempted to have her needs met in an appropriate manner.

The following well-known assertive format can be useful in communicating a personal perspective.

| | |
|---|---|
| When . . . | (description of the action, issue, etc.) |
| I felt . . . | (description of the feeling or emotion) |
| because . . . | (explanation of importance or relevance) |
| I'd prefer . . . | (indication of an alternative) |

Using an assertive statement can assist in handling a range of disagreements and differences, and prevent them from building up into more major disputes. If the assertion does not achieve the desired outcome, a further assertion can be valuable which lets the other person know that you empathise with their position but still require a modification of the issue. A comment such as 'I can see your point of view but I'd still prefer . . .' can communicate an intention to pursue the matter further. While it may be necessary to repeat the assertion a number of times, there comes a point where it is necessary to recognise that this technique for resolving the issue is not working. A different strategy needs to be selected.

## Negotiation

If being assertive does not achieve a satisfactory resolution of the conflict, it is useful to move to a position of negotiation. In this step, the unsatisfactory nature of the situation is highlighted along with the motivation to achieve a mutually acceptable solution to the problem. This is important for situations where the aim is to both achieve goals and maintain harmonious relationships. It is essential to communicate a cooperative intention, highlighting the costs of continuing the conflict and the benefits of resolving the conflict.

When negotiating a conflict, planning and timing are important. A meeting to discuss the issue needs to be set for a time when both parties are free and there is sufficient time to work through the issue. The first step is to obtain a joint definition of the conflict that is precise and does not exaggerate the problem. Both parties need to be fully aware of and communicate understanding of the other person's perspective and feelings about the conflict. Argumentative approaches and threats should be avoided. Concrete outcomes or alternatives should be emphasised. When moving towards an agreement, it is essential that the agreement be mutually acceptable and not the desired outcome of the dominant party. In situations where there has been difficulty in achieving a negotiated agreement, it can be useful to spell out the ways the two parties will behave differently in the future, how any breach of the agreement will be dealt with and the way in which the two parties can check on how well the agreement is meeting both their needs.

Punctual return from tea breaks is an example of how a negotiated agreement can work. For example, Susan has been assertive with Peter, who consistently returns late from morning tea. She has asserted, 'When you return late from morning tea, I feel angry because the children are late in packing up and getting ready for lunch. I'd prefer it if you came back by 11 o'clock.' But this has not resolved the problem. Susan then moves to a position of negotiation, saying, 'I'm really concerned with how we are coping with the transition from morning routine into lunchtime. I'd like us to discuss it in our planning time on Wednesday.' In the planning session, Susan empathises with Peter's position—for example, 'I know it's a rush to get to the shop for what you need. There's no time left to have a cup of coffee. But I'm having trouble coping with all the things that have to be done to get the children and the room ready for lunch when you are not back on time. I can see that my stress is having an effect on our work. If we can sort this out, we'll both be more relaxed for our own lunch and the afternoon with the children. Have you got any ideas about what we might do?' If a negotiated agreement is reached, Peter will agree to be back at a certain time and will understand the consequences of breaking the agreement. Susan and Peter will also discuss the smooth transition from morning to lunchtime in their planning meetings.

## Problem-solving

In cases where one party refuses to negotiate an agreement about a conflict, or where a negotiated agreement does not work or breaks down, it is essential to move quickly to a problem-solving strategy. It is possible that the three steps—assertion, negotiation and problem-solving—are employed in the same interaction. However, a number of attempts at assertion and negotiation are often employed before moving to a problem-solving approach. An assertive communication style is appropriate when using problem-solving strategies where conflicts are defined as mutual problems to be solved.

When employing a problem-solving approach, the following steps are helpful:

- Clarify the problem: What is the real issue? Where does each party stand on the issue?
- Gather the necessary facts and information.
- Generate or develop a number of alternatives by brainstorming.
- Evaluate and set priorities for the alternatives in order to determine the best solution. Create solutions by considering all alternatives.
- Plan the best means of evaluating the most acceptable solution following a period of implementation.
- If the first solution chosen does not work (which can be a real possibility), return to the first step and begin the process again.

The problem-solving approach incorporates a collaborative perspective on conflicts. If one person has a problem, then we as a team have a problem. Blame is not apportioned. It acknowledges that all parties have the expertise to resolve problems that arise. It focuses on the intention to reach resolution rather than permitting the defence of particular positions. A problem-solving approach is a 'win–win' situation in which everyone's needs are respected and where people are invited to cooperate and contribute to the resolution of the issue. An attitude of 'we can work it out' communicated by the leader to the educators and families can stimulate new levels of trust, more supportive relationships and greater commitment to the team and the job.

To resolve differences and find solutions:

- use active listening
- look for and observe non-verbal cues and information
- help those involved to understand and define the problem
- allow feelings to be expressed
- find common ground
- look for alternative solutions
- encourage all parties to work out how they will cooperate to put an agreed solution in place, and
- expect and reward cooperative attitudes and behaviour.

## Mediation: From discord to accord

Many early childhood leaders recognise the value of mediation in moving from discord to accord or from conflict to cooperation. Mediation tends to be employed when negotiation and problem-solving break down.

Mediation involves working towards settling difference by inviting a third party, who has no vested interest in the situation, to bring those who are entangled in a seemingly unresolvable exchange to the discussion table in the spirit of collaboration and creativity. However, the leader can assume the role of mediator in some circumstances, demonstrating that working cooperatively as a team is a high priority and a worthwhile investment of their time and energy.

The mediator's role is to:

- facilitate communication
- promote understanding
- focus those involved on the specific matter being discussed
- encourage creative problem-solving, and
- help those involved cooperate to reach an agreed solution.

It is important that those in conflict are not pressured into mediation, but voluntarily agree to participate actively. Early childhood educators are more likely to agree to mediation if they understand its benefits, the difficulties associated with ongoing discord and unresolved conflict, the role of the impartial facilitator, the importance of having the courage to communicate honestly, openly and respectfully and the centrality of confidentiality in the process. Effective mediators offer objective feedback, focus attention on progress towards harmony, cooperation and accord, and facilitate the empowerment and self-esteem of the individuals involved.

Successful mediation usually requires a number of meetings, including an introductory session to determine the nature and depth of the problem, and a number of follow-up meetings that focus on listening to and appreciating different perspectives, identifying common ground and working towards an agreed and harmonious settlement.

When early childhood leaders accept a role in mediation, it is important to do so when team morale and work productivity appear to be threatened. Leaders set an example to others regarding ways of moving from discord to accord through cooperative and constructive conflict resolution.

Because it often necessitates the involvement of a skilled, impartial and paid facilitator, mediation tends to be used as a last resort when other approaches to addressing conflict have not been successful. However, it is an important tool in this sector, which seems prone to both petty and major conflict. Addressing conflict takes courage by early childhood leaders and educators but, when handled constructively, it increases self-esteem and confidence, builds cohesiveness and creates a problem-solving atmosphere that is so important to raising quality in early childhood services.

## Bringing it together

Effective early childhood leaders place great emphasis on developing their own skills for addressing conflict, and on encouraging educators to view conflict as normal and as an impetus for personal and professional growth. They implement recognised practices for handling disputes and encourage educators to assume responsibility for handling their own problems. In addition, they encourage a professional climate where colleagues are aware of and understand one another's expertise and where individual differences are valued. Early childhood leaders appreciate their ethical responsibility for addressing conflicts constructively and, together with educators, are aware of the role of conflict in team development (see Chapter 8) and the need to take responsibility for assisting a team's progress to more harmonious, cooperative and productive working relationships.

# CHAPTER 7

## LEADING DECISION-MAKING: TRANSFORMING VISION INTO ACTION

*Leaders are good decision-makers and feel empowered to speak out ...*
DIRECTOR, EARLY LEARNING CENTRE

### THIS CHAPTER EXPLORES

- decision-making as a critical leadership skill
- transforming vision into action
- thinking styles for decision-making
- types of leadership decision
- methods of decision-making
- professional ethics and decision-making
- guidelines for leading decision-making
- problem-solving

Decision-making is the crux of the leadership process, and the means by which leaders plan, organise and guide early childhood services towards accomplishing agreed goals. This core skill can be difficult for many early childhood leaders, particularly those who are new to the position and role. However, it is an extremely important skill for early childhood leaders because the decisions they make affect the lives of children, families, educators, the community and the early childhood sector.

Decision-making refers to making a choice between two or more alternatives, guided by professional standards, and is one step in the larger process of problem-solving. The quality of decision-making directly affects the quality of the service provided in terms of productivity and team morale, and is what separates an able leader from a mediocre one. Decision-making is effective to the extent that resources—including time—are fully employed and well-managed, the decision is of high quality, implementation is supported by relevant staff and the team's problem-solving ability is enhanced.

Decisions are a focus of daily activity in all early childhood services. While many day-to-day decisions are more mundane and routine—for example, arrange-ments for a social function—others are challenging, infrequent and involve complex decisions about vision, values, policies, goals, budgets, pedagogy, recruitment and selection, family engagement and ethical issues. In addition, working in multi-disciplinary teams and multi-agency services poses further challenges for decision-making. Here, team members must value and respect each other's contributions, communicate openly and honestly, refrain from being judgemental and avoid letting different perspectives and loyalties interfere with decision-making. Decisions should be guided by a shared vision on which all team members agree and to which they are committed.

## Transforming vision into action through decision-making

The most critical leadership role is to build and communicate a vision that early childhood educators and families endorse and support. Transforming a vision into action is a product of skilled decision-making that results in focused activity. A vision is a catalyst for action (Yaverbaum and Sherman, 2008), which brings together the decisions made about a group's shared aspirations, hopes, ideals, inspiration and motivation.

*Our vision is for early childhood to reach its potential.*
Gowrie South Australia

*A society where all children and families receive the best-quality care and learning that enables them to reach their full potential.*
National Day Nursery Association

*To create a community where all children and families are valued and thrive.*
Gowrie Western Australia

A vision represents the core understanding of the purpose of early childhood services and bodies. It is the communicated direction—the 'why we exist' or the 'big picture'—from which early childhood services are developed. Vision, mission and consequent policies, goals, objectives and targets are the infrastructure of early childhood services, and the means for transforming agreed values and principles into action or practice. They are created through the process of decision-making, a key leadership function.

Vision defines how early childhood services view the future—that is, what they want to be and why they are important. A vision is an inspirational product of clear and transparent decision-making. Creating a vision is a process of building under-standing about what needs to be done and why. A vision engages and connects people to something bigger and generally better, acting as a catalyst for bringing people and work together in order to achieve something that would not have happened otherwise. Vision statements vary in length, and some are considerably longer than the concise statements presented here.

*[W]e believe that childhood is a unique time of life to be valued and enjoyed in its own right ... it is a time where foundations are laid for future health, learning and well-being. We value children growing up with the understandings, skills and dispositions to be caring people and effective learners, able to contribute to the world and to enjoy rich and successful relationships with others.*
GOWRIE QUEENSLAND

*In every small community, there should be a service for young children under 5 and their families. This service should honour the needs of young children and celebrate their existence. It should also support families, however they are constituted within the community.*
PEN GREEN CENTRE, CORBY

Initiating a vision begins with deciding what values underpin leading practice. Values motivate, drive commitment and are empowering because they clarify principles, ensure engagement and set the parameters for decision-making. Values are shared beliefs and principles that drive every early childhood service's culture, structure and priorities. Values provide a framework for decision-making, and in early childhood they include respect, dignity, worth, diversity, fairness and justice for all. More specific values focus on child-initiated learning, active and experiential learning, and children as competent learners from birth, and include family, community, social and cultural values. Discussion and decisions about core values are essential first steps in the process of transforming a vision into action.

*We value leadership, advocacy for children and families, a culture of learning and respectful relationships.*
GOWRIE WESTERN AUSTRALIA

*The strong community culture fostered at Campus Kindergarten is built upon five core values: rights, trust, respect, compassion, responsibility.*
CAMPUS KINDERGARTEN, UNIVERSITY OF QUEENSLAND

*[The centre] ... upholds the following values—quality, reciprocal relationships, community participation, respecting differences, integrity and accountability, innovation, collaboration, leadership.*
GOWRIE TASMANIA

Many early childhood services write a mission statement that communicates the leadership philosophy—that is, the means to be used to activate the vision. A mission statement describes the decisions made about what the service wants to accomplish and how it intends to go about that process.

*Our Mission: To lead and model the way in the provision of childcare, advocacy and support services for Western Australian children.*
THE GOWRIE WESTERN AUSTRALIA

*Mission ... [we] will advocate to ensure quality, social justice and equity in all issues relating to the education and care of children from birth to eight years.*
EARLY CHILDHOOD AUSTRALIA

*[Our mission is] to support the delivery of best-quality care and early learning for children across the UK.*
NATIONAL ASSOCIATION OF DAY NURSERIES

Very simply, a mission is a considered plan of action for reaching goals. The mission defines the fundamental purpose of the service, describing why it exists and what it does to realise its vision. It usually defines customers, clients and critical processes. Other examples of concise mission statements are:

*A national collaborative approach to better practices which benefit children, families and the children's services sector.*
THE GOWRIE AUSTRALIA (SEE GOWRIE VICTORIA)

*[T]o build a diverse community of advocates and educators to promote and defend the rights of children, families and teachers of all cultures through a collaboration of colleagues inspired by the Reggio Emilia philosophy.*
NORTH AMERICAN REGGIO EMILIA ALLIANCE

Once decisions have been made about the mission statement, policies—that is, a set of coherent guidelines, systems and approaches—can be determined using strategic thinking and decision-making. Policies support the fulfilment of the vision and leadership philosophy. Policy development requires skilled decision-making because it is the process through which early childhood services deliver consistent quality practice and desired outcomes. Policies are decisions that inform and guide daily practice (Children's Services Central, 2011), and therefore need to be decided on and agreed by all those they affect.

A policy outlines a rational approach to thinking and decisions about what early childhood services want to achieve, as well as the goals, objectives, targets, strategies and resources needed to do that. A policy can be a stated intention, an action, an administrative practice or an indication of a course of action that is adopted and endorsed formally (Baldock, Fitzgerald and Kay, 2009). Policies may include statements of values and broad objectives, and belong to a specific agency that commits to a particular approach or course of action. In simple terms, policies detail specific ways of dealing with specific issues—for example, healthy eating, family engagement, bullying, behaviour management, recruitment and selection, induction and training, health and safety, discrimination, equity and diversity.

When key policies are in place, decisions about specific goals can be made. Goals are the long-, medium- and short-term aims that an early childhood service wants to achieve. Goals specify how a service intends to go about achieving its mission. Success is measured by the progress towards goals.

*. . . to improve professional practice and working conditions in early childhood education.*
NATIONAL ASSOCIATION FOR THE EDUCATION OF YOUNG CHILDREN

*[O]ur goal is clear—to promote quality in early years care and education for the benefit of children, their families and the local community.*
NATIONAL DAY NURSERY ASSOCIATION

Sometimes individuals have different, and often conflicting, goals. As a result, the goals that actually are pursued (informal goals) may be different from the officially stated and formal goals. Informal goals may be inferred from the actual decisions made and actions taken within a service. Early childhood leaders and educators may have their personal goals—for example, to earn higher wages, to achieve promotion, to gain social satisfaction, to achieve status by supporting the activities of the service. If service and personal goals pull in different directions, conflict will arise and performance is likely to suffer. An early childhood service is more effective when personal goals are compatible with organisational goals.

From the goals, explicit objectives can be identified. Objectives are decisions regarding specific planning about how to make things happen.

*[The objective is] to provide professional development opportunities and resources for those who work for and with young children.*
NATIONAL ASSOCIATION FOR THE EDUCATION OF YOUNG CHILDREN

Objectives are small steps towards achieving larger goals, and are often described as SMART—that is, **S**pecific, **M**easurable, **A**chievable, **R**elevant and **T**imed (Hunsaker and Hunsaker, 2009).

Targets are a means of managing performance by selected desired and agreed levels of performance. They define concrete achievements required by the service and staff and may specify minimum performance, define aspirations for improvement or help prioritise team activity by focusing attention, energy and resources. Targets are motivators and help develop a culture of lifelong learning.

Strategies are the tactical tools (e.g. thinking, decisions and actions) chosen to achieve ends, for example, goals and/or to as a means to an end, for example, as a policy. They are rules and guidelines by which the mission and objectives can be achieved. They usually relate to key areas, for example, teaching, advocacy, marketing, media and recruitment. A SWOT analysis can help identify possible strategies by building on **S**trengths, resolving **W**eaknesses, exploiting **O**pportunities and avoiding **T**hreats.

The last step for ensuring that vision is transformed into action is to decide how to monitor and evaluate progress towards objectives, goals and targets. Monitoring involves the systematic collection, analysis and use of information to learn from experience, to account for the resources used and the results obtained, and to make future decisions. Evaluation involves the systematic and objective assessment of an ongoing or completed project or policy to make judgements about relevance, effectiveness, efficiency, impact and sustainability. Such information can determine whether any changes need to be made and what they are—for example, what went well and where there is room for improvement. Evaluation reviews the implementation of policy and, based on objectives, targets and resources and identifies what has been learned and what changes need to be incorporated for future decision-making in terms of results (for example, strengthened capacity of a service), effects (such as improved services) and impact (for instance, improved standards).

Decision-making ability is grounded in and guided by shared values and a common vision. Being able to make good decisions and having the confidence to choose among different decision-making methods, especially in changing times, enhances early childhood leaders' credibility and integrity with the team.

## Thinking styles for leadership decisions

In recent times, leaders have been encouraged to make rational, cognitive and objective decisions rather than be influenced by more emotional and subjective elements. However, insightful decisions usually involve a combination of reason and emotion, fact and feeling, objectivity and intuition. New understandings about the brain—particularly the influence of emotions on perception, thinking, memory and problem-solving—have provided insight into decision-making processes. In addition, new approaches to thinking styles (de Bono, 2004; Maxwell, 2011b) have contributed to leaders adopting more flexible problem-solving strategies.

Decision-making is the product of thought processes used to select the most appropriate choice from among the available options. Maxwell (2011b) proposes that flexible thinkers draw on their vision and values as guides for decision-making in order to select the best thinking strategy for solving specific problems. Becoming a flexible thinker involves applying specific skills to achieve specific purposes—for example:

- *big-picture thinking*—for vision, mission, empathy, innovation, change
- *focused thinking*—for clarity, decisions, goals and targets, application, impact
- *creative thinking*—for imagination, inventiveness, novelty, challenge, fun
- *realistic thinking*—for credibility, problem-solving, learning from mistakes
- *strategic thinking*—for discipline, planning, processes, certainty
- *possibility thinking*—for the unknown, creating new opportunities, motivation
- *reflective thinking*—for perspective, direction, connections, learning, clarity
- *unpopular thinking*—for questioning, confronting outdated ideas and limits
- *shared thinking*—for synergy, commitment, partnership, collaboration
- *unselfish thinking*—for altruism, ethics, values, fulfilment, and
- *bottom-line thinking*—for decisions, success in terms of purpose and results.

Such thinking skills challenge leaders to engage in agile, visionary, lateral, creative and imaginative thinking in order to come up with new ideas, unusual or unexpected possibilities, connections and solutions. Access to different ways of thinking allows early childhood leaders to see the 'big picture', to experiment, to take informed risks and to try out new strategies. If early childhood leaders have the courage to be flexible in their thinking and to encourage educators to do likewise, they will profit from the team's ideas and innovations. Flexible thinking strategies contribute to better quality decision-making and differentiate effective from poor decision-makers.

However, while flexible thinking is important, it should not be at the expense of 'joined-up', cohesive and integrated thinking. Early childhood educators must view the leader's thinking strategies as accessible, understandable and coherent so that they find them easy to commit to and support, and are comfortable implementing decisions. Flexible thinking must be smart thinking that ensures decisions are congruent with the service's values, vision, goals and policies.

Although many leaders argue that they use a rational approach to decision-making, involving gathering the relevant information and making an informed choice, some problems in early childhood services do not lend themselves easily to rational decision-making—for example, behaviour management, ethical choices and staffing decisions. Factors such as lack of knowledge, time pressures, service structure or strong emotions often affect the ability to be rational.

Goleman (1996) argues that decision-making is easily flawed when emotions are not used intelligently. He points out that emotions can disrupt thinking—for example, in stressful situations we sometimes say that 'we can't think straight'. The inability to deal with strong emotions can impair decision-making about even mundane matters.

Faulty logic, a lack of analytical skills and abilities, and permitting emotional issues to cloud the situation can produce poor-quality decisions. A number of national early childhood professional bodies have developed codes of ethics that are designed as reference points to assist early childhood leaders and educators in making some of the more complex and difficult decisions. These resources that help guide ethical, rational decision-making continue to be under-valued and under-used by many in the sector.

## Types of leadership decisions

Early childhood leaders are responsible and accountable for the majority of the decisions required for the efficient operation of early childhood services, but judgements can be made in a variety of ways. The decisions may be routine, problem-solving or innovative in nature. The method of decision-making chosen by the leader will be influenced by the nature of the decision to be made, who is included in the decision-making process, the extent to which those affected by the decision accept it, and the level of support given to implementation. It also is linked to the personal characteristics and style of early childhood leaders, the characteristics of the team and the contextual factors. It is the quality of decision-making that distinguishes competent from mediocre leaders.

Decisions can be classified into two general categories: programmed decisions and non-programmed decisions:

- *Programmed decisions* are appropriate for routine, regularly occurring incidents and previously encountered situations, and minimise the need for the decision-maker to exercise discretion. Here, an approach that has been found to be successful in previous situations is applied. It is very much a case of 'if this happens, do that'. For example, if a family does not arrive to collect their child on time, the situation calls for a programmed decision because the decision-maker will follow policy and do what others would have done in the same situation. All early childhood educators make programmed decisions based on policies and previous experience every day. Pre-service and post-initial training provide a repertoire of programmed responses that can be applied to routine and frequently occurring situations. These manifest as goals and objectives, standards, policies and procedures.

- *Non-programmed decisions* are used in relatively novel, ambiguous, unstructured, spontaneous and infrequent incidents and circumstances for which policies and procedures may not exist. A more general problem-solving approach is required to customise the solution for the specific situation. The creation of a vision and mission, selection of a deputy or team leader and curriculum development are non-programmed decisions. Non-programmed decisions are based on flexible thinking, sound judgement, intuition and creativity, and consequently necessitate competent decision-makers. It is more likely that early childhood leaders compared with educators have specific responsibility for making non-programmed decisions. In early childhood services, where administrative responsibility for children, families and employees is less routine, more ambiguous and less amenable to programmed decisions, early childhood leaders will need to gain skills in effective decision-making.

Decisions can be based on intuition, judgement and/or problem-solving:

- *Intuitive decisions* are based on feelings and emotions rather than rationality or logic. Although some objective information is used to guide the decision, hunches, intuition and feelings are uppermost in influencing the leader to 'feel right' about the decision, regardless of information or advice to the contrary. Experienced early childhood leaders might come to high-quality decisions using the intuitive approach, but the disadvantages of being swayed by one's ego, lack of perspective and devaluing important information may lead to inappropriate decisions that may be difficult to explain or defend. Intuitive decision-making might be employed in the appointment of an educator where, qualifications and experience being equal among applicants, the leader simply has 'a gut feeling' that a particular applicant would fit in better with the existing staff team. In dealing with a particularly vulnerable family, the leader might intuitively feel that sharing information about their child's lack of progress would be detrimental to the family's well-being and decide to withhold the information for the time being.

## Reflections on leadership in practice

In my experience, leadership was displayed when a new manager was employed and quickly redecorated the nursery, changing it from how it had been for many years into a brighter place to work. She made the decision, told us what was going to happen and then followed through. That decision totally changed the atmosphere into one that seemed lighter and more energetic. We loved coming to work because it felt like a good place to be.

CHILDCARE WORKER

- *Judgemental decisions* are based upon expert knowledge and experience, where the early childhood leader can predict accurately the outcome of a particular course of action or decision. The leader's technical expertise means that little time is needed to reflect upon the decision because the problem has been encountered and successfully handled before. Quick judgements may be accurate, but there will be situations where basic assumptions or underlying conditions have changed and are no longer relevant. Judgemental decisions might be appropriate for ensuring that the service complies with the local regulations, deciding which educators will be allocated to a particular group of children or deciding on the best course of emergency medical treatment for a child whose family cannot be contacted.
- *Problem-solving* is a rational, thoughtful approach to decision-making where systematic, objective steps are undertaken in order to solve complex or previously unencountered problems for which there may be several possible solutions. It is useful for situations where more information is needed and where time is required to study, analyse and reflect upon the problem. Preventative decision-making is also included under the problem-solving approach where the leader looks ahead and, on the basis of existing information and conditions, anticipates what might occur.

The information available to early childhood leaders is a critical issue. Being flooded with information can delay the problem-solving process.

Poor-quality or irrelevant information will produce low-quality decisions. The amount of information accessed by the leader is not relevant; what matters is how central the information is to the decision to be made. Problem-solving as an approach for decision-making is appropriate for any major change, such as enrolment policy, curriculum development, hours of operation, staff changes or responding to complaints from families.

These types of decision highlight another aspect of decision-making: the relative effectiveness of the individual versus the group. While shared decision-making may promote a sense of ownership, it can be detrimental if it is inappropriate to the nature of the decision. Also, the quality of the outcome of individual leader-led decisions depends on their acceptability to the team—that is, the extent to which others will support and implement them.

Educators and families may accept the use of both the intuitive and judgemental approaches to decision-making on the basis of the early childhood leader's expertise. However, if the decision proves to be inappropriate or poor, the leader will be the focus of their dissatisfaction, resentment and diminished morale. The problem-solving approach may be undertaken by one individual but, given the nature of the situation and the time required to gather, analyse and evaluate information and develop possible solutions, the sharing of the responsibility for this process among the team is likely to result in higher quality and faster decision-making. Early childhood educators are cautioned about the over-use of intuitive and judgemental approaches because of certain limitations that are inherent in such approaches. These limitations are discussed in Chapter 11 as part of a fuller discussion about sources of information for decision-making. Familiarity with the range of available sources of information, other than intuition and judgement, is essential because it offers opportunity to create a better match between the problem to be solved and the decision-making method employed in order to come up with the most appropriate solution.

## Methods of decision-making

Johnson and Johnson (2008) outline a number of decision-making methods that vary according to individual and team input. In some circumstances, decisions made by teams can be superior to those made by individuals. However, they are rarely better than the best decision-maker in the team. They consume more resources, including time; therefore, any improved effectiveness in team decision-making must be counterbalanced against poorer efficiency. Finally, the type of situation, as well as the interpersonal relationships in the team, can impact on the quality of team decision-making.

The major decision-making methods involving individual and team input are outlined below.

### Individual decision-making by formal leader

Here, the leader makes the decision independently. This may not be the preferred style or choice of the leader, but may be adopted because of team apathy or the team's stereotyped beliefs about the degree of expertise, power and responsibility held by the leader. Many early childhood leaders report that they are expected to make most of the decisions because they are the formal leaders. Some educators do not participate in decision-making, relying instead on the leader, because they don't see it as their role or responsibility. This can lead to a lack of team commitment to the implementation of the decision, disagreement, resentment and hostility about lack of involvement in the decision-making process and under-utilisation of team resources.

It is not uncommon for educators and/or families to go along with the early childhood leader's decisions until an unpopular decision is made. This can generate overt or subtle conflict between those affected by the decision. Individual decision-making is appropriate in circumstances where the team may lack the skill to make the decision and where there is insufficient time to involve relevant members.

### Individual decision-making by designated expert

Here, an individual team member is acknowledged as an expert in a particular area and given the authority to make the decision by the formal leader. Appropriate use of this method is the delegation of the purchase of musical equipment to the team member who is most qualified and experienced in music. High-quality decision-making by individuals is associated with their expertise in specific areas. However, if it is essential for all to accept the decision, then having others participate in the decision-making process is logical. Apart from having the advantage of using the resources of the team, the advantages and disadvantages of this method are the same as those for decision-making by formal leaders.

### Decision by averaging the opinions of individuals

Here, team members may be consulted individually or at a meeting to find out what each person thinks. The final decision is based on the most popular choice or alternative identified by those consulted. For example, determining the most popular topic for a speaker at the annual general meeting could be undertaken using this method. However, this approach can produce a lack of team discussion and interaction with any unresolved conflict impacting on future group decision-making. It is possible that non-assertive educators will voice what they think the early childhood leader wants to hear or what they believe will obtain personal approval rather than what they really think.

This approach is useful when an urgent decision has to be made, when it is difficult to get the team together for a meeting (as with shiftwork and rosters, or geographical distances between staff in multi-agency services), when team or family commitment is necessary to implement a decision effectively, or when the team lacks the harmony, motivation or skills to make the decision in any other way.

### Decision by leader following group discussion
Here, the team is offered the opportunity to discuss the situation, but the early childhood leader reserves the right to make the final decision. In this method, the team is consulted by the leader and has the opportunity to provide input, but has no responsibility for the final decision. This method is appropriate for consulting with the team about the funding submission or details to be included in the annual report.

The level of discussion is an important factor in this method, with the leader needing to employ sophisticated communication skills to ensure active listening and facilitate open, respectful and honest discussion. This method benefits from team discussion, but the disadvantages associated with decisions by averaging individuals' opinions can influence the quality of the decision ultimately taken.

### Decision by minority
Here, the early childhood leader delegates the decision to the team or to a small committee comprising individuals with appropriate knowledge and skills who will consider the issue, take a decision and report back to the staff. This method can be useful for a routine decision, a problem-solving decision where not everybody needs to be involved in the process or a decision where only a few educators have the relevant resources. For example, a small group of educators and/or families could organise a service-based training event, an end-of-year function or the production of an induction handbook. Again, because of the lack of involvement of the wider team, the disadvantages inherent in the previous methods of decision-making also apply here.

### Decision by majority vote
Following a period of team discussion, a vote is taken either publicly or anonymously, and the alternative favoured by the majority is accepted. This is a common decision-making method in early childhood services, and has the advantages of permitting discussion and interaction, as well as using the resources of the team. Many routine decisions—for example, the purchase of resources, the choice of a particular speaker for a professional development or training event, and problem-solving decisions

such as the establishment of dispute and grievance procedures—can be made by majority vote following discussion. Again, the productivity of the discussion will be dependent on the communication skills of the person chairing or facilitating it. Indeed, the end result could be achieved without full participation of all team members, with those who are non-assertive being overpowered by the more vocal members. It is also possible to alienate the minority, whose needs and interests may be denied in the final decision, with the result being lack of commitment to implementing the decision. Decision by majority vote can be subject to lobbying by those individuals with vested interests in certain decisions that may not be in the best interest of the team or service.

### Decision by consensus

This method is considered by many to be the most effective means of decision-making, producing innovative, creative and high-quality decisions. In this method, the issues are discussed thoroughly, with each team member participating fully until a basic agreement that is acceptable to everyone involved is reached. The decision has been the responsibility of all members, who then each become partially accountable for its effective implementation. The development of a vision, goals, philosophy, general curriculum guidelines and discipline statements can be achieved using this method.

The advantages of the consensus method include full use of the team's resources, full commitment to the implementation of solutions to serious and complex problems and enhanced confidence in future decision-making by the team.

The disadvantages of this method are that it can be very time-consuming for a team to arrive at consensus; it requires a high level of motivation and psychological energy; and it is inappropriate for emergency, pressure or high-stress contexts.

Leaders who chose to delegate, share or distribute decision-making to and with team members also encourage and increase their self-confidence and empower them to make valuable contributions to a team. Early childhood educators who are committed to a shared vision and mission use strong values, beliefs and principles to guide their decision-making. They do not have to rely on the leader for direction; their values, vision and mission keep them focused so that they make ethical and sound decisions.

### Groupthink: Consensus through conformity

Groupthink refers to a mode of reasoning in which individual team members engage when their desire for consensus overrides their ability to assess a problem realistically or to consider a wide range of possible alternative courses of action. Critical thinking is sacrificed for consensus and a sense of unanimity. In groupthink, people refrain from offering opinions that do not appear to favour the thinking of the majority of the team and articulate views that are perceived to be in line with its direction. The result is a low-quality decision that often diminishes a team's confidence in its ability to produce innovative, creative, problem-solving decisions.

Effective early childhood leaders are aware that leadership style can impact on quality decision-making. Those who use a directive style and who push their own opinion strongly tend to inhibit exploration and the expression of opposing opinion. However, leaders who directly encourage participation by team members who are reserved and reticent, and who also curb the contribution of more dominant team members, appear to empower higher quality decision-making.

To avoid 'groupthink', leaders could adopt an initial stand of impartiality, assign someone to act as devil's advocate, develop alternative scenarios, re-examine previously discarded options, and hold second-chance meetings for everyone to express residual doubts and concerns. In this way, decision by consensus is more likely to reflect real consensus rather than the pressures of groupthink.

### Limitations of individual decision-making

While group decision-making has its disadvantages, there are a number of limitations to individual decision-making that early childhood leaders should consider.

First, some early childhood leaders tend to put off decision-making until it is too late for effective action. Hence the opportunity is lost or the problem has become so big that it is not easily solved.

Second, some leaders time decision-making so that, while not acting too late, no significant progress can be achieved. Equilibrium is maintained and the service is kept on track, but change and innovation are discouraged.

Leaders need to be skilled in timing, judgement, considered and informed risk-taking and the use of information to make quality decisions. Leaders who are informed and considered risk-takers are likely to make more effective decisions because they think about the prevailing circumstances at the time the decision has to be taken, assess the degree of urgency or the risk factor necessitating the decision and use the amount, type and quality of the information available at the time. They are flexible thinkers.

Early childhood leaders need to assess their personal tendencies, and gain training and experience in decision-making so their judgement, timeliness and skills of critical analysis can be nurtured. Confidence to make decisions and take acceptable risks is enhanced with training and experience. Until a degree of skill is obtained in decision-making, early childhood leaders should consider the benefits of team decision-making.

The issue of field-dependent versus field-independent cognitive processing styles can affect the quality of decisions made. Field-independent individuals tend to employ their own internal standards and values as sources to guide them in processing information—that is, they can separate and abstract objects from the surrounding field and use flexible thinking skills to solve problems that are presented in reorganised or different contexts. Field-dependent individuals, on the other hand, tend to focus on external points of reference and rely on authority to provide guidelines for information processing.

The attributes of field dependence are related to the formation of empathetic relationships with others—the ethic of care and respectful interaction with children and families and educators. However, the more analytical attributes of field independence are related to the cognitive flexibility necessary for quality decision-making and problem-solving. While most human beings possess some of the characteristics of both styles of information processing, leaders of early childhood services need to strengthen field independence to enhance their professional performance in this key leadership responsibility.

## Professional ethics and decision-making

Leadership involves making decisions that are sound because they are grounded in ethics as well as practice. Early childhood educators are continually confronted by choices about purpose, meaning, relationships and practices, which means that they make decisions that are ethical in nature (Cameron and Moss, 2011). Effective leaders explicitly apply ethical principles in decision-making and encourage team members to do likewise. Being an ethical leader is discussed more fully in Chapter 13. However, the relevance of a code of ethics to guide professional decision-making needs to be highlighted for early childhood educators, given their autonomy to exercise considerable discretion about how they interact with clients and consumers of their service, as well as how they operate and conduct that service.

A professional code of ethics offers a protocol for critical reflection about relationships and practice. It is a reference point for professional behaviour and provides guidance for making appropriate and valid decisions when ethical concerns are identified. A code of ethics can provide guiding principles for decision-making about obligations and responsibilities in daily practice. It can make decision-making easier because it provides a basis for action that is less likely to be challenged by those inside and outside early childhood, and it can play an important role in the establishment and maintenance of standards.

Existing codes of ethics offer guidelines concerning what early childhood educators are committed to provide in terms of quality services for young children and their families. While current codes do not provide prescriptive or 'right' answers to the complex questions, choices and ethical dilemmas faced in early childhood service provision, they do offer guidance for decisions about what is right and good, rather than expedient and simply practical, and point to attitudes and behaviours that are forbidden and should never be engaged in or condoned. As such, reference to a code of ethics can help expedite both day-to-day and long-term decision-making regarding what responsible early childhood educators should and should not do.

## Guidelines for leading decision-making

The following guidelines can be used by novice and experienced decision-makers alike, whether they are early childhood leaders, educators or teams, to improve the quality of decisions:

1. *Ascertain the need for a decision by defining the situation, problem or goal.* Does an unsatisfactory situation exist? Is there disparity between what is and what should be? For whom is the situation unacceptable? Is the situation a symptom of another underlying problem? What, if any, are the hidden agendas? In defining the situation, effective leaders attempt to gather the facts and feelings as close to the reality of the situation as possible.

2. *Establish the decision criteria.* Identify the characteristics that appear to be important in making the decision, collect and study the relevant opinions, facts and information, allocate weight to the criteria in order to develop priorities in the decision criteria, and know which criteria are central and which are peripheral to the decision.

3. *Develop alternative solutions and formulate choices.* Identify all available alternatives and avoid evaluation at this stage. The leader is responsible for exploring all existing possibilities to ensure a fair and intelligent decision, and to refrain from formulating preferences and expectations as alternatives are uncovered.

4. *Evaluate the alternatives in terms of their likely results.* The strengths and limitations of each option should be compared with the relative weightings established in step 2. Questions such as when, where, how, with whom and what the likely results may be need to be answered for each alternative. Feelings about each option need to be considered now because they can bias and alter rational reasons for particular choices.

5. *Select the best alternative.* Choose the solution that appears to be the most appropriate and that makes the most sense. Don't procrastinate and postpone the decision. Note that the 'best' alternative at the time is still a subjective choice and might turn out to be inappropriate later because,

despite the systematic and objective efforts of the leader and team, a poor or wrong choice can be made.

6. *Follow through to support the implementation of the decision.* Provide personal support to those who will implement and maintain the decision. Stimulate interest and enthusiasm in the process, ensure backup and sufficient time for implementation, and communicate shared responsibility and accountability for the success of the decision.

7. *Evaluate the effectiveness of the decision in resolving the initial problem.* Be flexible and keep an open mind in case the first choice was inappropriate. Be willing to modify the initial decision or engage in the decision-making process again using the present information to reach a new alternative.

## Problem-solving

In the more general process of problem-solving, the same steps are employed. Problem-solving is useful when elements of discord, disharmony or conflict exist in the situation. The situation can be defined as a mutual problem to be solved rather than a win–lose circumstance. Because discord, disharmony and conflict trigger emotional responses, it is important to channel the emotional energy towards constructive and harmonious ends by adopting appropriate win–win attitudes. Therefore, it is beneficial to focus on the positive results associated with the process of arriving at a solution. The team members need to have developed a positive attitude to discord, disharmony and conflict so that they are regarded as a healthy and normal part of work and life, and they need to be willing to communicate respectfully, honestly and openly with each other concerning the issue. Conflict resolution is discussed in detail in Chapter 6.

## Bringing it together

The challenge of leadership in early childhood is for aspiring and existing leaders and educators to develop vision and personal confidence in order to make professional, efficient and ethical decisions that advance the service towards achieving its goals while maintaining a sense of cooperation, loyalty and harmony. Early childhood leaders should focus attention on the shared vision and the 'big picture', and avoid becoming preoccupied with day-to-day details. Skill in non-programmed decision-making should be strengthened where flexible thinking, sound judgement, intuition and calculated risk-taking produce flexible and creative approaches to goal attainment, situations, issues and problems that emerge in any early childhood service.

# CHAPTER 8

# LEADING COLLABORATIVELY: CULTIVATING COLLECTIVE RESPONSIBILITY

*Good leaders build teams by making everyone feel that their contribution matters . . .*

EARLY EDUCATION TEAM LEADER

## THIS CHAPTER EXPLORES

- collaborating to achieve quality
- working as a collaborative team in a service
- working in multi-disciplinary teams
- working in multi-agency services
- the benefits of professional diversity in teams
- the processes and stages of team development
- collaborative leadership and collective responsibility
- a framework for team-building
- recruiting and selecting team members

In early childhood services, considerable emphasis has been placed upon the significance of effective leadership to ensure high-quality provision and to raise standards and expectations of and for all. To achieve these aims, leadership responsibility cannot be shouldered by one person, but needs to be shared with formal and aspiring leaders, and implicitly and inherently distributed throughout the team. In the early childhood sector, leadership is not a solo activity; one person cannot know and do everything that is required.

In quality early childhood services, everybody contributes to the service's operation and administration—for example, by answering the telephone, dealing with inquiries, making programmed decisions, managing their own problems and responding to the needs of situations that arise. Teamwork—in which individual interests and needs are subordinated in order to engage in joint, coordinated, collaborative activity to achieve the common goals and purposes of a group—is equally important, particularly in early childhood services that involve people, their relationships and feelings.

## Collaborating to achieve quality

The team approach is considered by many to be the most appropriate way of meeting the demands of the complex network of integrated, multi-disciplinary early childhood provision—for example, for the development of vision, mission, goals, policy, plans and operational procedures, as well as for effective day-to-day running of the current range of early childhood services. It is a means for helping others to learn about the roles and responsibilities of leadership and a vehicle for beginning to share and distribute leadership throughout early childhood communities.

Working as a cohesive, collaborative team is a key strategy and resource for the provision of quality early childhood services. Consequently, effective early childhood leaders devote time and resources to transforming a group of disparate individuals into an empowered, collaborative and accountable team. Teamwork is about creating a workplace culture that values collaboration and collective responsibility. A collaborative team displays a number of features, including:

- shared vision, values and personal experiences
- diversity and complementary knowledge, skills and experience
- open communication (active listening, assertion, problem-solving) and respect for the perspectives of others
- respect, consideration, friendliness, empathy and emotional intelligence
- honest and tactful feedback about achievement of common goals and agreed performance standards, and
- inclusion, collective responsibility and mutual accountability.

Collaborative leadership and collective responsibility—that is, teamwork—has a major impact on service quality. There is a strong connection between young children's development and stability in early childhood services. Instability, be it a result of frequent changes in a service or frequent changes of staff within a service, has detrimental effects on children's development and learning. The workplace climate can produce a lack of responsiveness and sensitivity that may lead to high turnover rates. Effective leadership, coupled with opportunities to contribute through teamwork, is a critical factor for increasing self-esteem, job satisfaction and morale, as well as reducing stress and potential burnout—all of which contribute to higher quality.

While some still enter early childhood assuming that the job is one of autonomous work with children, the reality is that the sector is increasingly multi-faceted, multi-disciplinary and integrated, requiring effective interaction with others from a range of agencies. Teamwork is considered to be such an important issue for working in early childhood services that ability to 'work as a member of a team' is an employment criterion specified in most job descriptions.

Collaborative leadership and collective responsibility facilitate participatory management and shared leadership, and operate as a vehicle for subtly distributing leadership and kindling collective responsibility throughout the workplace culture of early childhood services.

*Sharing distributed leadership throughout the service and emphasis on teamwork are key leadership attributes.*
EARLY YEARS/PRIMARY ADVISER

Most early childhood leaders and educators appreciate that effective teamwork is fundamental to quality service provision, and that synergistic teams generate momentum, enabling them to achieve more than would be possible for one individual. However, what constitutes a team can vary in different contexts. For example, in pre-schools the team may consist of two adults: the director or leader and an assistant. In long day or occasional childcare services, the team may consist of the entire staff group or of the educators who work together in a room or with a particular group of children. In family day care and childminding, the team may mean a coordinator, field workers, office staff and a large group of independent providers who are physically isolated from the centralised admin-istration. Depending on the meaning given to the concept of the team, families may or may not be included in the broader definition. Regardless of its definition, the essence of a team is that everybody works together collectively to achieve a common goal.

The size of the team is important. In small teams—for example, two or three people—it is more difficult to access the range of knowledge, skills and experience that contribute to creative problem-solving than with larger teams of five to seven people. As early childhood services become more complex, multi-disciplinary and multi-agency in nature, early childhood teams will grow larger and offer a greater pool of resources for effectiveness and efficiency.

Working in an effective team offers many benefits, including:

- a pleasant and stimulating work environment
- a sense of belonging
- open communication
- help and support
- increased commitment to the job
- coordination of collective work activity
- support for professional development, and
- a range and variety of learning opportunities.

Collaborative leadership and teamwork provide social support that softens the strain, stress and tension that can arise in the daily activities in early childhood services, and may lead to burnout. Interpersonal relationships can become a source of support, satisfaction and stimulation, thereby enhancing overall team morale. By using the unique expertise and resources that each member brings to the team, motivation and job satisfaction are enhanced, resulting in commitment to effective accomplishment of tasks.

While many early childhood leaders and educators recognise the advantages of teamwork, some still assume that it is the only the formal leader's job to keep the team on track, to make decisions and to solve problems. Apparently, the benefits of collaborative leadership and collective responsibility are not appreciated fully by all.

## Working as a collaborative team in a service

In early childhood services, a team is defined as:

a group of people who cooperate with each other to work towards achieving an agreed set of aims, objectives or goals while simultaneously considering the personal needs and interests of individuals. (Rodd, 2006: 149)

Collaborative teams in early childhood services offer opportunities for:

*   the pursuit of shared vision, values, mission, policies and goals
*   collective responsibility and mutual accountability
*   open and honest communication
*   access to a support system
*   on-the-job training, and
*   professional development.

Early childhood educators become empowered by working in collaborative teams because authority and responsibility are delegated and shared. When leaders retain much of the power and control, team members' initiative and motivation are dampened and decreased, and they increasingly become dependent on leaders for direction and instruction.

*I was told that I was responsible for organising a training day but the manager would not even let me send a letter out without seeing it first. I couldn't make one decision without referring it to her—she might as well have saved me the trouble and done it herself.*
Nursery officer

Teamwork usually is expected to be a positive experience. Yet experiences of working in teams are not always consistent with expectations. Teams are more than groups of individuals in a workplace, and not all work groups are teams. Effective teamwork evolves out of work groups that are transformed into teams by leadership that is shared and distributed. Teamwork in practice can be quite a different proposition from teamwork in theory, with a range of negative experiences reported by early childhood educators.

*The educators say they like working in a team and they seem to get a lot of positives out of it when it works well ... but often there are difficulties and differences that are not resolved.*
NURSERY MANAGER

Although many early childhood educators value the teamwork approach to service delivery, it is not easy to meld groups of individual educators into a functioning team (that is, build a team), and it requires ongoing attention and effort to maintain team spirit once team energy has been fired up. Although the formal leader ultimately is accountable for achieving agreed goals, team members need ongoing inspiration and motivation to assume particular roles and responsibilities and, when the agreed goals have been achieved, have their contributions recognised and rewarded by the leader.

*Leadership is exercised by the manager when getting the team to complete tasks.*
PRE-SCHOOL DEVELOPMENT WORKER

Most early childhood educators understand that teamwork is more than just turning up for work each day. It involves a special understanding of the collective roles and responsibilities of both leaders and team members.

## Reflections on leadership in practice

My head teacher calls meetings to 'brief' the educators on what he expects at the beginning of each school year. He raises morale because he encourages us to share ideas and he guides us through group activities. He shares leadership with us because he focuses on the team, not the hierarchy.
TEACHING ASSISTANT

For early childhood leaders, collaborative teamwork means acting as a facilitator and enabler rather than a superior and controller. For educators, it means taking an active role in fulfilling roles and responsibilities rather than being a passive follower of instructions and directions. The reported inconsistency between expectations and reality in teamwork suggests that some early childhood leaders have not developed sufficient skills in building and leading collaborative teams. The examination of the processes and stages of team development (see below) will clarify some of the issues relevant to effective teamwork.

## Working in multi-disciplinary teams

Today, child and family services are delivered by a range of professionals from education, social work and health, who bring their own values, philosophies, agendas, language and approaches to meeting the inter-connected needs of young children and their families. The different backgrounds of these professionals have hampered the development of effective partnerships with early childhood educators who traditionally have not worked within a multi-disciplinary team context. However, the trend towards the integration of services and multi-agency provision has necessitated the development of multi-disciplinary team approaches in the early childhood sector.

Multi-disciplinary teamwork offers an holistic approach to the provision of child and family services. It is an opportunity to maximise the use of professional expertise and improve the outcomes for service users (Wilson and Pirrie, 2000). Many governments and service providers argue that integrated services are more efficient, both economically and for users. Collaboration between professionals who work with and for children and families brings specific benefits (Australian Institute of Family Studies, 2011), including:

- increased willingness to access and use services (especially any that may be stigmatised within a local community)
- increased access to services (which can be restricted by a 'siloed' system)
- holistic and streamlined service provision
- concise and uniform information, and
- the opportunity for families to have a voice and be heard.

Where the health, education and social needs of children and families are met through the integration of services, additional benefits of effective delivery, consumer satisfaction and cost-effectiveness accrue. Consequently, early childhood educators currently find themselves working with professionals and para-professionals from other disciplines, such as community health workers, social workers, educational psychologists, family workers, community police officers, special education teachers, speech therapists, play therapists, learning support assistants, doctors, physiotherapists, community psychiatric nurses, trainers and researchers.

Multi-disciplinary teams are formed for specific purposes and can have different structures. They may be centre-based service delivery teams but they also may be decision-making groups or consultants and trainers. They can differ to the extent that roles are distinct or blended. However, in order for multi-disciplinary teams to be effective and run smoothly and efficiently, certain commitments must be met. It is essential that professional diversity and specialised expertise are valued and respected by all. This requires that everybody involved must engage in establishing and maintaining good interpersonal relationships. There must be a willingness to explore and consider diverse perspectives, regardless of professional status. Tensions arising from questions such as 'Who is the expert?' can lead to destructive conflict. There is no place for a professional 'pecking order' in multi-disciplinary teams.

Team activities and service delivery need to be on the basis of shared values and language. Not all professions share the same values that underpin early childhood practice, and different professions may have competing priorities. Strategic leadership is vital for finding common ground and compromise. Multi-disciplinary contributions should reflect each professional's core competencies and expertise, and be guided by clear, agreed objectives, role definitions and decision-making processes.

To be successful, members of multi-disciplinary teams need to commit to collaboration, be willing to share information and maintain confidentiality as appropriate, be honest and open and work towards common goals. Team members need good communication skills—especially listening, assertion and negotiation.

## Working in multi-agency services

Multi-agency teams bring together professions from different sectors to support young children and families through integrated service delivery (Children's Workforce Development Council, 2010). The aim of integrated service provision is to reshape children's and family services to make them more flexible, responsive, efficient and effective (Anning et al., 2010). Multi-agency services are considered to offer many advantages, including:

- individualised, tailor-made support for children and families
- easier, often 'one-stop', access to expertise or services for families
- contact with fewer specialist professionals and agencies
- holistic approaches to early identification and intervention, and
- reduced needs for more specialist services.

Multi-agency services can operate and interact at different levels of cooperation (Frost, 2005), from *communication*, a basic sharing of specific and focused information through to *cooperation*, a genuine blending and merging of structures, procedures, roles and responsibilities:

- *communication*—basic provision of information about intentions or actions
- *consultation*—asking for opinions, information, advice
- *collaboration*—mutual activity by relatively independent agencies
- *multi-lateral*—joint planning and action by agencies whose provision overlaps, and
- *cooperation*—working together to plan and operate a mutual course of action.

Multi-agency services aim to provide seamless, joined-up thinking, policies and delivery to meet the joined-up needs of children and families (Fitzgerald and Kay, 2007). An intended outcome and benefit is the reduction in the number of professionals with whom each child or family has contact. Multi-agency services have different forms, structures and protocols according to local need and context. For example, a multi-agency service may form a team to address the needs of a particular child or family. Alternatively, it may create a panel of professionals to deal with needs of individual children or families based on an area or organisation where services work together. Such services may be sited within a single unit, co-located or virtual, with regular meetings across services (for example, fortnightly or monthly).

Working as a team in multi-agency services is not always easy. Many challenges need to be addressed. Early childhood leaders and educators who become members of such teams need to understand the barriers to and benefits of working collaboratively in multi-agency service delivery. Collett (2010) identifies specific professional dilemmas arising from structural, procedural, inter-professional and ideological differences that have to be overcome for multi-agency teams to work effectively. The resolution of such dilemmas requires skilled leadership, where leaders aim to create a flat hierarchy, a culture of distributed leadership and a sensitivity to the emotional needs of all (Gasper, 2010). Effective leaders encourage open dialogue, inclusive representation, shared values and agendas, and recognition of collective professional requirements. Team members may develop increased confidence about and skills to work in a multi-agency team through reflective practice (Walker, 2010).

## Benefits of professional diversity in teams

A diverse team values and respects difference and variation, and appreciates that different professional backgrounds, attitudes, skills and experiences contribute new ideas and perspectives to a team's work. A diverse team capitalises on difference and variation to make its service inclusive, relevant and appropriate for all who use it. Professionally diverse teams offer numerous benefits, including:

- promotion of a sense of belonging, increased morale and commitment
- empowerment of 'lower status' professions through distribution of power and leadership
- decreased marginalisation and under-representation of 'lower status' professions
- improved communication and working relationships as well as reduction in resistance to change among collaborative professions
- encouragement of flexible thinking, and improved decision-making and problem-solving
- opportunities to learn from each other
- greater creativity and innovation through the use of all of the talents and resources available, and
- better satisfaction and outcomes for service users.

Given increasing multi-professional and multi-agency collaboration, many early childhood leaders and educators will find themselves working in multi-disciplinary teams. Members of such teams will need to overcome a range of barriers to effective inter-professional collaboration, and work together cooperatively to develop shared vision, values and philosophy, goals and objectives, and quality measures and evaluation protocols. Rather than defending the approach of individual disciplines, they need to work on understanding and reconciling any differences to create a multi-disciplinary ethos and culture by establishing mutually agreed principles, priorities, protocols, procedures and objectives.

## Processes and stages of team development

Team development at the service, multi-disciplinary or multi-agency levels is not an easy task. It requires concerted, ongoing effort on behalf of each member and an even greater effort from the leader who nurtures the team from birth to maturity. Teams—including multi-disciplinary teams and those created through multi-agency service provision—commonly move through a sequence of stages at different rates and over different periods of time. The speed with which each group accomplishes the demands of a particular stage and moves to the next is related to the leader's skills. Consequently, early childhood leaders need to understand the stage of team development at which their group currently functions, and to possess the skills to facilitate transition to a higher stage of development as quickly as possible.

The processes and stages of team development are outlined in terms of the task and relationship requirements for early childhood services.

### Stage 1: Connecting—getting together as a team

The first stage in the development of a team is when a group of people becomes aware that they are going to be working together. This may be when a new service is established and a completely new group of educators is employed to work together. More likely, a new person or persons will join an existing group of educators or a person may resign. Whenever there is a change in the group composition, the start of a new team has been signalled. This requires assimilation of a new person into the team and accommodation by the existing educators to the new conditions, especially if the team is smaller. The early childhood leader must address the demands of the work and relationships in order to help educators to be productive and feel comfortable in this initial stage of team development.

The early childhood leader's major concern in terms of work is with orientation to task demands where structured activities such as articulating values and vision, information-sharing, organising roles and responsibilities and goal-setting are important because they act to alleviate educators' apprehension about change and anxiety about competence to undertake the job. Educators will focus on the formal authority figure for guidance about their work and may ask a variety of questions— for example, 'What are we supposed to do?', 'What happens next?' and 'What are our goals?' Conformity to the leader's approach will be high and few challenges can be expected. The leader needs to provide clear directions and guidelines at this point, communicate values and vision, and general objectives and expectations about participation and performance, and express confidence in the team, thereby increasing commitment to the goals. Educators should be encouraged to set personal goals for professional learning and development, self-evaluation and career progression.

The relationship and team morale aspect can be difficult to manage at this initial stage because many educators are concerned about belonging, inclusion and rejection, and some may be unwilling to disclose their personal concerns, vulnerabilities and aspirations. They are likely to be concerned more with self-protection in what is perceived as an unknown situation, so may keep feelings hidden, display little concern for others and be unlikely to listen effectively because their own needs dominate their attention. The early childhood service's climate may be characterised by politeness and a wish to avoid contentious issues or anything that might result in discord, disharmony or conflict.

Educators focus upon getting acquainted with others, assessing others' strengths and weaknesses, and generally testing out the situation to determine the written and unwritten ground rules that operate. Early childhood leaders need to provide opportunities for educators to get to know one another professionally and personally. Introducing some kind of informal social function such as coffee after work or a shared meal before a meeting can help to facilitate understanding and acceptance of others and the formation of initial relationships. The leader needs to be available and accessible, non-threatening, supportive and observant of interaction patterns and styles.

When early childhood educators feel sufficiently comfortable with one another because a level of trust and security in the people and the task has been established, a degree of risk-taking emerges where challenges to aspects of work and the expertise of others to undertake it may arise. Small indications of discord or disharmony may be noticed. The team is now in transition to the next stage of development.

## Stage 2: Confronting conflict in the team

It generally comes as some surprise, both to early childhood leaders and educators, when the team that initially appeared to get along so well disintegrates into one marked by discord, disharmony, open and covert displays of antagonism to one another, disputes and dissent. In terms of team development, the honeymoon period is over. The challenges for team members at this second stage are establishing a niche in the pecking order and negotiation of roles and responsibilities. The direction and activities of the leader are likely to be evaluated and possibly challenged by team members, who now feel more confident about their position in the team.

With regard to the work aspect, early childhood educators become concerned with aspects of the administrative organisation of the service. Rules, procedures, policies and agendas become the focus of attention, with queries raised about who has the power to direct, control and change the administrative structure. Commitment to team goals may appear reduced as educators debate the team's vision, overall direction and specific goals. As team members get to know each other better, they also can identify one another's strengths and limitations. This can bring about confrontation regarding values, beliefs and appropriate practice that can produce a climate characterised by criticism and confrontation. Questions and statements such as 'What authority have you got to make that decision?', 'Who makes the rules here—the team or the leader?', 'Who are you to tell me what to do? I only take directions from my manager!', 'How is my performance going to be appraised?' and 'The committee can't tell us to do that!' may be heard from early childhood educators as they attempt to clarify where the power lies.

In this second stage, relationships between team members become more significant and can be influential in terms of how emerging team differences are dealt with. Early childhood educators' need for their unique contribution to be recognised can be met only in an atmosphere of mutual support and respect. These individual needs, and subsequently overall team morale, can be undermined by a climate that is marked by criticism. In order to bolster self-esteem, educators may form cliques and alliances to pressure the leader and other team members to meet their demands. Increased stress is likely to be experienced by all those connected with the service, including children and families, if in-fighting, power struggles, disputes, confrontations and destructive criticism are not managed appropriately.

Early childhood leaders need to have a thorough understanding of conflict and its role in organisations. This was addressed in Chapter 6. In the process of galvanising a group of disparate individuals into a cohesive team, conflict is inevitable, normal and healthy. It is a sign that the team is developing. The constructive resolution of differences can clear the way for more cooperative and productive endeavours on the part of the team. Ignoring or avoiding conflict now will hinder the team's progress towards a more advanced and harmonious stage of development. In teams where conflict and confrontation are not resolved, decision-making and problem-solving ability is poor, commitment is low and team members do not enjoy being part of the team, psychological and/or physical withdrawal may occur, which in turn will diminish productivity and morale.

Effective early childhood leaders whose team is in this second stage of development need to employ sophisticated communication skills to manage any conflict in order to move educators towards greater acceptance, increased trust, accord and harmony, and commitment to the task. Active listening, assertion and conflict-management skills are essential, and the leader may need to provide guidelines for handling differences between educators in a professional manner. In addition, early childhood leaders need to be confident about their ability to manage the situation constructively and communicate confidence in the team regarding the ability to clarify any issues of concern while maintaining respect for others. Holding individual, small and large team meetings, where information, expectations, standards and boundaries are clarified, and established goals are focused upon, can be useful at this point.

Unfortunately, teams can get 'stuck' in cycles of conflict, resulting in high levels of stress for all involved, decreased morale and commitment and high staff turnover. As well as the extra energy required to survive working in conflict-prone environments, leaders may need to respond to other issues such as resignations, recruitment and selection. In such circumstances, the leader needs to facilitate a sense of closure and reorient the team to the fact that it will be re-forming. The team will return to the first stage of development and begin the initial process of getting together as a team again. If the leader does not possess the confidence and skills to deal with conflict, the same scenario will probably be repeated when the new team moves into the second stage of confronting conflict. Without competent intervention, the cycle is repeated with the resultant perception that the team is conflict prone, or trapped in a destructive cycle of discord and disharmony.

Early childhood services that experience a high rate of staff turnover as a result of unresolved conflict in this stage cannot capitalise on the training and experience gained by educators. The level of service quality expected by early childhood educators and families is more difficult to achieve with high levels of staff turnover. Over time, individual educators develop knowledge and expertise that is specific and relevant to the children and families with whom they work. Such distinctive expertise is not easy to replace. This places an added burden on early childhood leaders because they continue to be involved in orientation, induction, training and supervision until new educators attain competence levels to work more independently. Early childhood leaders therefore have less time to devote to other important aspects of administering a high-quality service. In addition, continuous staff turnover keeps team development at lower stages, requiring more input from early childhood leaders to ensure that the team grows and advances.

If early childhood leaders manage the challenges of this second stage, the team will begin to resolve personal animosities and to focus back on improving activities and performance related to achieving the agreed goals. It now is advancing to the third stage.

### Stage 3: Cooperating as a team

When a group starts to evidence consensus and cooperation, it has begun to work collectively as a team. While the team may appear to be operating in a more dynamic manner, some members are yet to collaborate in a unified or methodical way. However, having worked through some of the important issues in the previous stage, the team is now willing to take some risks and to experiment with new practices, to debate values and assumptions, to review and discuss operational methods and matters, and to examine leadership issues. New confidence gained from resolving the earlier conflicts can produce receptivity to new ideas and informed risk-taking. If a leader has skillfully handled the first two stages, the team will move quickly through this third stage.

The challenges surrounding task performance issues focus on information-sharing, win–win attitudes to problem-solving, a willingness to take calculated risks and receptivity to change. These task-related activities are anchored in the new level of trust and confidence that has developed through the management of conflict. Early childhood educators trust both themselves in the job and the other team members. This may motivate previously inactive team members to become more involved with a broader range of responsibilities. Change has begun. A breach of trust at this stage will reverse the team's progress, however, and it is possible that the team will regress to the previous stage. Skill in decision-making and problem-solving is needed by the leader as well as team members in order to capitalise on the team's potential at this point.

The formal leader's style becomes more important because now the team is interested in participation, contribution and collaboration. Therefore, a participatory, democratic or distributed style is appropriate for meeting team members' needs. Some team members will be interested in sharing responsibility with leaders, so effective delegation also becomes an important leadership skill. Where distributed leadership and collective responsibility are infused throughout the workplace culture, who leads and who follows depends on individual choices about the nature of the task or work to be undertaken (Talan, 2010). The relationship between early childhood leaders, educators, tasks, and workplace culture and climate determines the extent to which leadership and teamwork are understood as collaborative and collective responsibilities.

The focus of the team at the third stage of development continues to be on relationships. Having earlier been fragmented by conflict, early childhood educators now are interested in achieving community and cohesion. The beginning of a 'team spirit' is evident, with educators spontaneously referring to themselves and their colleagues as 'the team'. Team members are more open-minded, more willing to listen to and support one another, and able to focus on the needs of the team rather than their own needs. Mutually accepted team norms begin to guide the work and relationships. The word 'we' is heard more often than 'I' or 'you' when discussing work. The workplace climate is more lighthearted, with professionally appropriate humour illustrating good-natured attitudes in everyone.

Although discord, disharmony and conflict still may occur, they are perceived as less threatening by early childhood educators and addressed differently. The problem-solving approach to conflict and decision-making is evident because the team now wishes to protect its positive relationships, cohesion and interdependence.

At this third stage, the early childhood leader's role is to promote consensus and cooperation by encouraging and supporting educator involvement, participation in goal-setting, development and implementation of policies, as well as any meaningful and practical contribution. A willingness to identify and to address potential problems is essential. Open communication, constructive feedback and acknowledgement of contributions to teams facilitate team consensus and cooperation. As the team begins to take pride in its achievements, it starts to function effectively and is ready to advance into the fourth stage.

### Stage 4: Collaborating as an effective team

The rate at which a team proceeds to this stage depends on the effectiveness of the leader in facilitating the transition through the previous stages. It is not until this stage that the group of individuals who committed themselves to working together in the first stage can be said to be operating truly as an effective team.

Now all team members are making a unique but equal and valued contribution to the work and share with the leader collective responsibility for the efficient operation of a quality service. Leadership is enacted flexibly and openly. Regular review and evaluation of vision, policies, goals and practice are undertaken with a view to constant improvement of the service. Appraisal—either with the leader or through self-appraisal—is accepted as a form of professional development. The team adopts a creative problem-solving approach to its operation and engages in preventive decision-making. Change is anticipated and planned for, and the team is prepared for and included in phased implementation. The team may reward its own performance by articulating a sense of pride concerning its achievements.

Relationships are based on mutual respect and support. Team members recognise their interdependence as well as their independence. Individual differences and successes are valued. People are now able to 'agree to disagree' if mutually acceptable solutions to problems are not forthcoming. The climate is marked by concern for other team members, warmth and friendliness.

The team is working efficiently and early childhood educators are enjoying their work. The leader is able to relax and enjoy the fruits of previous efforts. However, early childhood leaders need to keep close contact with the various teams and ensure that any small quality control adjustments are made and shared. Opportunities for contact and relationships with outside groups are pursued, and team members welcome assistance from outside agencies. The team is willing to extend its energies beyond the confines of the service. Leaders have opportunities to facilitate the development of appropriate educators through the mentoring process, thereby contributing to the development of future leaders and taking responsibility for capacity-building and succession planning. These aspects are discussed in Chapter 9.

A team that reaches this stage of mature development can operate productively for a long period of time, as long as attention is given to ensuring effective working methods and the maintenance of relationships. While self-evaluation should be encouraged in all early childhood educators from the time they join the service, formal evaluation of the team and its performance needs to be introduced at this point. This will ensure that questions such as 'How are we going?', 'Where do we want to go next?' and 'What are our needs now?' are addressed in order to keep the team at its maximum operational efficiency. However, if any of the conditions change—such as promotion, resignation or the dissolution of the team because its purpose no longer exists—the team enters the final stage: that of separation and closure.

*Stage 5: Closure*

This ending of a team tends to be ignored by many leaders who, in their haste to move the team back to a more productive and positive stage, fail to acknowledge the team's need to celebrate or mourn its existence and track record. A change in or the disbanding of a team can occur at any stage in a team's development. The sensitive leader will ensure that the team has an opportunity to experience some form of closure so that educators can deal with any unfinished business that might prevent them from approaching their future working situation positively.

When a team ceases to be operational, the members have to come to terms with two issues: disengagement from work and separation from and/or closure of relationships. Usually there is a period of time for the team to work these issues through. It is the leader's responsibility to ensure that the team has access to a means of debriefing and bringing closure to the experience. Comments such as 'Remember when David was here? He would have known what to do' or 'Didn't we work well together before all the changes!' suggest that the educators have not had sufficient time to come to terms with the demise of the previous team. These nostalgic memories may interfere with commitment to the new team and acceptance of any new team members.

If the team has worked well and it has been a satisfying experience for those involved, everyone will be able to celebrate the end of the team by reviewing and evaluating individual development, work and relationships. The team should recognise and celebrate its accomplishments and express its satisfaction with the process. Emotional reactions to the team's closure need to be acknowledged and dealt with. Some frustration and anger may be expressed to the leader, who appreciates that this is part of the normal process of separation. There may also be some confusion about emotional reactions, with educators vacillating between feeling happy and satisfied about the team's achievements and sad and angry about the team's break-up. The stress associated with the closure of the team may produce lower quality performance. However, leaders need to de-emphasise task-related aspects at this point and focus upon meeting educators' social and emotional needs in preparation for establishing a new team.

If the ending of the team is marked by a lack of achievement and/or poor relationships, it is more difficult—but even more important—to engage in a process of closure. Each team member's contribution should be reviewed and evaluated, as well as the overall team dynamic, in order to identify the problems that prevented the team from operating effectively. In this way, the leader and team members should gain a basis for planning for the next team experience.

## Collaborative leadership and collective responsibility

Becoming an effective leader in early childhood involves an inherent difficulty that few leaders in other professions have to deal with. Many formal early childhood leaders have to adapt on a daily basis to moving from the position of administrative leader to being a member of a team with collective responsibility for the early learning and education of young children. The way in which an early childhood leader's time is allocated officially in order to combine administrative and pedagogical duties ensures that both leaders and team members have to adapt to the constant changes in the leader's position in the team. This can place a great strain on the resources of early childhood leaders, who are required to relinquish the authority of leadership when working as an equal member of a room team but resume legitimate command and authority when undertaking administrative functions. Team members can become confused about the appropriate way to interact with early childhood leaders when they participate in work with children as equal team members. This constant fluctuation between the roles of leader and team member requires sensitive management by early childhood leaders. Collaborative leadership has some advantages for early childhood leaders who find themselves in this position.

To review the leader's role in relation to a team, core functions are to build and articulate shared values and vision; to develop a team culture of collective responsibility; to set agreed goals; to monitor, communicate and reflect back the team's achievements to the team and relevant others; and to encourage and facilitate the professional development of team members. These functions can be fulfilled using the various styles of leadership outlined in Chapter 3.

Collaborative leadership can be understood as one strand of a cooperative web of interdependent individuals with shared values and vision, where the boundaries of leadership are open, permeable and flexible, and leadership capability and responsibility are available to and inherently distributed across and assumed by the many. Collaborative leadership is enacted through the leader's and team members' ability to listen to each other, to ask key questions, to make cogent arguments, to move discord to accord, to negotiate agreements, to reach consensual decisions and to commit to agreed plans of action. A workplace culture of distributed leadership values and nurtures the spontaneous enactment of leadership, whereby formal leaders make space by relinquishing some control, open up choice and encourage the autonomy of early childhood educators who aspire to such opportunities.

Early childhood leaders nurture a culture of collaborative leadership and collective responsibility by being:

- adaptable (responsive and innovative)
- energetic (action-oriented and committed to work)

- people-oriented (valuing people and communicating openly)
- quality-conscious (attending to standards of excellence, needs and expectations)
- uniting (clarifying common purposes, promoting community and cooperation)
- entrepreneurial (autonomous and able to articulate the uniqueness of the service)
- focused (self-disciplined, consistent and predictable), and
- informal (displaying a relaxed, straightforward approach to people and situations).

Collaborative leadership and collective responsibility are fundamental for increasing the engagement, participation and contribution of early childhood educators and families for the efficient operation of quality early childhood services.

In collaborative leadership, the ability and desire to delegate to and share responsibility with other suitable team members, as well as to distribute leadership functions throughout workplace culture, are vital. Sometimes, early childhood leaders become so concerned about achieving success and excellence that they become overly involved, excessively hands-on or preoccupied with attention to detail. When this happens, it is a signal that the leader has fallen into the trap of micro-management. Over time, team performance will deteriorate because educators become discouraged, disengaged and disempowered when they do not have sufficient opportunities to learn, develop and contribute.

Micro-managers will delegate, but they do so in ways that do not empower delegatees to take responsibility for completing the work in their own way. Micro-managers tend to hover, give advice, worry about fine detail, intrusively supervise work in progress and insensitively intervene to correct any errors or improve the final outcome. They generally discourage and frustrate educators' initiative and independent decision-making.

To avoid micro-management, early childhood leaders should delegate, share or distribute work appropriately, agree a timeline, offer support if requested, then stand back and trust that the person to whom the work was delegated is capable, responsible and accountable for delivering results in the time agreed. Failure to deliver may be a result of ineffective delegation or micro-management by early childhood leaders rather than the inability of educators to complete the work satisfactorily.

When building and leading a team, in a service or with a multi-disciplinary team in multi-agency provision, early childhood leaders need to be conscious of the positive impact that collaborative leadership can have on a group of individuals who are working together, and incorporate appropriate aspects of this approach into their repertoire. In addition to a leader's individual style, a systematic, step-by-step approach to team-building can progress the team's relationships and productivity.

## A framework for team-building

The process of galvanising a group of individuals into a cohesive team is not always a quick and painless one. Becoming a team demands energy, effort and commitment from everyone, and requires that early childhood leaders relate to teams in a certain way. However, helping a group of educators evolve into a collaborative team can be a very rewarding experience for early childhood leaders. Although numerous obstacles to team-building exist in early childhood services—such as varying skills, interests and values, the fragmentation of staff through physical environments and shiftwork, and the increasing integration with different agencies—the process can be implemented gradually, with educators encouraged to provide feedback about their satisfaction or otherwise with the process.

Team-building processes basically focus on the two dimensions of any team: productivity and relationships. In order to build relationships and subsequent morale, a team needs to provide social support for the interpersonal demands that evolve in any work group. This support may consist of emotional, informational, instrumental or appraisal support. Early childhood leaders may need to help teams to identify how members may be able to assist and support one another. The accomplishment of the task requires an analysis of work demands and the development of role profiles based on the collective expectations of leaders and educators. Early childhood leaders need to respond to educators' desire for increasing participation in and a growing contribution to decision-making as well as increasing responsibility for and personal control over how the job is performed. Attention to these two dimensions produces cohesive teams that collaborate to accomplish and assume collective responsibility for specific tasks in supportive workplace environments. Early childhood leaders can encourage, support and facilitate team-building with the following strategies.

- *Setting achievable goals* that have been mutually agreed by team members. It is important to ensure that assertive team members do not dominate, especially during discussion at meetings.
- *Clarifying roles.* Team members work most effectively when their roles are clear to all and free of ambiguity and conflict. Each team member should be aware of who is responsible for what. While it will be easier to clarify the formal roles that need to be fulfilled, the informal roles that relate to the internal functioning of the team should not be forgotten. Johnson and Johnson (2008) identify these as task roles (initiating,

information-gathering, opinion-seeking and giving, clarifying, elaborating, energising, summarising and consensus-testing) and team maintenance roles (encouraging, harmonising, compromising, gatekeeping, observing and standard-setting).

- *Building supportive relationships.* Providing opportunities for feedback and developing trust stimulates a cooperative team spirit. Teams where members feel supported are more likely to deal with (rather than ignore) common team problems such as role ambiguity, role conflict and conflict between members.
- *Encouraging active participation* to capitalise on the knowledge and skills of individual team members. An atmosphere of acceptance and collective responsibility encourages team members to contribute ideas, opinions, energy and action. Being part of a collaborative venture can be extremely motivating, and increases commitment and productivity.
- *Monitoring team effectiveness.* There is little point in putting time and energy into team-building if the team does not achieve its goals effectively or is unhappy with the process. Early childhood leaders should provide regular opportunities for teams to assess the extent of goal achievement and how well they are collaborating. This review process helps identify any problems and establishes their cause, as well as assisting with future planning.

The success of collaborative leadership and collective responsibility relies on open communication, democratic organisation and processes, and effective problem-solving skills. An effective team should fulfil early childhood educators' needs for participation, contribution and support, and result in efficient and effective approaches to working with and for children and families.

## Recruiting and selecting team members

Forming an effective early childhood team is a complex process that involves the recruitment and selection of the best person available to complement and improve the quality of the existing team, and to work sensitively and effectively with children and families. Most early childhood services have written recruitment and selection policies that guide these processes. Early childhood leaders and key team members usually are involved in the decision about who to appoint, yet few have had training in the human resource management processes that are vital for identifying and choosing the right person for their service and existing team, as well as identifying and rejecting those applicants who are unsuitable or who pose a risk for working with young children.

Leading practice for the recruitment and selection of quality personnel is grounded in values that safeguard and protect children and families, promote their welfare, and guard against neglect, maltreatment and abuse. To ensure that unsuitable applicants are prevented from working in early childhood, everyone associated with service provision—regardless of capacity—needs to be familiar and comply with current statutory guidance regarding legal and mandatory obligations and responsibilities.

The appointment of a new team member involves choosing someone who is suitable to work with young children, who truly endorses and openly commits to the existing values and vision, and who will fit into and complement the existing team. Written position and person specifications define the required professional and technical qualifications, experience and expertise as well as the needs and scope of the work. Because existing team members understand the complexity and demands of the work in early childhood services, they can make an important contribution to identifying the parameters of the position, including essential personal and professional qualities, attributes, capabilities and skills.

Most early childhood person and position descriptions make reference to:

- professional qualifications and experience
- specific personal qualities
- interpersonal and communication skills
- ability to work independently and as a collaborative team member
- problem-solving skills
- ability to work under pressure and manage stress
- support of and commitment to early childhood values and goals
- strengths that could be offered to the team, and
- commitment to diversity and inclusion.

In addition, all early childhood services must give priority to safe recruitment—that is, to identifying, rejecting and deterring applicants who are unsuitable or who might pose a risk in terms of working with young children (Department of Children, Schools and Families, 2010). Safe recruitment practice includes:

- ensuring position descriptions emphasise responsibility for guarding and protecting children's welfare
- ensuring person descriptions emphasise suitability to work with children
- obtaining, scrutinising and verifying all requisite information about applicants (including qualifications, employment history and experience, health and physical capacity), and investigating and fully resolving any discrepancies and concerns

- obtaining professional character references, and
- completing all mandatory documents regarding statutory checks on those who wish to work with children.

As well as written information, early childhood leaders and selection teams must conduct face-to-face interviews that further explore suitability to work with children by examining applicants' motivation for working with children, attitudes to children, willingness to support early childhood values, and goals and communicative ability. Following appointment, early childhood leaders and educators need to be aware of, alert to and responsive to any evidence of unsafe or poor practice and any concerns expressed by children, families or colleagues.

For teams to collaborate effectively, a high level of mutual trust is essential (Hunsaker and Hunsaker, 2009). Every team member needs to know that they can depend on others to undertake their work with children and families in ways that meet the early childhood sector's values, principles and ethical standards, and comply with statutory requirements.

## Bringing it together

Collaborative leadership usually result in teams who assume collective responsibility and display high-quality interaction between team members and leaders, thereby enhancing trust and openness, encouraging the development of interpersonal relationships, joint goal-setting, clarification of potentially fluctuating roles and responsibilities, and analysis of the appropriate processes related to achieving the team's purpose and development. Early childhood leaders who understand team-building processes build collaborative teams that, even when the leader is absent, continue to pursue and achieve agreed goals confidently, accountably and professionally. The collaborative approach to teamwork in early childhood services also contributes to professional development and helps to meet the challenge of change because it provides the backdrop of support for and commitment to quality service delivery.

# CHAPTER 9

## LEADING PROFESSIONAL DEVELOPMENT: SUPERVISION, MENTORING AND COACHING

*It is essential that leadership development programs are set up but that doesn't necessarily mean training courses. Leadership potential can be nurtured through putting the right people together in supervisory and mentoring meetings.*

HEAD TEACHER, EARLY EXCELLENCE CENTRE

### THIS CHAPTER EXPLORES

- the leader's role in supervision
- supervising educators as adult learners
- the leader's role as a mentor
- the leader's role as a coach
- the deputy: a special opportunity for leadership

The quality of early childhood services is related directly to the quality of the personnel who operate them, from the formal leader to the educators who work with children and families, whether they are trained or untrained, more experienced or less experienced. Early childhood leaders face many challenges in fulfilling professional support responsibilities so that educators continue to learn and develop their potential, and the team continues to move towards leading practice. The development of the potential and capacities of both individuals and teams is included in most leaders' visions because the development of human resources is an investment in the sustainability and future of early childhood services.

Supervision, mentoring and coaching are leadership skills that support the development and learning of professional potential in individuals and teams. Because many early childhood educators think they learn better from colleagues than from more formal training opportunities, effective implementation of these strategies for development of professional potential is increasingly important. In addition, the shift towards a culture of distributed leadership means that many early childhood educators assume responsibilities that are additional to their normal roles. Consequently, they need focused support, guidance and development opportunities to enable them to aspire to and successfully meet these challenges.

Supervision is no longer regarded as a form of control or surveillance; rather, it is viewed as a means of supporting, encouraging, guiding and developing the potential and capabilities of others. When early childhood leaders enact their supervisory responsibility from a perspective of support and guidance, they can encourage educators to become lifelong learners who are self-evaluative and reflective about their practice, and help them to develop as confident and capable educators who are motivated to provide quality early childhood services for young children and families.

## The leader as a supervisor

Supervision is a professional responsibility of early childhood leaders in which early childhood educators are helped to use their knowledge and skills effectively in the performance of their daily work, and to deepen their understanding of professional values, vision, philosophy and practice. The range of supervisory responsibilities is complex, and leaders need to address both personal and self-development potential as well as professional and team-building issues.

The aims of supervision are for early childhood leaders and educators to:

- be clear about their roles and responsibilities
- plan and monitor progress towards meeting service objectives
- receive support for their work effort and outcomes, and
- access planned opportunities for learning and professional development.

Effective supervision ensures that both early childhood leaders and educators' work is of high quality and complies with local and national guidelines; that they are challenged and developed professionally; and that they are supported in times of stress and change (Caruso and Fawcett, 2007). It can focus on service delivery issues (practice, standards, performance), educational issues (individual learning and development of potential) and support issues (relationships and morale). Supervision is useful in attending to issues around diversity, collaboration, multi-agency teamwork, performance, development and evaluation practices, and leadership succession.

Every early childhood educator is entitled to regular one-to-one meetings with a supervisor to ensure that they are meeting service, professional and personal goals. Effective supervision provides professional support that encourages educators to listen to and accept constructive feedback and learn to reflect upon and critically evaluate their own practice. In fact, supervision can stimulate learning through which educators can become 'praxiologists' and contribute to the creation and synthesis of new knowledge, understanding and practice (Pascal, 2011).

Supervision involves offering early childhood educators positive feedback, constructive and encouraging criticism, information on professional development and training needs and options, and guidance regarding work-related matters. It needs to be undertaken in such a way that difficult issues—for example, inappropriate dress, levels of personal hygiene, inappropriate use of information and communication technologies, inappropriate interaction with children and/or families or unsatisfactory and/or unacceptable performance—are raised and discussed openly and in confidence.

Good leadership is based on delivering effective feedback (Marrin, 2011). Feedback informs people about how well they are progressing towards agreed goals. Positive feedback is encouraging and constructive feedback helps improve understanding, commitment and performance. When offering feedback, effective supervisors:

- are clear, specific, goal-oriented and avoid generalisations
- emphasise the positive and are non-judgemental
- focus on behaviour or work, not the person
- focus on behaviour that can be improved or changed and is attainable
- use detailed descriptions and reasons rather than vague evaluations
- own the feedback by using 'I' statements
- check that the feedback has been understood, and
- avoid offering advice or solutions.

Good feedback helps educators to reach a better understanding of an issue, how it developed and how to find other ways of addressing it. The best supervision develops as ongoing, respectful collaborative conversations between colleagues.

Reflective dialogue is a specific type of collaborative conversation between supervisors and colleagues through which early childhood educators evidence, illustrate, monitor and evaluate their practice. Collaborative conversations shape how early childhood educators develop understanding and practice (Kuh, 2012). Through reflection, these conversations facilitate professional learning, understanding and practice because they offer opportunities for sharing insights, exchanging information, constructing knowledge, gaining broader and deeper understanding, and exploring roles and responsibilities.

Supervision therefore becomes a way of assessing quality because it involves goals, target-setting, and monitoring and evaluation. It can reduce isolation by connecting early childhood educators with the leader and team by questioning, talking about and scrutinising the what, why and how of practice, and reflecting about new possibilities.

## Reflections on leadership in practice

Early childhood educators benefit from having the opportunity to take on leadership roles, especially where supervisors help them to understand what is involved and recognise when they are displaying leadership qualities and actions.

DEPUTY SUPERVISOR

Some leaders are required to engage in supervision when they are still novices in their own professional development and themselves in need of supervisory support. Responsibility for supervising the training of new and future staff through practical experience and guiding untrained employees, para-professionals and professionals from other disciplines in the values, vision, philosophy and practices of early childhood has been assumed by early childhood leaders who in the past usually had little or no training themselves in supervision, and had limited access to support and backup if problems arose during the process. Quality assurance initiatives require that early childhood leaders assume greater responsibility for on-the-job training, development and supervision of educators, as well as greater input into the support and education of families in child-rearing. It is evident that supervisory responsibility continues to grow, as does the need for early childhood leaders who are trained properly and adequately prepared to undertake the leadership role.

Perceptive early childhood leaders reflect upon their attitudes to and capabilities for supervisory responsibility. Many educators still regard the process of supervision with suspicion, which can be difficult for leaders who are responsible for ensuring quality standards and competent personnel. Reluctance by either leaders or educators to engage in supervisory dialogue may reflect the traditional fears about disguised control and surveillance by employers. Today, supervision is viewed as a form of continuing professional development in which learning, growth and competence are the overriding objectives. Given the increasing participation of educators in operational and administrative roles, supervision is no longer considered to be the sole responsibility of one individual—that is, the leader—but more appropriately is regarded as a collaborative process between leader and educators. Moreover, it can be conducted formally and informally, and on a team basis, as well as using the traditional one-to-one format. Supervision is a means of communicating to educators that they are important assets and that they are valued for their special contribution.

> ## Reflections on leadership in practice
>
> My supervisor displayed leadership when she encouraged me to apply for this position. She gave me fair and open feedback about my strengths and limitations, and that helped me succeed. Her leadership was about creating an enriching environment that valued each person, their contribution and not being threatened by people's ambitions.
> DEPUTY SUPERVISOR

The diversity of policies, contexts, personnel and services within early childhood services makes the creation of a supervisory profile for early childhood leaders difficult. However, training and experience are important variables in improving this aspect of leadership responsibility. Effective supervisors possess a range of attributes that are regarded as desirable rather than prescriptive, offering direction for further professional development. They include:

- possession of professional values and attitudes relevant for early childhood
- expertise in technical and professional knowledge and skills
- the ability to transmit knowledge and skills in a manner conducive to adult learning
- communication skills—especially the ability to listen empathically and offer feedback that shows appreciation and recognition
- decision-making skills
- the ability to resolve discord, disharmony and conflict
- the ability to involve educators in setting team and individual goals, objectives and targets for short-, medium- and long-term achievement
- the ability to monitor progress on a regular basis
- confidentiality
- the ability to anticipate and prepare educators for impending change, and
- openness and receptivity to new ideas, flexibility and accessibility.

## Supervising educators as adult learners

One of the most important aspects of supervision is the leader's ability to work with educators in ways that optimise adult learning styles. Sensitive early childhood leaders understand that adult learners—such as early childhood educators—possess unique traits that differentiate them from children as learners. Examples of these characteristics are readiness, attitude, motivation, previous experiences and autonomy. Adult learning is grounded in experience—that is, it is focused on problem-solving and on the relevance of process. When leaders employ supervisory approaches that incorporate essential principles which underpin adult learning, they help educators (and families) to become better learners by encouraging them to be self-directed, think critically and become reflective.

Supervisory styles that highlight the links between theory, research and practice, and encourage immediate application of new learning, help reduce the frustration that many adult learners (including educators) experience while acquiring new knowledge and skills. Adult learners experience less frustration when mastering new knowledge and skills if they are intrinsically motivated, appreciate the need to learn something specific and understand its relevance to their work. Early childhood leaders who are open, respectful and collaborative encourage educators to move beyond basic understanding of concepts and practices to more sophisticated approaches to information-processing, such as analysis, evaluation and praxis—that is, synthesis of ideas and practices. In other words, they encourage educators to become reflective.

In summary, early childhood educators learn more effectively when:

- they are involved in the learning process, responsible for meeting their own needs, and have opportunities to build on existing skills in self-direction and decision-making
- their previous knowledge, skills and experience are used, with the leader encouraging team members to help others
- their immediate concerns and problems are focused upon in ways that result in new information, skills, insights and solutions, which can be applied to and integrated into their current circumstances
- appropriate and varied instructional methods are used, such as feedback, group discussion, brainstorming, role-playing and problem-solving
- a democratic and participative atmosphere is cultivated through the leader's emphasis on equality, shared responsibility, cooperation and mutual respect, and
- they actively participate and learn by doing, as well as by critical analysis and reflective thinking.

Capable supervisors match the model of supervision to early childhood educators' experience, needs and the stage of professional development, as described in Chapter 3, because training and supervisory needs differ with background and history and change with exposure to and time spent working in early childhood services. Novice and less experienced educators require more concrete support and technical assistance than those with more experience. Those who have more experience benefit from exchanging information and observations with other experienced educators from their own or other contexts. Consultation with specialist staff, such as psychologists and curriculum advisers, can extend the knowledge and skills of educators who are maturing in the job. Those who have considerable experience benefit from networking with colleagues from other agencies and disciplines, and by participating in conferences and specific professional preparation and development programs.

Effective supervisors consider the form of supervision to which educators will be most receptive. For some, the one-to-one tutorial model might be the most effective way to support their development. Novice and less-experienced educators benefit from supervisors who impart information, listen to concerns and anxieties, and show support and understanding in a private consultation. An extension of the tutorial model is a supervisory model where educators or a team whose members are at a similar stage of professional development meet with the supervisor.

Both less experienced and more experienced educators may find the peer model of supervision more stimulating. Peer supervision involves the objective observation of a colleague's practice without making inferences, interpretations or assumptions about the interaction, and later having a reflective dialogue or conversation about those observations. It is an appropriate form of supervision when staff relationships are based upon mutual trust and respect. Educators may choose to work in self-selected pairs; or, alternatively, small groups of educators may wish to participate in regularly scheduled peer conferences to discuss aspects of observed practice and interaction. The peer model provides an opportunity independent of the supervisor to discuss decisions, solve problems, share responsibility and support one another. Peer supervision can encourage educators to engage in reflective thinking and dialogue about practice, and therefore provide a continuing opportunity for professional development.

The team model of supervision enables members of defined teams to evaluate the relationship and task aspects of their performance in order to work more effectively. When early childhood leaders share supervisory responsibility with teams, they need to ensure that the necessary professional knowledge and skills—especially essential communication skills—are well developed so that this delicate task is managed properly. Willingness to request outside help is essential if any problems are identified that are beyond the team's resources.

Today, there is an acknowledged need for more effective leaders in early childhood. One way to develop leadership potential and capacity is through improved supervision of students and current educators. The position of deputy offers considerable scope for early childhood leaders to mentor a suitable educator so that they gain valuable on-the-job training and experience, which will nurture emerging leadership potential and capacity, and ensure that succession planning is in place.

## The leader as a mentor

Mentoring as a means for supporting the growth of personal and professional potential is recognised as an essential tool for supporting professional development and career progression in early childhood. Unfortunately, the proliferation of early childhood award-bearing courses and increasing numbers of students has resulted in poorer quality vocational preparation. The trend towards increased lecture-based training with concomitant reduction in tutorial opportunities, coupled with drastic cuts in the number of supervised hours that students work in early childhood contexts, means that many novice graduates begin work ill-prepared to meet the needs of young children and families and the demands of quality service provision.

Because current qualifications and training do not guarantee quality practice of fledgling employees in the sector, mentoring is regarded as a leadership strategy for enhancing learning and professional development over a sustained period of time for both beginning and experienced early childhood educators. Mentoring essentially is an ongoing relationship between a more-experienced educator and a less-experienced one, where the less-experienced person is helped to gain competence, improve performance and achieve personal and professional goals (Hunsaker and Hunsaker, 2009). It is a peer-support strategy based on processes of review and reflection that enable both mentor and mentee to feel valued, respected, supported and encouraged. Mentoring supports a culture of learning by exploring the potential of educators to deliver quality practice.

*A few weeks after I joined the nursery, I asked the head teacher if someone could be my mentor to help me develop the skills I didn't learn in my last job. She asked one of the more experienced teachers and we met for about an hour every fortnight. We talked about all kinds of professional issues and also some personal ones. It helped me feel more confident, especially knowing we were due for an inspection.*
EARLY CHILDHOOD TEACHER

When early childhood leaders assume responsibility for mentoring a less experienced educator, they enter a special ongoing personal relationship that is based on the development of rapport, mutual trust, respect and openness to learning. Mentoring is not a supervisory relationship; it is an opportunity for colleagues to engage in reflective dialogue that can enhance feelings of empowerment and success and promote dispositions towards lifelong learning. The mentor becomes a critical friend in a supportive, non-judgemental and non-threatening professional environment.

The quality of the learning relationship between mentor and mentee is fundamental to its success. Successful mentors display:

- empathy and understanding
- an interest in lifelong learning and professional development
- sophisticated communication and interpersonal skills
- sensitivity to gender, ethnic and cultural issues (Elliott, 2008)
- understanding of the role of a mentor
- appreciation of the benefits of reflective practice, and
- considerable early childhood knowledge and expertise.

Effective mentors are active listeners, insightful observers, reflective conversationalists, critical friends and are responsive to different learning styles. They share their knowledge and experience to help others learn, grow and develop (Alred and Garvey, 2010).

To gain the most from a mentoring experience, the mentee needs to commit willingly to the process; trust and have confidence in their mentor; be open, honest and take responsibility for their own learning; be prepared to be challenged; and be willing to take informed risks (Alred and Garvey, 2010). They need to take an active role in their progress and be committed to lifelong learning.

According to Zachery (2009), the key elements for successful mentoring are:

- *reciprocity*—equal engagement of both parties in the process
- *learning*—active and reflective
- *relationship*—trust, honesty and authenticity
- *partnership*—equal involvement of and contribution by mentor and mentee
- *collaboration*—sharing knowledge, learning and building consensus
- *mutually defined goals*—articulating and clarifying agreed aims and targets, and
- *development*—expanding new knowledge, thinking and abilities.

A good mentor leads through empathy and example, communication and guidance, and supports the mentee by being an advocate. If undertaken inappropriately, mentoring will be perceived and experienced as an authoritarian leadership style, with the mentor dominating and imposing their ideas and the mentee submitting to and following their authority. Mentoring is not about controlling or foisting one's ideas, values and behaviours on another, but rather encouraging mentees to explore possibilities and collaborate in an array of decision-making opportunities.

Some forms of mentoring activity are more useful than others, including having a mentor from the same sector, having common planning time or time for collaboration with others, regular and supportive communications with administrators and being part of an external network.

One of the dangers of mentoring is that mentees become compliant through perceived powers of mentors, who may have control over important aspects of employment, such as pay awards or promotion. Mentors therefore need to set up a supportive framework of expectations, targets and assessment timelines that is neither overly ambitious nor undemanding, and both mentors and mentees need to be clear about goals and obligations in the agreed timeframe.

Early childhood leaders also benefit from acting as mentors. New understanding and insight can be achieved, better relationships can be developed, professional competence can be enhanced and careers progressed, and professional renewal and reinvigoration can be experienced.

*Aspiring leaders need to be mentored by other early childhood leaders with recognised expertise.*
ASSOCIATE PROFESSOR, EARLY CHILDHOOD

The early childhood sector has endorsed informal and formal mentoring as a key leadership strategy because it focuses on helping educators to realise their personal and professional potential. Most early childhood educators are passionate about their work, and are keen to help others learn by sharing their own knowledge, understanding, practice and expertise. Mentoring is a strategy that promotes self-awareness and self-assessment in a collaborative, non-threatening atmosphere.

Formal mentoring programs have been established in many early childhood services to assist with induction, to promote reflective practice, to support leadership development, to build leadership capacity, to plan for succession and to sustain change. To be effective, such programs require the input of high-quality, trained mentors. Structured mentor training contributes to the development of leadership capacity because it produces heightened awareness of the complexity of early childhood. Successful mentors are recognised for their knowledge and expertise, as well as for their ability to critically examine and reflect on their own and others' practice. Unfortunately, at present only limited preparation and training are available for would-be mentors in early childhood.

## The leader as a coach

Coaching is another collaborative process designed to promote early childhood leaders' and educators' ability to deliver quality services for children and families. Early childhood leaders may be coached themselves while simultaneously mentoring aspiring leaders or educators.

Coaching is the facilitation and management of day-to-day individual and team processes, and is based on questioning and listening. Effective leaders use coaching to help educators and teams to achieve goals and objectives, and to achieve their potential by asking questions, listening, supporting, advising, guiding and suggesting. Effective coaches know when to challenge and when to support (Osborne, 2008). They help unblock limiting or constricting beliefs and confront unhelpful behaviours. Coaching can help deepen both leaders' and educators' learning, build specific skills, boost performance and enhance the quality of services.

Coaching and mentoring share many similarities, and both are vehicles for questioning, analysis, reflection and action (Alred and Garvey, 2010). Both mentors and coaches help early childhood leaders and educators to construct a mental image of themselves as effective in the roles and functions to which they aspire, and use this as a vision to inspire and motivate them to commit to learning, development, growth and change. However, there are important differences.

Mentoring is a longer-term, protected relationship in which a more experienced colleague enables a less experienced colleague to make significant transitions in professional knowledge, understanding, skills, experience and opportunities. Mentors usually have had direct experience of the roles and responsibilities of the mentee, and wisdom is shared and received.

Coaching is a process that may not be based on direct experience of others' occupational roles, and coaches do not necessarily benefit from the activity. In early childhood, coaching tends to be related specifically to maximising leaders' and educators' potential within a specific timeframe—for example, six weeks or six months—while at the same time achieving a balance between professional aims and objectives, and individuals' personal needs.

Coaching is a continuing but time-specific partnership that begins with individual leaders and educators' personal and professional goals and uses questioning, reporting, exploring and choice to help them move forward and make transitions to new self-perceptions, competencies, roles and responsibilities. Through a series of regular meetings or contact, a good coach can help early childhood leaders and educators to improve their confidence and self-esteem; to enhance relationships with children, families and colleagues; to develop communications skills; to understand stress and time management; and to balance work and personal life, and personal and professional direction and purpose.

A coach is someone—not necessarily from within the sector—who acts as a catalyst for early childhood leaders and educators to find the answers themselves by asking challenging and thought-provoking questions and focusing attention on the action that is needed for realising potential. A coach doesn't tell someone what to do, but helps them to challenge assumptions and explore different perspectives and alternatives. An effective coach can help early childhood leaders and educators develop greater self-awareness, purpose, well-being and professional competence, thereby empowering them to use their skills and abilities better and thus improve job satisfaction.

## Reflections on leadership in practice

I have a life coach and he's brilliant. Generally, I find it hard to set goals in my life and I tend to procrastinate, putting off doing things that are difficult or unpleasant, and these issues have cropped up at work too. A friend recommended that I contact this particular coach. I have met with him a couple of times and I phone him up when there is something that I really need a push to get on with. He asks me questions and won't let me get out of answering them properly, and he sometimes suggests another way of seeing the problem. I found that talking to him has helped me see solutions to situations that I hadn't thought of. Knowing he is there and that I need to report back on my progress means I get on with doing the things that need to be done. It's worked for me in my personal life and I now use his strategies for dealing with issues at work. My manager noticed that I seem more assertive and confident in tackling certain work difficulties, especially delicate communications with colleagues and families, and I feel a lot more satisfied with the state of my personal and professional life.

DEPUTY SUPERVISOR, DAY NURSERY

Coaching can be conducted in a number of different ways and via a variety of media—for example, in one-to-one meetings or team coaching sessions, in person, on the telephone, by email or using video-conferencing. This means that leaders can coach people both within and outside their own context and at times that are convenient. The length and frequency of coaching sessions are decided together to meet individual needs and schedules.

Goleman, Boyatzis and McKee (2002) observe that leadership is a competency that can be developed through coaching. For them, leadership development is self-development. They argue that the self-knowledge accessed through coaching helps leaders improve their confidence and skills, clarify their values and guiding principles, and strengthen their initiative to reach their goals. Leaders who believe in themselves can achieve whatever they want to achieve.

Early childhood leaders and experienced educators have a wealth of expertise and experience to offer in coaching because they possess contextual knowledge and understanding, as well as the appropriate communication and interpersonal skills and techniques to successfully engage in the process.

## The deputy: A special opportunity for leadership

The position of deputy (sometimes referred to as the second-in-charge) has the potential to be a valuable training ground for becoming a formal leader in an early childhood service. However, the role can be as challenging as that of the official leader.

The position of deputy is an administrative one that often is characterised by role ambiguity and possible conflict, and where the level of responsibility fluctuates between shared and sole responsibility. It is a position where the deputy is sometimes the formal leader (on a short-term or longer term basis when the formal leader is absent) and sometimes a member of the team. An educator who is chosen by the leader often fills the position. This is a good example of a situation where the leader should apply the principles of delegation to ensure that the most suitable educator is selected for the role. The demands of the position of deputy call for sensitivity, flexibility and understanding on the part of the incumbent, the leader and the rest of the team.

The deputy's main roles include:

- supporting the leader by encouraging team members to cooperate and collaborate in the early childhood service's operation and administration
- supporting the team to achieve agreed goals while maintaining positive working relationships and morale, and
- meeting one's personal needs for affection, belonging, self-esteem and competence.

At times these roles may appear mutually exclusive and contradictory, as well as impossible to achieve. However, the essence of the deputy's position is commitment to the delivery of efficient and effective early childhood services. It is not about fulfilling power needs by controlling the team or sabotaging the leader's efforts or getting involved in workplace politics. It is an opportunity to make a positive contribution at an administrative level for those educators who aspire to and are interested in leadership responsibility, as well as a means of preparation for career progression.

The position of deputy is an opportunity to gain a broader perspective on the operation and administration of early childhood services, and to develop a broader background of skills and experience that may further career openings. Any educator who is interested in building trust and workplace relationships, shared decision-making, collective responsibility and team-building, and supporting an early childhood service's administrative structure is a potential candidate for the deputy position. Assuming the role of deputy is important from the perspective of professional career progression because it is a designated position, and aspiring leaders often are expected to have some experience at this level of formal responsibility.

Changes in the structure of early childhood services as a result of increasing integration have altered early childhood leaders' roles and responsibilities, with a greater emphasis on long-term planning, policy formulation, professional preparation and development, and anticipating and responding to the need for change. This can leave little time for any leader to have a significant input into the day-to-day running of a service, with the deputy often assuming greater responsibility for daily operation, administration and service delivery. This may leave formal leaders more isolated from the daily concerns of services, so the deputy needs to ensure that links are maintained between the leader, the team, children and families, and to keep the leader informed about tasks, resources, opportunities and problems.

As with other aspects of work in early childhood, little opportunity for preparation and training is available for those educators who wish to or undertake deputy positions. Most have to 'learn on the job' in order to discover what the position actually involves, what roles and responsibilities it entails, and what skills are needed. In some cases, the deputy has to fulfil allocated educational duties as well as take on extra duties associated with this administrative position. It is not surprising that many educators who hold the position of deputy experience high levels of stress and diminished morale when they think that their performance is not up to standard, or if their relationships with their colleagues appear to deteriorate. The deputy and the formal leader need to communicate, cooperate and collaborate in order to enact their roles effectively.

The lack of opportunity for preparation and training and the absence of a standardised job description or specification can create problems for early childhood leaders and their deputies. Some leaders willingly share authority, power and information, and provide a time allocation for the extra administrative duties assumed by the deputy, affording them a genuine experience of formal leadership roles and responsibilities. However, some leaders micro-manage the deputy's role by not delegating appropriately, refusing to share real responsibilities and information, and expecting any extra duties to be absorbed as part of the normal workload. The deputy becomes a token, powerless and ineffectual leader in the formal leader's absence. The lack of formal channels of communication between the leader and deputy can contribute to difficulties in the mutual understanding of roles and responsibilities, including expectations about possible financial remuneration for the higher duties and responsibilities.

The following support is necessary for a deputy to be successful in the role:

* appropriate orientation, induction and training for the position to develop a thorough understanding of the range of administrative duties
* a standardised job description, with appropriate levels of financial remuneration if possible
* allocation of a minimum time allowance for administration in addition to educational planning time
* an operational definition that defines the parameters of delegated authority
* the employment of a reliever or cover in the leader's absence to ensure statutory staff:child ratios are observed
* continuing collaboration with the formal leader on certain policy and decision-making issues, and
* ongoing opportunity to participate in the wider early childhood sector.

Without such support, the potential for conflict between the formal leader and the deputy is considerable, and is associated with:

* lack of leader support for decisions made in the leader's absence
* poorly defined roles and responsibilities
* different ways of doing things
* insufficient information
* unwritten expectations
* different values, ethics and interpretations of situations
* micro-management by the leader, and
* the leader feeling threatened by the deputy's initiatives.

Lack of role definition and authority creates the greatest potential for conflict with the rest of the team when the deputy is elevated to the position of responsibility in the formal leader's absence, with two major difficulties identified. First, team members may not accept and therefore may challenge the deputy's authority and decisions. They may refuse to recognise the deputy as the legitimate leader, covertly choosing someone else as their unofficial leader and spokesperson. A team may bestow on their chosen person unofficial power and status, and the prerogative to represent and make decisions on their behalf. In addition, an unofficial leader may have recourse to unquestioning support from team members, which is an invidious situation for formal leaders.

The deputy—like any formal leader—needs to earn the respect of the team by demonstrating relevant knowledge, skill and expertise, and by gaining the team's support by virtue of the genuineness of their personal qualities, resources and relationships. Simply assuming the formal position and title of deputy leader does not necessarily mean that the team will acknowledge and support an educator as legitimate in that position. In some cases, authority over, respect from and the support of the team are earned through the way in which the role is embodied and enacted.

The second issue is confidentiality. There are instances when a team member has confided in the deputy who later decided that they had a moral obligation to inform the leader. This is an example of an ethical dilemma for which a professional code of ethics should provide guidelines. An apparent breach of trust can have destructive outcomes on a deputy's future relationship with a team, with the deputy being rejected as an equal member of the team when no longer in the leadership position. The impact on the deputy's relationship with a team as a result of varying levels of trust, support and authority is an important concern.

Although some difficulties arise with the position of deputy, there are many positive aspects to the role. Participation in a team in this capacity helps to build self-esteem and enhances job satisfaction through opportunities to provide input at a different level. The opportunity to develop leadership potential, demonstrate leadership capability, gain experience and knowledge, and change perceptions about personal capacities are positive outcomes of accepting this additional role and responsibility.

Awareness about the possible pitfalls and pressures of leadership responsibility is important because it allows early childhood educators to develop the knowledge and skills necessary to undertake the position in the future. In terms of the overall team, a competent deputy is essential to act as a backup in any emergency or unplanned absence by the formal leader. It is a logical and rational way of purposively sharing and openly distributing responsibility for the provision of quality early childhood services, as well as for growing the future leaders of these services.

## Bringing it together

Supervision, mentoring and coaching provide on-the-job opportunities to advance the professional development of early childhood leaders and educators. Creating a climate for personal and professional growth is critical for ensuring ongoing quality in early childhood services. Such opportunities and experiences help improve educators' confidence, communication, respect for others and teamwork, and develop broader professional perspectives. The most effective on-the-job professional development experiences provide both the motivation and opportunity to learn from positive role models, mentors and coaches in supportive, encouraging and collaborative environments.

# CHAPTER 10

## LEADING IN CHANGING TIMES

*An effective leader can harness the necessary expertise to push forward*
*an agenda for reform and change that has been jointly constructed.*
SENIOR LECTURER, EARLY CHILDHOOD

### THIS CHAPTER EXPLORES

- change as a crucial leadership challenge
- types of change
- change and the individual
- sources of resistance
- converting resistance into commitment
- effective implementation of change
- helping educators cope with change
- leading change
- features of successful changes

The ability to lead change is regarded by theorists, researchers and successful leaders as the critical responsibility of a leader's role and functions. Contemporary leadership is a dynamic endeavour that demands personal capacity for vision, commitment, innovation, flexibility, shrewdness, decisiveness and action to ensure that organisations and employees remain responsive, relevant, current and possibly even ahead of their time. These qualities and skills are the driving force behind continuing improvement, innovation and transformation of organisations and people. Leading change requires early childhood leaders to draw on their insight, energy, determination, persistence and resilience to ensure that quality services are sustained and progress.

Change is a natural and necessary phenomenon, and one of the few certainties in all aspects of human life. Given that human beings experience considerable change in day-to-day life, and throughout the course of their lives, it is perplexing that the process of change presents such a threat to some people. Indeed, one of the realities of change is that it will be resisted by many of us. Change occurs in individuals, organisations and societies. Change at any one of these levels will necessitate change in the others. Decisions usually involve change because the process of implementation requires change in individual attitudes and skills, as well as organisational policies and procedures. Change is an inevitable and continuing process in life and work (Carnall, 2007), and as such should be approached positively and confidently by all.

From conception, change is an essential part of human life. Growth is a result of change, and illustrates the capacity of an individual or organisation to respond to the environment, to adapt, to be flexible, to question traditional or established practices, methods or ideas in order to innovate, and to develop new knowledge and ways of applying and integrating that knowledge with practice. It is a means of creating opportunities that sustain individual and organisational survival and advancement. Any formal leader who is not willing or ready to accept and embrace change as an essential responsibility is not an authentic, legitimate or appropriate leader.

Early childhood continues to experience acute and chronic change where pressures for rapid and extensive adaptation, innovation and transformation have occurred over an extended period of time. Considerable levels of uncertainty and unpredictability still exist as the sector attempts to accommodate rapid social and economic changes by creating and developing services that are adaptive, flexible, integrated and responsive to family and community needs. Therefore, leadership in early childhood services is grounded inextricably in change, with leaders and educators functioning as active agents of change who initiate and respond proactively to demands for improvement and change. Given the complexity of current and potential future changes, early childhood leaders must develop robust attitudes to and skills for leading change.

While some early childhood educators view the demand for change as challenging, stimulating and ripe with future benefits, others see it as a threat to themselves and service provision, and as something to be avoided and resisted where possible. Both responses to change arouse people's emotions. Positive emotions are associated with favourable responses, with change perceived as beneficial, stimulating and useful. Negative emotions are associated with pessimistic and resistant responses, with change perceived as stressful and destructive. Leaders are responsible for ensuring that early childhood services remain viable under current and anticipated circumstances. Therefore, they need to encourage, support and strengthen positive, optimistic attitudes, emotional responses to and willingness to engage with change in all team members. Listening—that is, hearing and understanding what is important to and of concern to team members—is an essential tool for empathising with yet overcoming negativity and resistance.

As part of their professional identity, role and responsibilities, early childhood leaders need to become skilled as agents of change, to be instrumental and responsible for anticipating, inspiring, communicating, enabling and managing change in services for children and families. Early childhood leaders as change agents are expected to ensure efficient use of resources to meet present, short-term demands while simultaneously finding ways to guarantee the long-term survival and effectiveness of early childhood services. Planning for and implementing change are two of the major challenges facing today's early childhood leaders. Leading change requires skill in:

- inspiring vision and motivating commitment
- effective communication and interpersonal relationships
- decision-making
- forward planning
- confident conflict resolution, and
- sensitive people management.

The extent to which change is well planned, carefully managed, appropriately timed and sufficiently resourced (as opposed to it being a vaguely conceived, loosely implemented project) will depend on the leader's understanding of the process of change and its implementation in early childhood services. Peterson and Baker (2011) propose that lasting improvement in early childhood service delivery and provision hinges on leaders' understanding of the complexity of the change process, with their ability to build a sense of readiness to change in educators the first and fundamental step in the process.

The following features pinpoint the essence of change, as well as where and how it fits into personal and professional life. Change:

- is inevitable because it is an intrinsic part of life
- is necessary and a stimulus for growth and improvement
- occurs in individuals, organisations and societies
- can be anticipated and planned for
- is a process, best put into action in small incremental steps
- is highly emotional, and can cause tension and stress
- is resisted by many people
- can be adjusted to by individuals and teams with a leader's support
- entails development in attitudes, knowledge and skills, policies and procedures, and
- is best facilitated on the basis of diagnosed need for improvement.

When considering change, sensitive early childhood leaders appreciate that their service does not exist merely for the purpose of testing out new ideas. Prior experiences with ad hoc approaches to change, where change has been introduced for its own sake, have left many of those involved feeling ambiguous about or resistant to future change. It is rare for early childhood service effectiveness and viability to be enhanced through the introduction of ad hoc changes. Sustainable change grows out of early childhood services' diagnosed needs for improvement, visionary and innovative thinking, and inspirational and motivational leadership, which generate a sense of commitment, feelings of control and involvement, and perceptions of challenge and attainability in the team.

Successful services adjust continually to social, political and economic demands in terms of opportunities presented and constraints experienced. Early childhood leaders understand that quality services are created and sustained by educators who follow and fulfil their shared vision and mission, and who want to achieve agreed goals and objectives. Therefore, change should be considered only when it is deemed to be effective in furthering a service's vision, mission, goals and objectives.

The strength of any early childhood service is a function of the mix of and balance between two major forces: bureaucratisation and innovation. Bureaucratisation refers to the need to establish ritual, routine and predictable ways of doing things, and is a means of ensuring stability. Rules and regulations, standard procedures, division of labour and the internal structural hierarchy are examples of bureaucratic forces. Over-emphasis on traditional and established ways of doing things can result in a failure to perceive the need for change and a lack of, inadequate, delayed or overdue action. Sometimes policies and practices are upheld not because they are the most effective or efficient ways to do things now—or even because they were the best ways to do things in the past—but simply because they *were done* in the past.

Leading change is linked intrinsically with innovation—that is, the leader's ability to respond creatively to environmental demands for adaptability and flexibility. Changes in structure (for example, new teams), communication channels and processes (such as who reports what to whom, when and how) and considered changes in behaviour (such as building a culture of distributed leadership) illustrate innovation in a service. However, over-emphasis on innovation can lead to a haphazard approach to change, premature change or blind imitation of certain policies and practices of similar services (an attitude of 'if they're doing it, it must be right, so we'll do it too'). Early childhood leaders must ensure that innovative decisions are based upon diagnosed need as well as adequate bureaucratisation in order to achieve goals and objectives, and sustain team relationships and morale. Leaders who adopt flexible thinking styles are more likely to anticipate, stimulate and bring about innovative and transformational change.

## Types of change

Change happens in a variety of ways, and involves different levels of significance for those affected by it. Early childhood services are dynamic in that people, hierarchies, structures and systems continually evolve through the pursuit of new knowledge and experiences, more efficient practice and more effective functions. This is *incremental change*, where small modifications are introduced into and absorbed by early childhood services on a day-to-day basis. These small changes often go unnoticed until someone becomes aware that a substantial difference has evolved. Simple and small changes to the curriculum or routines are examples of incremental changes to which little attention is given. Incremental change can be effective, especially when a bigger change is broken down into smaller do-able steps. However, a series of incremental changes that is not monitored properly, whether planned or unintentional, can lead to a major shift in an unwanted direction:

- *Routine change* is very common and is effected by the leader and team members in response to problems that arise on a daily basis. Such routine changes—for example, alterations to the staffing roster, mealtimes and menu, toileting, indoor/outdoor experience and activity schedules— are designed to improve quality, to meet the needs of children and families, to enhance team cooperation and collaboration, and to avoid or reduce conflict.
- *Induced change* results from a conscious decision to implement changes in people, processes, schedules, structures and systems. The decision to change an aspect of an early childhood service, such as curriculum, behaviour-management practices or family engagement approaches, can be a result of participation in a conference or training event. The introduction of new government frameworks or qualification standards can bring about induced change, where services deliberately make changes in order to comply with mandated national guidance. Induced change can involve different levels of significance: it can be routine, intended to cope with a crisis, innovative or, more rarely, transformational.
- *Crisis change*, as the name suggests, is any response to an unexpected occurrence in a service. Due to the time constraints of a crisis situation, early childhood leaders may make an individual, quick decision without consulting the team. Team members usually do not object to the demands of change in a crisis, and are willing to accept an authoritarian decision by the leader in order to meet the needs of a crisis situation. If the leader has procrastinated about or deferred necessary decision-making prior to a crisis, early childhood educators may support a fast, executive decision

but with an expectation that consultation and collaboration with team members will occur in the future. Crisis change can occur because of unexpected resignations, illness or absence, unexpected changes in structural or financial conditions or unexpected needs of children and families. Crisis change arises unexpectedly from, for example, issues around quality, ethical matters, inappropriate information-sharing and confidentiality. Indeed, failure to anticipate and recognise the need for change can precede and precipitate a crisis change.

- *Innovative change* results from creative problem-solving, or trial and error, where the early childhood leader and team seek easier, faster and more successful ways to further vision and mission and meet goals and objectives. Innovative change is more likely to occur through the collaborative leadership of highly supportive, committed and goal-oriented educators. Altering a service's opening hours to meet the needs of local families is an example of innovative change. Decision-making for innovative change involves initiation and implementation. Initiation arises out of knowledge awareness, the formation of positive attitudes towards the change and the actual decision to change. Implementation refers to the initial introduction and planned execution of the change plus continued, sustained integration of the change. However, the decision-making processes for the initiation and implementation of change rarely follow a rational and logical sequence from problem recognition to evaluation of alternatives to the adoption of a solution. Early childhood leaders and educators need to merge understanding about decision-making processes with awareness about factors that can make innovative change appear a chaotic event.

- *Transformational change,* where the form of a service is radically altered, occurs at crisis point when survival calls for drastic action. This type of change is most likely to occur if an early childhood service fails to respond to the demands of the environment due to an over-emphasis on either bureaucratisation or innovation. The leader and team may have ignored cues about the need for routine, minor crisis and innovative changes. Transformational change is most obvious in early childhood services with the creation of multi-disciplinary teams, integrated services and multi-agency service provision. Transformational change can occur in pedagogical thinking, organisational structure, staffing patterns and reconceptualisation of early childhood practice. The pressures on early childhood educators involved in transformational change are enormous, and the potential for stress and burnout is high.

## Change and the individual

Effective leaders understand that any change can have a major impact on the lives of those involved or affected by it. It is not uncommon for people to react to change with anxiety, uncertainty and stress—even those who are fully committed to change. The magnitude of the change determines perceptions about the amount of stress generated. Stress and its management are very important for the successful implementation of change. Conflict is often the impetus for change, and should not be avoided in professional situations. However, both conflict and stress need to be managed intelligently by early childhood leaders because of the links between these and self-esteem and performance. While some stress can challenge and motivate individuals, too much lowers performance and self-esteem. Early childhood leaders and educators should learn how to manage stress levels to ensure optimal perform-ance and high levels of self-esteem.

Change at work can challenge early childhood leaders' and educators' sense of professional identity. The competent accomplishment of tasks becomes routine with experience, and change can threaten perceived competence and mastery at work. This may lead to educators questioning the meaning of their roles, responsibilities and achievements, and evoke defensive reactions, active and passive opposition and resistance to suggestions about and the implementation of change. Early childhood leaders need to present any impending change in ways that permit educators to see it as a new opportunity consistent with existing views about professional identity. Where change questions established perceptions about and practices in work or threatens routines, sensitive early childhood leaders make sure that educators appreciate the need for and benefits of change and make it clear that support will be available to all throughout the implementation process.

In any team, the possibility of change will evoke a range of reactions on a continuum of emotions from negative to neutral to positive. Early childhood leaders should be aware of the reactive tendencies of individual team members and draw on communication and interpersonal relationship skills to turn any negative or neutral responses into positive ones that commit to and support change. The following descriptions illustrate some common reactions to change from team members.

- *The victim* has a very narrow view, with any proposed change perceived as a direct attack on their personal abilities, role, responsibilities or job, and is concerned only about how it will affect them personally.
- *The critic* attacks, challenges, condemns or opposes any change as a matter of principle and as a means of galvanising support from others to prevent it.
- *The resister*, for a range of reasons identified below, openly or subtly tries to obstruct, disrupt, derail or sabotage proposed change.

- *The detached bystander* is neither for nor against, positive nor negative about change, does not actively or passively criticise or resist but will not commit proactively.
- *The enthusiast* views and approaches change positively and energetically, actively advocates for and engages others with change, and supports initiation and implementations processes.

It is important for early childhood leaders to recognise such reaction tendencies to change by team members early in the change process and, along with any enthusiasts, communicate, educate, involve and support them to convert negative, oppositional and neutral reactions into positive ones.

## Sources of resistance to change

Every early childhood context is unique, and therefore resistance to change will arise from different sources. However, the following are some common sources of resistance, and early childhood leaders are responsible for recognising and finding antidotes or ways to overcome them:

- *Fear about personal future* in a changed environment. Educators may fear the unknown, be anxious about losing their jobs, having their salary reduced, losing status, being unable to perform a new job, taking on new responsibilities, undergoing new training, changes in social relationships or possible relocation from the integration of services.
- *Ideological factors*, such as changes in values and belief systems. These may affect vision, mission, goals and objectives—especially if working in a multi-disciplinary team, integrated or multi-agency service.
- *Individual personalities* such as negative and pessimistic educators with low self-esteem and those who prefer routine and predictability.
- *Misunderstandings* about the need for, purpose of, scope and ramifications of change.
- *Lack of trust in the leader* where the educators do not believe that the leader has their best interests at heart.
- *Different assessments or points of view* about proposed changes and effects on the established team culture.
- *Self-interest*—'what's in it for me?', where an educator perceives the change to involve loss of benefits or little personal pay-off.
- *Lack of knowledge* about proposed changes.
- *New technologies* that require new skills or different ways of doing the job.
- *Lack of ownership*, where change is imposed from outside.
- *Excessive change* in the immediate past or demands for sudden change.

Resistance to change is less likely to occur where leadership style is collaborative, shared or distributed, and where joint and consensual decision-making approaches are adopted. Everybody performs better when they take charge and feel in control of change. However, effective early childhood leaders are aware that some educators engage in covert and subtle ways of resisting change and sabotaging its efficient implementation.

## Converting resistance into commitment

The ways in which early childhood leaders approach resistance to change are an important issue in implementing any change. Fighting resistance by trying to overcome it with information, data, reasoned argument and power usually is unsuccessful because it goes underground and is not visible. Overcoming resistance by resorting to force or pressure often generates a desire for revenge, where educators wait for an opportunity to get even. A better way to handle resistance is to bring it out into the open and encourage full expression of concerns. This can help resisters to start expressing any concerns, fears, unease and anxieties directly to the leader and team, thus preventing pointless attempts at subterfuge and sabotage.

The following approaches for converting resistance into commitment are helpful for early childhood leaders because they draw on communication and problem-solving skills that are usually well developed and well received by all.

### Communication and education

This approach is useful prior to and during the implementation of change where lack of, or inaccurate, information increases stress levels and hinders appreciation of the benefits of change. If the rationale behind change is understood, early childhood educators may be persuaded to accept it. The provision of accurate information to others encourages educators to participate actively in the implementation phase. Unless most educators are involved in communicating with and educating team members, families and even the local community, informing and bringing others on board can be a very time-consuming activity for leaders, especially if large numbers of people and groups are involved.

### Participation and involvement

This approach is useful prior to and during the implementation phase where a leader wants to ensure team commitment to the proposed change, where the leader needs more information to design or tailor the change or where there are numerous potential resisters. Collaborative, shared or distributed leadership includes the team by inviting advice and help with designing and activating the change. Participation helps reduce stress and allay fears, and acts as a motivator by increasing self-esteem and self-confidence. Resisters are more likely to contribute if they believe that they can have some control over the process. Educators who actively participate and are involved can contribute to the integration of available and relevant information into proposed change, thereby assisting in refining and enhancing commitment to the final outcome. The only disadvantage is that poorly supervised participants may design an inappropriate change that can be costly and time-consuming to rectify should it be implemented. The leader needs to monitor the team's direction and contribution to ensure that the change is consistent with the service's vision, mission, goals and objectives.

### Facilitation and support

This approach is helpful where early childhood educators openly resist change. While it is time-consuming, costly and ultimately may be unsuccessful, it is an important option for dealing with adjustment problems. Attention is focused on educators' concerns about task performance and relationships. The early childhood leader uses listening, conflict-resolution, problem-solving and stress-management skills to strengthen the level of trust in the team. Acknowledgement of and empathy for the difficulties of undergoing change are essential. Support needs to be made available through training and access to other resources.

### Negotiation and agreement

This approach is useful where it is obvious that someone is likely to forfeit certain existing benefits or experience extra burdens, or when the team has a lot of power to resist the change. The early childhood leader needs to offer incentives to actual or potential resisters, or work out some form of trade-off where special benefits are guaranteed if the change is not blocked. Unfortunately, most early childhood leaders have little to offer in terms of special incentives and benefits because they do not have the power or resources to provide financial and/or time-in-lieu rewards. Prestige in terms of nomination for the position of deputy or for special responsibility may be a reward for some educators.

If early childhood leaders have personal concerns or a lack of confidence about their own ability to facilitate change, they may enact a more autocratic style of leadership, hampering the team's ability to respond positively to change. Early childhood leaders and educators with positive self-concepts and high levels of self-esteem are more likely to have positive attitudes to change and to respond to the demands of change in creative ways. Those who perceive change as an opportunity for growth and development will approach new situations with confidence and enthusiasm, and a willingness to learn new skills to become competent in the unfamiliar circumstances. Energy and time are devoted to preparing for change, thereby enhancing personal effectiveness and creativity, and developing more positive attitudes to change in the future. To survive the demands of constant change, a culture of learning and communities of lifelong learners need to be encouraged and supported so that people are receptive to each other's ideas and are committed to learning and growing together.

## Reflections on leadership in practice

Our team wanted to instigate High Scope as part of a government initiative. The lead person was the manager but she encouraged different people to take the lead on different aspects. She showed leadership because she supported each team member to sustain this area of practice.

EARLY CHILDHOOD COURSE LEADER

Where early childhood educators believe that change threatens their security, or demands skills that they cannot attain, or where they erroneously believe that change can be avoided, forestalled or even stopped, energy and time may be devoted to opposing and resisting change. Stress levels escalate, and discord, disharmony and conflict can increase. A corresponding deterioration in performance, relationships with others and self-esteem is inevitable, with eventual outcomes being withdrawal and alienation from the team and its goals. In such circumstances, early childhood leaders need to bolster up everyone's self-esteem and confidence to meet the new demands.

## Reflections on leadership in practice

I have seen some very innovative educational programs being implemented in early childhood services. For example, the head teacher and teaching staff rewrote the Foundation Stage curriculum with an emphasis on skills. The changed curriculum also required moving one teacher out and replacing her with someone new. It was very impressive how they worked together constructively to make such a huge change happen.

PRIMARY ADVISER

A commitment to personal and professional development on the part of all educators is essential to meet the requirements for change in early childhood.

Thoughtful leaders accept that early childhood educators have the right to be cautious about something new, but they do not have the right to become complacent or apathetic, to stagnate or to become inept. Furthermore, nobody has the right to stop others from learning, growing and developing. Professional development opportunities help foster self-esteem and the ability to cope with perceived threat from change. The leader needs to encourage everybody to develop dispositions for lifelong learning so that resistance to change is overcome and they are open to approaching change with interest and enthusiasm.

## Preparing to implement change

Effective early childhood leaders motivate and prepare educators to be receptive to change by explaining the need for change and confirming confidence in the team's ability to meet new demands. Educators must be convinced that the present situation is no longer viable, and that they have a professional responsibility to act to restore the service to expected levels of quality. Early childhood leaders who convey confidence in everyone's ability to cope with change tap into their sense of psychological safety. The leader must address any barriers to and sources of resistance to change at this point. A common mistake many leaders make is to introduce change when the team has not been prepared sufficiently and consequently is not yet receptive to change.

People often move through stages of coping with change. First, they may deny that a need for change exists and may try to defend the status quo. Much energy can be devoted to resistance if educators have not been prepared adequately for the change or given enough time to adjust to the realities of the situation. As they come to perceive that change is inevitable and necessary, with sufficient support from the leader they begin to let go of the past and focus on the future. Educators will then start to adapt to the new requirements and circumstances, but could find this period frustrating because they may not have the level of skill and competence to meet new or different demands. Ongoing mutual support from the leader and team members is essential to move through this stage and to ensure the long-term success of the change. Finally, as the change is incorporated into educators' personal skill repertoire and into the service, it becomes accepted as a normal and routine part of work.

### Effective implementation of change

Change begins to be implemented when new attitudes and behaviour, new information or cognitive reframing become evident and affect practice. The essence of changing is to ensure that the educators engage in new behaviour, or with the new circumstances, and to start to experiment with the change. This is a transitional stage where learning, risk-taking and creativity are required. The more educators interact with the change, the faster it will be integrated into and embedded in accepted, normal patterns at work. The early childhood leader should provide feedback about how well the team is effecting improvements in achieving its vision, mission, goals and objectives, improving the strategies, tasks, structures and learning culture.

Early childhood leaders set the conditions for the successful implementation of a change by appreciating that it is a people-oriented process requiring specific groundwork to stimulate and encourage receptivity to change. Implementing change requires that everybody concerned takes appropriate action. Stabilising, embedding and sustaining change all require ongoing attention and activity by the leader and team members.

### Stabilising and embedding change

When educators have accepted the change to a point where they support and enact it as a normal and routine part of daily work, it has become stabilised and embedded in practice. Change becomes stabilised, embedded and sustained when a sense of equilibrium is restored in the work environment and team culture. The process of stabilisation helps eliminate the feelings of chaos and lack of control that some educators experience during the process of change. Early childhood leaders need to provide support for the change, reward educators for their efforts to meet the demands of change, and review and evaluate its effects so that any adjustments can be made. Efforts need to be made to ensure that educators are supported in the rebuilding of their self-esteem and self-confidence. If work conditions are not stabilised following the introduction of a change, some educators might revert to the old ways, and the change will be short-lived or abandoned. The leader's inability to stabilise, embed and sustain the changed circumstances accounts for many failed attempts at change.

## Coping with change

Fear and uncertainty about change can lower performance level and team morale. However, sensitive early childhood leaders can support teams through periods of change by easing adjustment to new demands and enhancing self-esteem using the following techniques:

- Encourage the team to perceive change as a challenge, not a threat, through open communication, encouraging mutually supportive, cooperative and collaborative approaches to work, and keeping team spirit and morale high.
- Keep the team up to date and informed. Fear of the unknown, lack of information or misinformation can lead to resistance and lack of trust in

the leader; empathise with rather than ignoring or trivialising real experiences and problems with change.

- Involve the team in the diagnosis of the need for change, as well as the planning, design and implementation of the change. Participation and involvement in decision-making and problem-solving ensure high levels of commitment. In this way, team members 'own' the change and do not feel that it has been imposed from above or from outside.

- Encourage team members to feel they are not powerless in the face of change and that, through involvement, participation and negotiation, they have some control and are able to influence the timing, pace and course of the change. Allow for some flexibility to incorporate their ideas and feedback.

- Build confident, resilient team members who do not read any implications about their personal worth into change. Help them to be realistic and comfortable with their assets and strengths, as well as their limitations and vulnerabilities. Focus on promoting self-awareness and self-acceptance, while at the same time encouraging personal and professional development.

- Network with and seek assistance and support from colleagues, other professionals, services and agencies who are experiencing change to help the team develop awareness about the inevitability of change and a more sophisticated approach to adapting to change.

## Leading change

Leading change is a core role and function for early childhood leaders who are committed to the continuing provision of quality early childhood services. Although leading change might appear complex, it is a relatively simple process that employs specific skills. While many of the factors that relate to effective leadership have been outlined in previous chapters, the demands of leading change in early childhood require that leaders possess the ability to:

- *anticipate and diagnose the need for change*—a cognitive skill for assessing the gap between the present situation and future needs
- *communicate*—a process skill for articulating vision, mission, goals and clear objectives to others
- *identify and work on and with reactions from team members*—an emotionally intelligent and empathic skill for appreciating and turning the reactive tendencies of others from negative and adversary to positive and committed, and

- *adapt*—a behavioural skill for adapting, modifying or transforming practice and bringing a range of resources to solve the demands of meeting future needs.

Effective early childhood leaders take into account the service's previous history of change when considering introducing change. The timing and pace of change can act as barriers to the efficient implementation of necessary changes. Positive or negative experiences with change in the past, as well as the length of time for which change has been ongoing, and the significance or magnitude of change that has been required, affect team members' readiness to accept and implement further change.

Given that early childhood has experienced an extended period of continuous change, with many educators poorly prepared and with few skilled agents of change, high levels of resistance to demands for further change can be expected. Effective early childhood leaders analyse the critical barriers to change and plan any innovation in small, unintimidating steps to help reduce the stress levels of those who are involved with or affected by the change. To implement a change successfully, early childhood leaders will:

- ensure that team members clearly understand the need for and the benefits of change
- communicate vision, mission, goals and objectives so that team members have a clear sense of purpose
- provide broad guidelines for achieving the objectives (such as a step-by-step plan)
- encourage team participation to clarify the needed change and provide detailed information relevant to the change, and
- offer feedback and some form of reward for those who supported and participated in the implementation of the change.

The essence of leading change is to communicate, clarify and focus on the vision and values that underpin the needed change, to encourage the team's task accomplishment through informed risk-taking and problem-solving, to design processes and procedures that scaffold and reinforce manageable action, and to support people in the development of confidence and skills. This is not an easy task, but it is an essential one.

Change is about learning by both the early childhood leaders and educators. It is possible that some changes will not be achieved, or that they will be short lived. Effective leaders will not be deterred by failure or avoid becoming involved with possible future change, but will reassess the situation and try again. Commitment to leading change in early childhood is another hallmark of the effective leader.

## Reflections on leadership in practice

Our service was given a new identity when a new manager took charge. She developed courses and events to meet local government targets, and existing and known community needs. Her leadership skills are not reflected in her job description or salary and that needs to be reviewed. But her leadership has improved her own job prospects alongside the enhanced quality of our service.

TEACHER, EARLY EXCELLENCE CENTRE

### Features of successful change

To complete this exploration of leadership and change in early childhood, the following summary encapsulates features of successful change:

- Anticipation, assessment or diagnosis is needed before change is initiated.
- Adopt a realistic and limited scope—start small and build up; when small changes are successful, teams become more receptive to bigger changes.
- Team members are informed about and aware of the role of change in personal, professional and service development, survival and sustainability.
- Select appropriate intervention strategies that are consistent with the service's culture.
- Good timing and appropriate pace are crucial—ensure that change is not introduced too early or too late, too slow or too fast.
- Support competent educators to optimise the probability of success.
- Support is needed from the majority of team members to lessen resistance.
- All those affected—especially resisters—should have a sense of ownership, created through participation.
- Training and other necessary resources need to be put in place.
- Existing power structures, such as the deputy and lobby groups, should be involved in the change process.
- Support is needed from key power groups—especially top management.
- Scaffolding of new policies, procedures and practices is important until they are integrated with existing and established ones.

- There should be a protocol for continued evaluation.
- Adequate rewards are required to embed and sustain the change, such as feedback and public recognition.

## Bringing it together

Some early childhood services have been criticised for their apparent inability to meet demands for change. While many are responsive to change in times of crisis, more needs to be done to improve overall capacity to engage in innovative and transformational change. Effective early childhood leaders need the courage and motivation to overcome barriers and obstacles, and to counteract sources of resistance to change, and to mobilise both internal and external resources that support change. The traditional conservatism within the early childhood sector could jeopardise its long-range survival and viability. However, if attitudes to change become more positive and educators feel confident about voicing their opinions and experiences of change, as well as participating in and supporting it, the future can hold exciting possibilities for children, families and early childhood services.

# PART III

# SPECIAL RESPONSIBILITIES OF EARLY CHILDHOOD LEADERS

Given that early childhood is dynamic in that it must be responsive to social, political and economic changes, most early childhood leaders appreciate the necessity of incorporating four additional functions into their leadership repertoire.

The ability to undertake research is an important aspect of the contemporary professional identity of early childhood educators. In the quest for quality improvement, early childhood leaders need to acquire research skills as a means of ensuring that services remain relevant and sustainable. This means keeping up to date with developments in thinking, research design, findings and practices appropriate for early childhood services, researching and reflecting on their own practice, investigating and trying out new and innovative approaches, and creating and disseminating new understanding and thinking to other early childhood educators, professionals and agencies.

The ability to lead partnerships by engaging families and the community with the values, vision, mission, goals and activities that underpin service delivery and provision is another key leadership function. Effective early childhood leaders prioritise the values of collective understanding, participation and contribution between and with services, families, local communities and other related agencies.

The importance of ethical practice and responsibility in early childhood has been highlighted for many years. Early childhood leaders must be aware of ethical boundaries, the demarcation between what is right, moral and non-negotiable and what is wrong, unethical, unacceptable or forbidden when faced with the difficult and complex decisions that arise in early childhood practice.

Finally, it is essential to identify, develop and support future leadership capacity, given that leadership is temporary and transient. Insightful leaders create capacity-building strategies and succession plans to train and mentor aspiring leaders and those who yet have to be inspired to aspire to leadership.

# CHAPTER 11

## LEADING RESEARCH: MOVING QUALITY FORWARD

*Effective leaders possess a desire to know more and they want to pass on their knowledge widely to others in the early childhood sector and/or the public arena.*

<small>Associate Professor, Early Childhood</small>

## THIS CHAPTER EXPLORES

- research and its benefits for early childhood
- attitudes to research in early childhood
- encouraging a research culture
- action research for critical inquiry
- reflective practice

Early childhood has made considerable progress in developing its own research ethos, culture and community, with specific research agendas that focus on the application of findings to services for young children and families. Some high-quality formal research has been conducted—sometimes in partnership with government departments and higher education organisations—and some early childhood educators have acted as consultants to external research studies. Certain pedagogical approaches, such as that espoused by Reggio Emilia, define educators as researchers, with research embedded as an integral part of everyday educational practice. Practitioner research is now standard in early childhood, with educators regularly engaging in systematic critical inquiry and reflection about their work. However, the study of research—like that of leadership—usually is not included until the final stages of pre-service training, which contributes to the reluctance of some early childhood educators to incorporate research as an integral aspect of professional identity, roles and responsibilities.

Historically, early childhood relied on academic researchers from a variety of disciplines within universities and colleges to pursue new knowledge and apply it to the early childhood context. A professional and discipline divide between research and academic staff and early childhood educators led to the latter becoming recipients of others' advice, and consumers rather than producers of research. Today, however, greater understanding about research processes has led to early childhood educators becoming more active and skilled in their own research community.

With their earlier reluctance to regard themselves as intellectuals with a responsibility and capacity for scientific inquiry, many early childhood educators have perpetuated the outdated stereotype that they hold lower professional status, concerned more with practice than theory. However, with increasing numbers holding a range of accredited qualifications and the growing professional opportunities for inquiry-based research, the nature of early childhood educators has changed. Early childhood now grows its own researchers, who innovate, activate, lead quality improvement, interpret research findings and apply them to leading and contextually relevant practice.

Effective early childhood leaders possess the ability to understand and apply research findings to early childhood services, and to design and implement research within a service. Research inquiry—especially action research—is considered to be one of the most effective ways to improve quality, to advance service delivery and its provision, and to enhance early childhood's professional status and credibility. It is now accepted that early childhood educators themselves can and should set their own research agenda and priorities, and apply relevant research findings to improve the quality of services for young children and families. Early childhood leaders and educators are making a critical contribution to their profession's transformation by engaging in research that applies professional knowledge to practice and grows theory out of practical expertise.

Early childhood educators who continue to opt out of the research role deny themselves a valuable tool for change, and do not become empowered to influence others to think and act. Their ability to initiate and implement change on their own behalf and from their specialised knowledge base is diminished too. Early childhood's credibility as a true profession is threatened by any lack of involvement in research, especially if the essence of professional practice in early childhood is underpinned by a knowledge base generated by researchers from other disciplines or professions.

The early childhood sector has a responsibility to meet the challenge of effecting change—that is, inquiry needs to go beyond the descriptive (what is) to the predictive (what ought to be) to be appropriately responsive and improve quality provision. However, many early childhood educators display a tendency to resist changes that are guided by research findings. This has come about because much of the tradition and practice in early childhood is based on professionally socialised attitudes, beliefs and values that are ingrained and hard to change under any circumstances, let alone on the recommendation of research conducted by an 'outsider' who would be unlikely to empathise with contextual and perhaps idiosyncratic constraints.

Early childhood educators need to jettison outdated fears of professional inquiry, discourse and discussion, and to scrutinise carefully and question traditional and accepted practice by developing basic research skills in self-evaluation, analysis, reflection, articulation and dissemination. When critical reflection is used as a research tool, the constraints of traditional knowledge and practice are broken down, allowing more effective practice and thereby transforming professional practice, growth and development.

With a limited sense of ownership of research, a gap has formed between those who conduct research and those early childhood educators who could and should apply the findings to their practice. Early childhood educators play a vital role in initiating and implementing change in local communities, where informed action is based on contextualised critical inquiry and reflective judgement. Assuming responsibility for conducting research helps early childhood educators to move away from traditional conceptual simplicity—which is concrete, particular and not necessarily valid—to a scientific multi-disciplinary approach to knowledge and thinking—which is theoretical, general and rational.

Fortunately, many early childhood educators now understand the relationship between research and innovation and change, with more collaborative relationships, overlapping roles and blurred boundaries emerging between those engaged in practice and those engaged in research. Early childhood leaders and educators increasingly participate in a range of collaborative multi-disciplinary research projects, and no longer find themselves caught between the pressure for change and the pull of tradition, reactive to trends and counter-trends. The early childhood sector continues to experience rapid change, and is pushed continually to address the many pressing problems faced by children and families. Finding new ways to encounter, understand and respond to the issues and demands evident in the sector has become early childhood educators' greatest challenge. Willingness and ability to be innovative in the application of new knowledge assists early childhood leaders and educators to improve the quality of services and to enhance the quality of life for young children and families.

Specialist resources are available for those who wish to undertake research and learn how to apply research to practice. They are useful tools for assisting early childhood educators to identify more closely with the research aspect of their work.

## Research and its benefits for early childhood

Research is a basic tool for advancing knowledge and stimulating change in attitudes, values and practice—all of which are essential means for empowering early childhood educators and progressing early childhood generally. It can help explain current status by looking at and reflecting upon the past, and contributes to the generation of new ideas, direction and activity. Research is a means of evaluating the impact of a variety of ecological contexts upon children's development and learning, as well as professional practice. It can be used to influence the design of broad social policies. In short, research can provide early childhood with a comprehensive, systematic, rational basis for understanding young children and families, both in a broad sense, and for practical action. It is also a means to stimulate professional development through increased learning and insight.

Demands on early childhood educators are many and varied because they are required to provide quality services that meet the range of needs of children and families in ways that are inclusive and socially and culturally relevant. Early childhood is recognised universally as a critical period for growth, development and learning, with society and local communities holding certain assumptions and expectations regarding the types of experience to which young children ought to be exposed and from which they should be shielded. Early childhood educators are expected to extend their contribution to the development and welfare of children by meeting families' needs for information, support and education. They are charged with responsibility for making decisions about the experiences and resources that optimise young children's development and learning in diverse contexts, and are expected to be responsive to the challenge of constant change in society. The key to quality is the basis on which early childhood educators make decisions about young children and families, especially the information they use to do so.

Early childhood educators draw on many sources of information and resources to ensure responsible decision-making and be appropriately responsive to the challenges of change. Increasingly, early childhood leaders have a large impact on the sources and variety of information that are available to educators, particularly those with little or no training. However, some early childhood educators still are reluctant to use research as a basis for decision-making, relying upon other sources of information as guidelines and reference points. Some of these sources have limitations and disadvantages, and are likely to result in poor-quality and perhaps even inappropriate decisions.

One of the most common sources of information for decision-making is *personal opinion and intuition*—that is, the use of a subjective viewpoint, usually derived from personal values and experience, as a guide to action and decision-making. This approach needs to be treated with extreme caution because some early childhood educators justify decisions using irrelevant, unsuitable and invalid opinion and personal knowledge. The more popular justifications include 'intuition', which may or may not have some basis in theory but which is often little more than a gut feeling that cannot be justified on rational and logical grounds; 'common sense', which can be vague, often incorrect and fallible; 'in my experience', which may have been limited and/or unrepresentative of general experience; and 'in the best interests of the child/family/educator', which usually describes a personal opinion or dogma.

This subjective approach is unhelpful as an information source for decision-making because it is influenced by the prevailing moral and social climate, personal values, convictions and stereotypes, the psychological characteristics and personal histories of the decision-maker, and other political and ideological considerations. The basis of decision-making is personal mythology. Inexperienced early childhood educators tend to rely on this source of information as a basis for action that is often well-intentioned but non-professional.

*Tradition*, or the justification of decisions and action by reference to *historical or established practices*, is another source of information used—often to create barriers to and to resist proposed changes. Early childhood educators justify decisions using expressions such as 'That's the way I was brought up and it didn't hurt me', 'We've always done it that way' and 'Why change something that's working well? Leave well enough alone!' However, insightful early childhood educators appreciate that considerable differences exist from one period of time to another, as well as from one place to another. Attitudes and practices that were fashionable at one time or in a particular place lose popularity as more information becomes available and societies and communities change.

While traditional and established practices may have been defensible at one time, this approach rarely employs rational, logical or scientific evidence as the basis for decisions. Rather, its basis is bold assertion of subjective assumptions and preconceptions about what is 'the best way'—and there is usually little room for debate. Fear about the uncertainty of change may evoke this tendency to hold on to what is known or familiar. However, educators who use this as a basis for decision-making may find themselves in a vulnerable situation professionally, with their ideas and practices out of touch with current information and thinking.

Reference to 'the expert' as a source of information for decision-making is a common strategy used by early childhood educators. There are many experts who have contributed to scientific knowledge about and understanding of young children, families and the early childhood period, such as Bowlby, Bronfenbrenner, Freud, Katz, Piaget, Spodek and Tizard, to name just a few. Then there are other experts who have professional credentials and background, but who often rely on their personal charisma or reputation to capture the imagination of ordinary people. These experts, such as Dr Benjamin Spock, Dr T. Berry Brazelton and more recently Gina Ford, Tanya Byron, Steve and Sharon Biddulph and Supernanny Jo Frost, have become influential regarding information, attitudes and practice in popular culture.

In the main, their contributions have been helpful and informative; however, it is essential that early childhood educators do not simply take for granted the wisdom of these so-called experts, whose thinking may be guided by subjective personal experience, and theories and principles that may not fit with ethical contemporary early childhood practice. Instead, early childhood educators should examine and evaluate closely the sources of so-called experts' information and recommendations.

While early childhood educators have assumed that their interests can be represented by contributions from more prestigious individuals and groups of professionals, their background and training lead to different perspectives on early childhood practice, and take decision-making and change out of the hands of educators. In addition, an expert's information and recommendations equally can be a mixture of personal opinion and intuition, guesswork and informed hunches, folklore, work with small numbers of clinical cases and sometimes their own child-rearing experience. The proportion of reliable and valid scientific information from which claims are asserted may be small.

*Research* is an important source of information for decision-making that is available to, but generally under-used by, early childhood educators. Research is defined as the systematic investigation of a problem or issue. In early childhood, research can be a form of audit, examining, analysing and evaluating systems, structures, behaviour and practice as a means of developing leading practice, improving quality service provision, and benefiting clients and consumers. The information and knowledge acquired from research has clear advantages compared with other sources of information. Research is:

- *Empirical*—findings and conclusions are based on direct observations of relevant phenomena or from verifiable experience available to all
- *Systematic*—data are collected according to an explicit plan not on an ad hoc basis, dependent on personal biases or tendencies
- *Basic and applied*—the purpose of basic research is to develop a base of knowledge upon which theory can be built. Applied research is designed to answer practical and useful questions, solve specific problems or provide information that is of immediate use.
- *Qualitative and quantitative*—qualitative studies provide descriptive data, whereas quantitative data enable comparisons between groups or conditions. Qualitative data, used in conjunction with quantitative data, can help educators understand and interpret what the numbers mean. Quantitative research usually is controlled: studies are designed in such a way as to rule out all possible explanations except one.

- *Public*—the methodology and findings of studies are available for public scrutiny so that the work can be critically assessed and subsequently replicated by other researchers.

Research provides early childhood educators with valid and reliable information from which they can confidently make new decisions, reaffirm previous decisions and initiate change. Such changes will not be on a whim, an ad hoc basis or 'change for change's sake', but rather will have a rational and logical basis. Early childhood educators need to value and incorporate research as a valid source of information for decision-making to avoid becoming rigid, stereotyped and outdated in their attitudes. Engagement in inquiry- or research-based practice enhances professional development and effectiveness because personal bias is reduced and mistakes are minimised.

Research does not provide magical answers, however, and there may be no one right answer to the questions asked or the problems posed. More often than not, the answer may be that 'it depends'—that is, factors such as the individual, the context, the type and composition of the group, the kinds of intervention and the local conditions will affect the interpretation of research outcomes. In addition, more questions and problems are generated for future investigation than are resolved by research. Fortunately, this helps expand the pool of knowledge relevant to early childhood.

In Chapter 3, the relationship between stage of professional career development and leadership was explored. In relation to research, early childhood educators who are more advanced in professional career development use more complex and sophisticated sources of information in their daily practice. They tend not to rely on common sense, personal experience or simplistic applications of basic empirical knowledge and theory, but rather demonstrate progressive thinking by using an inter-disciplinary knowledge base (underpinned by scientific research), which is interpreted in the light of their experience and practice.

Although some early childhood educators may not regard themselves as researchers, in practice that is what they are, because they continually process information gathered as they work with and for children and families. Pascal (2011) refers to early childhood educators as 'praxiologists' because they can contribute to the creation of knowledge, practice and policies by translating practice into and integrating it with theory. Using data collected prior to, during and following decision-making, they construct their own implicit theories on which to base future action. These grounded theories are extracted out of their own experience and practice, and are not developed and tested by researchers for other disciplines. Effective early childhood leaders embed practice in information gleaned from scientific research as well as praxis—that is, theories constructed from personal experience and practice in early childhood contexts.

## Attitudes to research in early childhood

Although some progress has been made in the incorporation of 'researcher' into early childhood educators' professional identity, the role, importance and value of research need to be endorsed by early childhood leaders and more fully appreciated by politicians and the general public. Unfortunately, limited awareness of and interest in research by some of the key stakeholders are major obstacles to the meaningful application of any research findings and recommendations in early childhood contexts.

Any discontinuity between research and practice limits the potential of research for improving the quality of early childhood services, especially if educators continue to under-value the need for and the benefits of new knowledge in relation to the improvement of professional practice. Such a situation would be untenable in other professions, where it is an inherent expectation that professionals keep abreast of current research and developments in practice. Imagine how a medical practitioner or an engineer would be perceived if they were ignorant of, disregarded or discounted new research findings and failed to incorporate them into their work! It would be considered totally unacceptable by other members of the profession, consumers and the general public. Fortunately, increasing numbers of early childhood leaders appreciate that well-designed research is a reliable source of information where new ideas can be identified, developed, transformed or created, and more early childhood educators appreciate their professional responsibility to keep up to date with relevant research and related literature. However, research remains under-valued and under-utilised by some early childhood educators for the following reasons.

First, many pre-service training courses offer a cursory examination of the role and value of research, and it remains a low priority on the training agenda for the preparation of early childhood educators. The key priority is skill development for the practical aspects of working with children and families, and for operating services with little focus on the development of the skills required to understand and conduct research. The predominantly practice-oriented priorities in early childhood training have impeded the inclusion of training in basic research understanding and skills.

Second, because of the practical orientation and limitations of current training, early childhood educators often are unaware of different approaches to research. For some, the lack of training and information is a barrier. Many educators simply lack knowledge about what research is available because in general they do not subscribe to or read research-oriented journals, do not read theoretically and conceptually demanding books, and do not attend professional development opportunities that have a research orientation. The personal libraries of early childhood educators tend to be filled with popular literature on practical aspects of child development, child-rearing and psychology, with some dated texts from pre-service training courses.

The inability of researchers to disseminate and communicate research findings in an accessible form for educators is another factor in the under-utilisation of research. When early childhood educators do read research reports, they often complain that the theory, findings and recommendations are incomprehensible, and therefore irrelevant. Because they lack training and skill in research methodology, the technical and abstract language of the researcher can be difficult to understand and interpret. To overcome this obstacle, researchers need to communicate their findings in the language of the educator. Unfortunately, many researchers find this a difficult task given their limited familiarity with the practical contexts of early childhood services, and prefer to pursue their own research interests rather than become a translator and interpreter for those who may not be particularly receptive to what research has to offer.

Researchers tend to write for specific audiences—usually other academics and colleagues in higher education. Researchers often favour academic journals over applied publications because publication in these journals is related to career advancement. However, access to academic journals has become easier via the internet and for those who are enrolled to study for higher education degrees. Other possible audiences—such as educators, families, the general public, the media and policy-makers at local and national levels—are perceived by many academic researchers to have less status compared with their colleagues. Consequently, research findings may not be disseminated and communicated to these audiences.

Some early childhood educators actually distrust research findings and new ideas, and are reluctant to accept them because their personal security is grounded in the known and familiar. Some are resistant to change, regarding it and innovation as unnecessary. Ongoing and persistent demand for change has generated some negativity towards it—especially if the adoption of new practice is required. Consequently, some educators have become suspicious about embracing innovations too quickly. Research findings alone are unlikely to overcome such prejudices and stimulate change in established practice that has been created from attitudes, values and beliefs built up over many years.

The implementation of research findings and new ideas usually involves extra work for early childhood educators who already have demanding jobs. Those who wish to implement applied research findings may find it necessary to persuade management committees, school governors and employers of cost-effective benefits; may need to devise new strategies and techniques; and may need to clarify and restructure their value systems. All of this takes time and energy. Time is the most valuable, but also the most scarce, resource for most early childhood educators, who argue that lack of time is a key reason that they are not able to remain abreast of or implement new developments.

Most early childhood educators consider themselves to be autonomous, and may use their traditional right to independence to justify poor practice. Some are suspicious that academic researchers (who often are assumed to have little knowledge of and experience in actually working with young children, families and services) try to dictate what should be done in early childhood services. Consequently, contributions from academic research may be ignored. When researchers do not collaborate with educators, and where educators are not involved in research, they do not have a sense that it relates to them, giving rise to the problem of 'ownership'. Genuine collaboration enhances ownership and helps to diminish any perceived threat to autonomy.

Some early childhood educators regard their work as essentially practice oriented rather than as a theoretically based science. A dislike of theory that often starts in pre-service training can persist in workplace attitudes. Some find theory difficult to grasp because they have not developed the sophisticated conceptual and analytical skills required to comprehend the relevance of theory to practice. They have not grasped that theory and research are rich sources of knowledge which can be used as guides to practice or as a resource, but alone are insufficient to act as a foundation or directive for developing pedagogical frameworks.

Current training and career structures in early childhood rarely emphasise the skills of understanding, implementing and producing research as an integral aspect of early childhood professional identity and practice. More intelligent consumers of research as a basis for nurturing producers of research are needed in early childhood. However, unless early childhood educators themselves take responsibility for extending the boundaries of knowledge and ideas, the present reliance on non-early childhood professionals to conduct research and shape its future will continue—a factor that ultimately will disadvantage the sector.

The obstacles to interest in and incorporation of research into decision-making and change will not deter effective early childhood leaders, who—while acknowledging these structural difficulties—work towards overcoming them through the creation of a special ethos or climate where research is valued for its contribution to professional learning and development, and to early childhood service provision.

## Encouraging a research culture

Effective leaders need to embrace a research orientation and make research and reflection an inherent part of their own activity while encouraging educators to do the same. One way to elevate the status of research as a source of information for professional decision-making and the initiation of change is to foster a culture where research is valued.

Basically, a research culture is a matter of personal and professional attitude, an environment in which intellectual interest and scientific curiosity exist, are evident and are supported. A research culture should prevail at all levels in early childhood, from pre-service training to service provision and delivery, where individuals are motivated to seek additional knowledge on which to base choices, be they researcher, educator or family member. A research culture values theoretical and research-based knowledge to inform all aspects of early childhood service provision for young children and families.

The following strategies are useful for creating and enhancing a research culture in early childhood.

First, early childhood is acknowledged as distinct, unique and possessing its own traditions, values, assumptions, experiences, practices and training, and therefore capable of extending its own knowledge base. A shift in attitude is necessary—from deference to the opinions of experts and authorities from other professions to a healthy, questioning scepticism of the input from others and increasing respect for the contributions from early childhood educators.

A greater acceptance of the validity of different theoretical perspectives on which research can be based should be encouraged. Research in early childhood was grounded in psychological theory, particularly developmental and educational psychology. However, in order to gain a deeper and broader understanding and influence of social contexts and realities, sociological theory has become significant. Other perspectives—ecology, biology, anthropology, history, philosophy, politics, curriculum theory and economics—need to become as familiar to early childhood educators as psychological and sociological viewpoints. Early childhood needs up-to-date information on a wide range of issues, problems and options to advance the provision of a range of quality services that will meet the needs of a changing society.

A research culture should be supported with training at all levels, from students to executive leaders, so that research becomes an accepted and valued part of professional identity. In this way, aspiring early childhood educators will develop the skills to be intelligent consumers of research and to perceive their role as one that may include the production of research. As more educators complete higher research-based degrees as part of their own professional development, the face of early childhood is changing from a predominantly practice-based orientation to one of evidence-based practice where scientific and practical needs are balanced.

Early childhood educators should participate as equal partners in collaborative research in order to blur the boundaries and narrow the gap between so-called researchers and educators in the multi-disciplinary teams that currently conduct research. The inclusion of educators in research teams sensitises them to the entire research process in ways that promote effective use of resources and improvement of practice. Collaborative investigations begin with dialogues concerning values, beliefs, assumptions, local contexts and conditions in order to establish the basis of the research project. Skilled delegation by research team leaders can encourage individual responsibility, initiative and direction in research inquiry.

Collaborative research teams overcome the problem and effects of lack of 'ownership' in research. Lack of involvement can lead to important findings remaining unknown, and consequently not being applied in appropriate circumstances by early childhood educators. Collaborative processes promote communication and understanding, and help to ensure that jargon-free research findings are made available and presented in simple and intelligent ways, so that they are easily understood by decision-makers and consumers.

From their day-to-day practice, early childhood educators gain intimate knowledge about and understanding of questions and problems that need to be addressed through systematic investigation. These educators can provide the clear link between real-life issues and the needs of early childhood services, and the research questions that are defined for examination. Nevertheless, there are some difficulties associated with being an 'insider', including confidentiality, information-sharing and power issues (Mukherji and Albon, 2010). Reflective leaders and educators use their drive and initiative to initiate and conduct necessary research themselves, or to establish collaborative—possibly multi-disciplinary—research teams with the goal of changing, improving and transforming practice.

While the research activities of developing, testing and confirming scientific knowledge are not pursuits that can be carried out in spare time at work, early childhood educators can engage in action research in various contexts. Research needs to be incorporated as a routine problem-solving exercise that contributes to new knowledge and understanding, as well as to practical outcomes.

The prevailing professional culture in early childhood is changing, but effective leaders continue to reinforce and emphasise the positive outcomes of valuing research as much as practice. Leaders who value and are committed to research promote a culture of inquiry aimed at improving pedagogy and outcomes for young children (Watson and Williams, 2011). Consequently, early childhood educators should increasingly be active in research because of the added value brought about by systematic inquiry into practice. Collaborative research plays an important role in enhancing critical reflection and co-construction of professional understanding because it offers educators opportunities to engage in conversations about pedagogy and change in knowledgeable and meaningful ways.

Early childhood educators who want to engage in research can begin to do so by making the time and space to:

- reflect on their practice
- talk about pedagogy—that is, learning and teaching
- relate professionally and collaborate with colleagues, and
- use evidence-based practice as a means for improving quality.

In early childhood, a research culture develops when educators appreciate that:

- research is a professional responsibility for those working in learning communities such as early childhood services
- collaborative inquiry is fundamental to the development of inclusive professional learning communities
- collaboration ensures that knowledge, understanding and leading practice are shared, and
- evidenced-based practice builds on success and improves quality.

A research culture is stimulated and fostered by early childhood leaders who support educators to accept some responsibility for defining questions to be investigated by themselves or others, for verifying research results reported in professional literature, and for ensuring cogent interpretation and practical application of relevant recommendations.

## Action research for critical inquiry

Action research is a research approach as well as a recognised means of professional development for early childhood educators (MacNaughton and Hughes, 2008). It is a tool for bridging the gap between research and practice that enhances professional learning and fosters reflection (McNiff, 2010). Early childhood leaders and educators become more effective when they are willing and able to conduct action research in their places of work. Early childhood educators who undertake action research often display leadership in their ability to diagnose and respond to problems and the need for change in a systematic manner. Action research is a legitimate means of enhancing professional development because, through its processes, educators begin to value research and to develop a culture of inquiry that values reflection.

The term 'action research' refers to a way of thinking that uses reflection and inquiry as a way of understanding the conditions that support or inhibit change, the nature of change, the process of change and the results of attempts to change. Action research entails action disciplined by inquiry, and combines the research procedure with a substantive act (Hopkins, 2008). The goal always is to improve practice, which is an ongoing concern for all in early childhood. In order to optimise successful outcomes for action research undertaken by early childhood educators, the issues chosen to be explored need to be significant for the leader and team in terms of the vision, mission, goals, objectives and quality of the service. The issues must be actionable and manageable within a realistic timeframe, and appropriate for the research skills of those involved. A healthy attitude within the team to problem-solving, risk-taking and experimentation is also helpful, but needs to be tempered by the leader with realistic expectations about the unpredictability of change and the probability of immediate success.

The action research process commonly involves seven steps.

1.   *Identifying issues of mutual concern.* Current issues are brought into focus through the processes of observation and reflection by all team members.

2.   *Analysing problems and determining possible contributing factors.* The ability to diagnose the determinants of an issue is required. The existing situation is monitored using recorded, uncensored and uninterpreted observations from members of the team.

3.   *Forming tentative working hypotheses or guesses to explain these factors.* At this point, questionable assumptions are eliminated. Decisions are made about the form and method of interpretation of the data that are to be collected.

4.   *Collecting and interpreting data* from observations, interviews and relevant documentation to clarify hypotheses and to develop action hypotheses. Accurate details of events need to be recorded in order to avoid erroneous or superficial influences.

5.   *Formulating plans for action and carrying them out.* Plans are experimental, prospective and forward looking, and may require the acquisition of new skills or procedures for implementation.

6.   *Evaluating the results of the action.* Observation and reflection are used to critically assess the effects of the informed action and to make sense of the processes and issues that emerged during implementation. Collaborative reflection provides opportunities to reconstruct meaning out of the situation and establishes the basis for a revised plan.

7.   Introducing a revised cycle from steps 1 to 6.

Without support, encouragement and commitment from colleagues and research project participants, undertaking action research can be a threatening, demoralising and time-consuming experience. The interpersonal aspect of action research makes it particularly attractive for early childhood educators, given the philosophical focus on the importance of positive and constructive interpersonal communication and relationships for all the children and adults who are concerned with early childhood services.

Consequently, successful action research is grounded in early childhood educators':

- *commitment*—giving and taking time, developing trust with participants
- *collaboration*—respect, sharing, listening, reflection, reciprocity
- *concern*—developing a support network of critical friends, risk-taking
- *consideration*—reflection about and critical analysis of professional action, and
- *change*—working towards growth, development and improvement in a nurturing, supportive environment.

Some academic researchers regard action research conducted by professionals such as early childhood educators in their own contexts as deficient in sound methodology and competent research skills. However, there is little doubt that skill in action research contributes to improvements in practice and raises the critical consciousness of those involved, thereby enhancing professional development.

In accepting the responsibility to systematically research solutions to common problems and goals, mutual respect and teamwork can be boosted. Action research provides another opportunity for leadership to be enacted by any team member. However, the formal leader retains the major responsibility for convincing the team of the necessity for and usefulness of action research as a means of problem-solving and responding to the need for change.

## Reflections on leadership in practice

Early childhood educators display leadership when they engage in action research and then disseminate its findings at an in-service, conference or through publication.

Associate professor, early childhood

One final issue related to action research—or indeed any type of research—is awareness of and adherence to the ethical principles that guide research involving children and adults. Those conducting research need to appreciate their moral obligations to those participating in or affected by any research project, and strike a balance between the pursuit of knowledge and understanding and the rights of children and adults who are included in the project (MacNaughton, Rolfe and Siraj-Blatchford, 2010). Ethical issues can arise in a range of research areas, including the nature of the specific issue under investigation, the context, research procedures, data-collection methods and the uses of and access to data (Cohen, Manion and Harrison, 2011). The following principles provide guidelines for would-be researchers about the types of ethical considerations that need to be addressed before beginning any research project, especially those where young children may be included as participants or affected in any way by research processes (Roberts-Holmes, 2011):

- *Informed consent*. Participants should be made aware of the focus of the research and any features of the research that might affect their decision to take part in the project. In the case of children, informed consent should be obtained from families or adults who act *in loco parentis*.
- *Openness and honesty*. Participants should be made aware of the specific purpose of the research. Deception is unacceptable, unprofessional and unethical behaviour.
- *Right to withdraw*. Participants should be informed at the beginning of the study that they may withdraw at any time, and may choose not to engage in specific aspects of the study, answer specific questions or provide specific information. Any verbal or non-verbal evidence of young children's or vulnerable adults' unwillingness or discomfort with participation must be respected and acted upon.
- *Protection from harm*. Participants must be protected from experiencing physical or psychological harm during the project. While it is unlikely that early childhood research would result in physical harm, some research may focus upon sensitive or delicate issues that participants may find stressful. Researchers have an obligation to minimise stress arising out of research projects and to provide support to alleviate any stress experienced.
- *Debriefing*. Participants have a right to have access to oral or written information about the procedures, processes and results following the conclusion of any research in which they participate.
- *Confidentiality*. Unless participants give specific consent regarding identification, researchers must ensure that confidentiality of the identity of individuals and organisations is maintained and protected during the project and in any ensuing publications.
- *Ethical principles of professional bodies*. Where professional bodies, such as the National Association for the Education of Young Children and the

Australian Early Childhood Association, have published their own guidelines and principles, these must be consulted and adhered to in the design and conduct of any research project.

These principles are designed to protect both participants and researchers from potentially difficult situations that can arise in undertaking research. Early childhood educators who wish to undertake research are encouraged to develop, interpret and extend such considerations in ways appropriate to early childhood services.

## Reflective practice

Reflection and reflective practice are research tools that engage early childhood educators in thinking about what they do in their daily work in order to reconsider, reconceptualise, make changes to and improve their professional practice on the basis of this thinking. Unfortunately, the realities of daily work in early childhood services can obstruct the development of theoretical understanding and attempts to integrate theory and practice (Hedges, 2011). However, the process of thinking about and critically analysing daily activities and practice helps to link and ground action in theory. In addition, reflective practice helps early childhood leaders to fulfil their role as change agents because it necessitates reflecting about what types of change might be productive, worthwhile, beneficial, viable and sustainable for improving service provision.

Reflective practice initiates and reinforces a cycle of ongoing learning during which early childhood educators are challenged to become more open in their thinking, to learn from professional experience, and to become more flexible and adaptable in their practice. Reflective practice stimulates educators' capacity to engage in continuous learning that in turn engenders a professional culture of inquiry and learning. Consequently, it is a key resource and starting point for professional development and capacity-building in teams.

Reflective practice can include reflection in action (while engaged in practice) or reflection on action (following practice). Regardless of when it is undertaken, reflective practice involves:

- describing the practice, feelings and associated factors
- analysing the factors that underpin the practice
- theorising, reconceptualising or formulating new thinking about the practice, and
- acting and applying new conceptualisations and understandings to practice, thereby engaging in praxis.

Reflective practice challenges early childhood educators to:

- keep an open mind
- question what they do
- look at practice from different perspectives, ask 'what if'
- search for alternatives
- try out and evaluate new ideas and possibilities, and
- implement those options that improve practice and quality.

Early childhood educators who engage in reflective practice usually keep a journal and ask for feedback, assess professional experiences and outcomes objectively and build in regular time and/or opportunity to reflect on practice.

## Bringing it together

Research activity is an effective way for early childhood educators to improve the quality of services and to shape their professional image and reputation. Early childhood educators need to establish their own research base that reflects balanced multi-disciplinary and collaborative inquiry into theoretical and practical concerns. Action research is popular because of its focus on improving practice in work contexts. In addition to fostering a positive attitude to research through valuing a research culture, the status and relevance of research can be elevated by encouraging the development of reflective practice in early childhood learning communities that focus on the idea and practice of shared knowledge. While it is acknowledged that research is a slow but effective tool for change and progress, early childhood educators should acquire knowledge about and skill in research approaches, processes and technology so that they can command legitimate authority and respect to play a central role in the advancement of early childhood.

# CHAPTER 12

## LEADING PARTNERSHIPS: ENGAGING FAMILIES AND COMMUNITIES

*Finding ways of working with families in genuine ways and as partners is one of the biggest challenges of my work.*
NURSERY OFFICER, DAY NURSERY

### THIS CHAPTER EXPLORES

- engaging families in partnership
- family engagement in early childhood services
- the challenge of engaging families
- advocacy for engaging communities
- participation in professional associations
- networking
- research and writing
- becoming politically aware and active

Early childhood leaders and educators today appreciate that their roles and responsibilities for improving the well-being of children and families in the community continue to evolve and change, particularly given that collaboration is an essential feature of contemporary leadership. Although work with families has been a priority for many decades, some early childhood leaders and educators—perhaps due to the breadth of other commitments, are reluctant to take an active leadership role with families.

Given the democratic nature of many societies, a lot of families expect to be involved and have a voice about the future direction, functions and operation of the early childhood services they use. Consequently, early childhood leaders and educators need to find incentives and meaningful ways of engaging all families—especially those who are difficult to reach or reluctant to become involved—in articulating and communicating their ideas, views and concerns in order to share in and help shape the structure and organisation of future provision (Small, 2010). In addition, early childhood leaders need to engage colleagues from other disciplines, related agencies, community groups and professional associations to generate shared understandings about how best to support young children in their learning and to nurture family well-being through quality service provision.

Today, early childhood leaders and educators generally accept local and national government input and action on behalf of children and families. However, they also expect to have a voice and be heard through collaborative engagement with government departments and representatives so that early childhood professional views and expertise are reflected in the development and implementation of new policies, frameworks and guidelines. Just as many families expect to engage with early childhood educators so that they can play a role in shaping relevant service provision, early childhood leaders and educators expect to engage with government departments and agencies in the shaping of their professional future.

Contemporary early childhood leaders are responsible for representing the views and expectations of the early childhood sector to governments in terms of the appropriate use of expertise in local communities, as well as for engaging families in real and meaningful opportunities to contribute to this process. Early childhood leaders must become vigorous advocates and activists for early childhood, children and families, responsible for public relations with the range of people and agencies that they come across in their position, including other professionals and the general public.

## Reflections on leadership in practice

Leaders in early childhood are people who have a 'public face' and who are committed to participating in professional activities in ways that achieve recognition and respect from families and members of the wider community.

ASSOCIATE PROFESSOR, EARLY CHILDHOOD

At the grass roots level, the early childhood sector needs leaders who take on the responsibility of informing families about the important role that early childhood educators have to play in the growth and development of young children. Every educator needs to take responsibility for helping raise the status of early childhood.

DIRECTOR, EARLY LEARNING CENTRE

Government and community understanding about the types of high-level skills and unique expertise required to satisfy the complexities of the early childhood educator's role is clearly linked to professional recognition by the general public as well as families. Therefore, it is essential that early childhood leaders consider how they will enact this aspect of leadership. Early childhood leaders and educators need to perceive families as allies rather than adversaries. In turn, through their contact with and involvement in early childhood services, families can provide feedback and information that will assist in enhancing community understanding about the roles and responsibilities associated with working in these services. Helping families to understand early childhood services' vision, mission, goals and objectives helps to demystify them, and increases public awareness about, support for and the status of early childhood.

## Engaging families in partnership

A strong relationship between families and early childhood service providers is essential for creating quality learning environments for young children (Draper and Wheeler, 2010). Research consistently shows that when families are involved positively in their children's early learning and education, children demonstrate higher levels of achievement and display more positive attitudes and behaviour (Thornton and Brunton, 2010). In addition, families who receive positive and frequent messages from early childhood educators participate more in their children's early learning and education. Early childhood leaders who appreciate families not merely as clients, but also as assets with the potential to become valuable resources, make a commitment to building a sense of community within their services.

*I have learned a lot from the families because they have known the child from birth and I have only known this child for a few weeks.*
EARLY CHILDHOOD TEACHER

Quality early childhood services engage families through opportunities for information sharing and dialogue, relationships with other families, mutually agreed developmental and educational goals, and shared decision-making about children's learning and education (Redding et al, 2011). The philosophies of shared and distributed leadership that currently are popular in early childhood support the development of family partnership and engagement as a way of openly or more subtly devolving power throughout services. Engaging families in partnership empowers them to have a say in and control over their lives. Most early childhood leaders and educators appreciate the benefits of inclusive and meaningful family engagement in service delivery and provision.

*Families have a lot to offer. They don't need a special skill or language; they just need to be ordinary people who will chat, help, share, read a story and sing songs with us.*
TEACHING ASSISTANT

Engaging families in various levels and types of collaborative partnership has always been a core component of early childhood service delivery, with previous interest focused on themes of:

- *partnership*—a philosophy of shared child-rearing
- *continuity*—the promotion of consistency between service and home, and
- *education*—the professional responsibility to support and educate families to enhance children's well-being, as well as family enjoyment and competence in child-rearing.

Early childhood educators' interest in helping families better understand young children and child-rearing illustrates the shift to a holistic approach to early childhood philosophy and practice, as well as an affirmation of traditional responsibility to work with and for families.

The adoption of a philosophy of partnership grew out of the recognition that early childhood educators and families held shared and complementary goals for children. Both are considered to be experts when it comes to young children and child-rearing, but each brings different understandings and expertise to the situation. Partnership acknowledges the impact of both home and early childhood services on young children, as well as the benefits of coordinating the efforts of families and educators through non-hierarchical, collaborative relationships. The willingness of early childhood leaders and educators to share power and responsibility with families in a partnership of equals affirms the advantage of shared leadership for achieving early childhood services' vision, mission, goals and objectives.

*If families don't have any real experience of what happens in the classroom, they can't really make any judgement about the quality of provision.*
EARLY CHILDHOOD TEACHER

A partnership approach to family engagement stresses collaborative rather than joint activity, and engages families on their own terms and at levels suitable for their priorities, commitments and circumstances. Genuine partnerships evolve when early childhood educators and families work together as informed contributors and collaborative decision-makers, rather than when families are simply visitors, helpers, experts or fundraisers. There are many excellent examples of services where families and educators are engaged in powerful partnerships—for example, the Pen Green Centre in England and the Reggio Emilia pre-school centres in Italy.

*Families need to know what goes on day to day in the nursery so they don't get confused or panicked by what they hear in the media these days. The best way to find out what goes on is to spend some time here.*
MANAGER, DAY NURSERY

Working partnerships are grounded in equal but different contributions from, and shared accountability of, families and educators, and implement a whole-family, multi-disciplinary approach to early learning and education. They offer a range of opportunities and a variety of ways for families to contribute. In a partnership, early childhood educators allocate time to help families understand how children learn and the families help them find out more about their children. Families may spend time observing children in the services and collect practical information about their children at home to share with educators. Documentation of children's learning and progress may be encouraged. In these ways, educators and families can enjoy mutually supportive, collaborative partnerships based on shared goals and understanding. The partnership is created from meaningful contact, connection and communication.

*I need families' help with monitoring the children's progress.*
NURSERY OFFICER

The development of partnerships between early childhood educators and families lies in fundamental values and beliefs about families—that families are:

- experts on their own children
- significant and effective teachers of their own children
- skilled in ways that complement those of educators
- different but have equal strengths and equivalent expertise
- able to make informed observations and impart vital information to educators
- inherently involved in the lives and well-being of their children
- able to contribute to and central in decision-making, and
- responsible and willing to share accountability with educators.

These values are useful guidelines for early childhood educators who wish to establish collaborative relationships with families, or assess the extent to which their relationships with and involvement of families constitutes a partnership.

## Engaging families in early childhood services

Early childhood educators historically have defined their client group broadly, and have considered relationships with families integral to their practice (Draper and Wheeler, 2010). Today, families are as much the clients of early childhood educators as their children. Given that it is the goal of every early childhood educator to assist the client to achieve a more meaningful experience in life, there is a lot of potential for early childhood educators to display leadership in work with families.

Family engagement refers to the creation of inclusive, collaborative and coordinated systems, structures and procedures that offer families opportunities for meaningful communication, commitment, connection and contribution. In practical terms, engagement means offering real opportunities for families to:

- access and use services
- have a voice and be heard
- play a legitimate role with significant functions
- work collaboratively with educators, and
- influence, contribute to and make decisions.

Genuine engagement encourages families to invest in, take an active role in, become partners in and contribute productively to early childhood services that support them and their children.

In order to successfully engage families in services, early childhood leaders appreciate that they first must attract and draw in families to services, and then involve, hold and sustain their interest and contribution. Engagement is more likely to occur where accessible opportunities for information, education, consultation, involvement, partnership and devolved power are offered in ways that are familiar to and meet families' expectations (Staffordshire Children's Trust, 2010).

Genuine family engagement is based on trust, open and respectful communication, and the valuing of others' knowledge, experience, opinions and contributions. In an inclusive and accepting climate, all members of a collaborative team are encouraged to share their perspectives and views and to participate in consensual decision-making. Successful family engagement in early childhood services is underpinned by ethos (vision, values and attitudes), expertise (educators' knowledge and training), systems (policies and procedures) and support (resources and help) (Staffordshire Children's Trust, 2010).

The ways in which early childhood leaders enact leadership will affect the development of genuine family engagement. Leaders build the willingness to engage though the relationships they develop with families by:

- being friendly, welcoming, approachable
- listening to and empathising with family concerns
- sharing information freely through a range of inclusive communication forms

- constructively addressing differences in opinion
- actively seeking family input into building a shared vision, mission and goals, and
- actively supporting participation in collaborative decision-making.

Today, family engagement in early childhood service delivery and provision is an essential feature of quality. However, early childhood leaders' and educators' efforts to transform family participation and involvement in early childhood services from the typically token level, to genuine partnership, through to inclusive engagement is one of the most difficult aspects of their role. In addition to benefits for children, family engagement (as members of collaborative teams) encourages families to act as advocates for children, other families and early childhood services. Early childhood educators who engage families in genuine decision-making about service delivery and provision have taken a political step towards initiating innovative change in the sector.

Families and educators may have different expectations, perspectives, views about and experiences with young children. Where shared understanding is achieved, their roles become mutually affirming, reciprocal and interdependent. Early childhood educators benefit from specific training to enable them to work effectively with the diversity of family types, circumstances and community members associated with early childhood services. Quality training in family engagement can relieve any anxiety and frustration that educators may experience in this complex role.

Strategies for encouraging family commitment, involvement, contribution, partnership and engagement include inviting families to:

- attend, participate and contribute in meetings to assist, for example, in reviewing and making decisions about early childhood vision, mission, goals, policies, standards, expectations and pedagogy
- work in conjunction with experienced educators on special skill-development projects with their own or other children
- create opportunities and activities related to family-initiated needs and interests, such as family education
- volunteer their expertise for special activities, such as music, movement, stories, inclusive and diverse perspectives
- contribute to policies—for example, health and safety, recruitment and selection, and
- contribute to financial and fundraising procedures and processes.

Where does family engagement in early childhood service delivery and provision leave early childhood educators? Where does professional expertise fit? How is professional standing with colleagues, peers, other professionals, agencies and the community affected when family engagement means mutual responsibility and accountability with people who are also consumers and secondary clients of early childhood services? Could professional efforts to maximise family engagement undermine early childhood leaders' efforts to realise their vision, mission, goals and objectives for implementing pedagogical practice in ways that are culturally, developmentally and professionally appropriate? The answers to these complex and challenging questions will determine the ways in and levels at which early childhood leaders genuinely engage families in service operation and delivery.

Families' ideas about how children develop and learn are by no means clear or straightforward. Families—like early childhood educators—hold differing implicit theories about children, constructed largely from their experiences in their family of origin and from the ways in which they have lived with and reared their own children. Early childhood educators developed their theories from their own experience in a similar way to families, but usually interpret this experience in the light of knowledge and skills gained during professional training and the experience of working with large numbers of children in a variety of services. Family theories and professional theories about the right way to work with children lead to differing perspectives on policies, procedures and practice. Early childhood educators need to bring all their expertise to finding a common ground between the two perspectives.

The answer to the dilemma of family engagement is through the negotiation of cooperative decision-making and shared agreements concerning the planning and implementation of early childhood services. Early childhood educators accept the responsibility to meet other people's needs (that is, those of the families) by making their expertise available to the families. Educators also meet their own needs by recognising the value of their training, experience and philosophy as information sources for making decisions about how, when and where young children's development and learning can be facilitated. Early childhood leaders who effectively engage families in collaborative partnerships possess the confidence to articulate philosophies concerning early learning and education while simultaneously acknowledging families' rights, information, theories, expectations, problems and pressures.

In this way, the complementary expertise of both families and educators is brought to meet the needs of the situation in mutually agreed ways. Engaging families begins with inclusion—that is, welcoming everybody, respecting all families, building up trust, encouraging dialogue with families about alternative perspectives on children, and learning to point out different ways of responding to or intervening in issues related to early learning. It is also essential to seek families' own ideas about how they might wish to engage with their young children's learning and education.

Families may wish to engage with early childhood services through outreach activities, home visits, diaries, chat sessions, short talks, workshops or whatever type of contact best meets their needs, interests and circumstances. Successful family engagement depends on early childhood leaders' and educators' skills to contact, connect and communicate with families.

Communication is the key to successfully negotiating relationships with families, and actively engaging them with early childhood services. Fostering shared understanding and partnerships with families depends on leaders who:

- clearly and unambiguously explain issues in egalitarian and inclusive language
- remain non-judgemental and overcome stereotyped and/or prejudiced attitudes
- listen with understanding to families' views and acknowledge their feelings
- respond in ways that will enhance collaborative teamwork
- respond professionally, managing and expressing personal feelings appropriately
- confidently assert their professional opinion
- recognise and respond to discord, disharmony and conflict appropriately, and
- validate families as active and equal members of the decision-making team.

## The challenge of engaging families

Successfully engagement of families with early childhood services takes time, experience and committed effort. Lack of time—for both families and educators—is a major challenge for building the respectful relationships that are the foundation of shared understanding, collaborative partnership and meaningful engagement. While some early childhood services have funding to employ family liaison coordinators, most do not. Work with families usually is an additional responsibility that educators assume because of its importance. Time constraints make it difficult for early childhood educators to fully integrate family engagement with other responsibilities for children, and many would benefit from specific training in innovative, accessible and inclusive approaches to family engagement.

Most early childhood educators become more comfortable with the need to include families in service delivery and provision when they have gained experience, feel competent and have developed considerable expertise in working with young children. This shift in professional maturity often is the stimulus for identification with families as well as children, and for appreciation of the need for and benefits of family engagement. At earlier stages of career development and professional maturity, relationships with families may be more authoritarian, paternalistic, patronising, token in nature and from a deficit perspective—that is, where families, even when parents and carers are considerably older than the educators, are not thought to possess the knowledge and skills necessary to bring up their children. Such attitudes are unlikely to engage and empower families to develop skill and competence in child-rearing or their own lives.

Successful family engagement in early childhood services depends on matching family needs, expectations, characteristics and circumstances to tailored opportunities for contribution and access to support. The initiation of any change in early childhood services should be on the basis of diagnosed need (discussed in Chapter 10). Effective leadership of families entails understanding family needs in order to tailor engagement initiatives that reflect specific needs expressed by families, their social and cultural diversity and levels of educational achievement. All aspects of family engagement should be evaluated objectively to ensure that both processes and outcomes are appropriate for families, thereby avoiding any unintended negative aftermath from poorly designed and implemented experiences. It is pointless to put energy and effort into family support, resourcing, education, partnership or engagement if it is not what families expect or want. Empathic early childhood educators offer opportunities for family engagement in ways that meet families' expressed or objectively assessed needs and wants.

Most early childhood educators report that some of the families who use their services would be classified as 'hard-to-reach' families. Hard-to-reach families usually are living with or temporarily experiencing a range of challenging circumstances, including financial difficulties, long-term unemployment, health problems, disability issues, separation or divorce, sole or teenage parenthood, or cultural and language differences. Working families also can be hard to reach because of time constraints in balancing work and family life. Many early childhood educators find it extremely difficult to attract and draw in, involve, motivate and sustain such families' engagement with services.

Special thought and effort are required to find sensible and authentic ways to establish contact and connect with hard-to-reach families. With integrated multi-agency provision, it may be possible to go to them using outreach activities and home visits. However, if families are persuaded to use services, those services need to embody and openly display a culture and ethos that is welcoming, friendly, accepting, inclusive, non-threatening, non-stigmatising, meaningful and relevant, and offer equal opportunity for all to engage at accessible times and in accessible locations.

For example, if families do not speak the dominant language, it is helpful if there is someone associated with the service—an educator, family member or colleague—who does speak that language. Providing 'family champions'—that is, trained family members or carers who make contact and connections with other families—can help to overcome fears, uncertainties and suspicion. Some men are nervous in the female-dominated environment of early childhood services, so the open display of a 'father-friendly' ethos, times and activities is helpful. Some families really appreciate the use of email for communication and dialogue. Others prefer to converse and communicate in a group at a coffee morning or informal lunch.

If early childhood leaders and educators seriously wish to engage families as collaborative team members and equal partners in the delivery of quality services for young children, then real power needs to be devolved by handing responsibility and control for specific functions to them. However, both early childhood educators and families need to understand the parameters of their respective roles and responsibilities as they explore and experience the effects of such shifts in the balance of power. Collaborative partnerships can be the starting point for growth, empowerment and change for families, early childhood educators and service provision. Of all the people with whom early childhood educators interact, it is families who, through their meaningful engagement with services, will advance early childhood's professional status and credibility in local communities and with the general public.

## Advocacy: Engaging communities with the early childhood sector

Although day-to-day leadership is enacted mostly within the micro-context of interaction between early childhood leaders, educators and families, leadership activity outside services and in community and public domains has become a responsibility and expectation for formal and aspiring leaders. The demand to exercise innovative leadership at local and national levels cannot be ignored. Early childhood educators currently need to extend their concern beyond the 'ethic of care' (Cameron and Moss, 2011), and combine their unique knowledge, expertise and communication ability to advocate for and champion the rights of children and adult in the wider context.

Advocacy can be described as leadership activities that are related to and enacted in the wider context. It is a term that refers to early childhood educators' personal and professional responsibility for raising the profile, value, credibility and status of young children, families and early childhood in the eyes of the general community. Most early childhood educators are advocates but don't use that terminology to describe their championing activities. Advocacy expresses the politically aware and active dimension of leadership, and it has become one of the key functions of leadership in early childhood.

*One of my families was in dire straits financially so I suggested they contact the Citizens' Advice Bureau which helps with this sort of issue. I also made contact with the benefits agency to see if they were entitled to any financial aid. I wouldn't call myself an advocate but I was told that was what I was doing, advocacy!*
CHILDCARE COORDINATOR

Advocacy is a political act aimed at improving the well-being of young children and families by influencing the attention, interest and decisions of the media, the general public, politicians, policy-makers and law-makers. Becoming politically aware and active simply means understanding how the policies of the public, private and voluntary sectors affect the lives of children, families and the early childhood sector. Early childhood leaders who are effective advocates keep abreast of local policy and other issues, know who is involved and how the political scene operates locally and nationally, and network with key people and agencies to champion early childhood within the community.

*Once I was so angry about proposed cuts to our funding that I wrote a letter to my local member. I got a reply but I don't think my letter made much of a difference. I think that more people needed to stand up and express their opinion about something that was going to impact on not only our service.*
HEAD TEACHER, NURSERY SCHOOL

Being an advocate means building support for a particular issue in different groups or audiences. Advocates 'lobby' elected government representatives to influence and change legislation and laws. They also communicate with and provide information to them about special work, topics or issues that are of concern in early childhood. Politicians are fond of visiting early childhood services, especially if they wish to announce policy changes that affect children and families.

With early childhood services frequently under the threat of closure, restriction and withdrawal of funding, survival depends on the abilities of leaders and educators to act as advocates in order to bring key issues to wider audiences. This requires creativity in approach, skill in respectfully and constructively articulating issues and concerns, and determined persistence (Ebbeck and Waniganayake, 2003). Given that most of the key people and audiences have little time to devote to discussing and becoming informed about complex issues, early childhood leaders must capture their attention and get the message, point or argument across as succinctly and concisely as possible. It is helpful to use different forms of communication, including personal, written, electronic and public formats.

*I think more politicians should be invited to speak at our annual conference. They need to explain their policies to us and we need to be able to hold them accountable by asking questions and expressing our views on their policies.*
EARLY CHILDHOOD TEACHER

Early childhood leaders need to keep abreast of national government policies and changes as they affect services and the profession, to network with relevant politicians in order to raise the profile of children and early childhood, and to keep them visible and high on the political agenda.

*It's become a paper war ... there are so many government papers and documents that I need to read to keep up with changes initiated by the government, sometimes I feel the weight of information overload but I know being well informed is part of my responsibility to the children and families that I work for, so somehow I make the time to go through them.*
HEAD TEACHER, EARLY EXCELLENCE CENTRE

Given the political attention that early childhood receives, it is essential that early childhood leaders are confident about voicing and sharing their expertise and insight with key people in the community as a means of moving forward.

*I found out that a fast food chain was applying for planning permission to build an outlet near our centre. Most families and all of the staff objected to it. I organised families to write letters and emails, one staff volunteered to be the media contact and I attended the planning meeting. I found the meeting totally overwhelming and I didn't have the confidence to speak out. But for the next meeting, I asked another educator to come with me. Because she was there, I felt supported and though it was scary, I did speak up and expressed our objections. It was hard and I was shaking but I felt fantastic afterwards.*
CHILDCARE COORDINATOR

Once early childhood educators appreciate that advocacy is the application of professional knowledge, expertise and leadership skills to benefit children, families and the profession, they can begin to engage in some of the wide range of activities that help enhance the status of children, families and early childhood. However, bringing about change through advocacy usually is a long and slow process that requires high levels of self-confidence and assertive ability to overcome the obstacles and setbacks inevitably encountered.

Activities that are related to advocacy as a dimension of leadership include participation in professional associations, research and writing, networking with other professionals, and becoming politically aware and active. Compelling advocacy takes time, effort and the development of special knowledge and skills in order to become influential in the arenas that hold the power to make decisions and change policy. While advocacy is the responsibility of every early childhood educator, it is a special responsibility of leaders because they usually have a broader perspective on current trends, issues and needs.

Collaboration with other relevant professional bodies also helps to solve complex problems in early childhood service provision. Bringing in other representatives who also advocate for children and families helps to facilitate systematic problem-solving, which can be difficult for one group or sector alone. For example, creating multi-disciplinary teams from child care, teaching, health and social services or from private, public and voluntary childcare agencies that share similar concerns about services for children is logical, desirable and time-efficient. Collaborative activity requires that contributors share mutual aspirations, common conceptual frameworks, and agreed goals and outcomes. Effective collaboration requires devolved power and responsibility—that is, work must be delegated and control shared.

Collaboration with other professional associations is a means rather than an end with regard to advocacy in early childhood. Messages from united collaborative multi-disciplinary teams or multi-agency groups have more weight and command more respect from powerful decision-makers than one lone organisation. Engaging professionals from diverse backgrounds to advocate for early childhood is an efficient means to use their knowledge, expertise and perspectives, as well as to encourage them to take responsibility for and to contribute to policy-making and planning issues in the sector.

## Participation in professional associations

As a leader, it is important not only to join but also to become active in the associations that are concerned with early childhood. With the publications, seminars and conferences offered by professional associations, such as Early Childhood Australia, the British Association of Early Childhood Education, the Association for Childhood Education International and the National Association for the Education of Young Children, opportunities are provided for continuing professional development. They are arenas where important matters that concern early childhood educators are identified, discussed and addressed. Professional associations also advocate regarding issues of concern in early childhood, bringing them to the attention of families, the wider sector, unions, politicians, government ministers, business and the media. However, their effectiveness depends on the commitment and efforts of the membership. The more professionals whose views are represented by an association, the stronger and more effective will be the impact of its advocacy and actions.

As well as through professional associations, early childhood educators can be influential in advocating for and accomplishing change as members of unions, advisory boards, committees and working parties at local, state and national levels. Such bodies offer direct access to influencing decision-making and change. Membership therefore allows early childhood educators to articulate and champion professional concerns, issues and perspectives.

> *I see it as part of my professional responsibility to sit on our local networking partnership. It takes a lot of time because I also sit on working parties and other sub-committees that are established to deal with particular issues. But I also learn a lot about what is happening in the sector so I am empowered and better prepared to deal with changes that impact on my service.*
> HEAD TEACHER, INFANT SCHOOL

In addition, membership of professional associations increases opportunities for professional contact with colleagues. Given the isolation in which most early childhood educators work, this is an important function. Those in positions of leadership often feel that they have less access to support than other team members in the service because of the distance needed to retain authority. In addition, team members often are unable to empathise with early childhood leaders—perhaps because their child-focused responsibilities may constrain access to broader perspectives and concerns. Membership of professional associations provides contact with colleagues who understand the early childhood leader's position and dilemmas and can offer the emotional support that may not be available within services. Membership of professional associations is a step towards building a support network.

## Networking

Professional networks offer opportunities to exchange information, share resources, test new ideas, reflect, develop relationships, support others, create new opportunities and build on existing practice. Leaders who act as advocates on behalf of early childhood need the support of others—such as families, communities, the public, politicians and law-makers—to help them achieve their goals. However, the probability of success increases if leaders engage the support of, and act in collaboration with, members of other professional bodies who are concerned with early childhood. Change can be accomplished more effectively if it is supported by a range of professional bodies rather a single professional group. Networking with colleagues from diverse backgrounds gives access to a greater range of knowledge and skills that can strengthen the weight of any argument. Colleagues outside early childhood can offer moral support, encouragement and feedback, which can help strengthen early childhood educators' resolve and commitment to pursue and advocate for issues of concern.

> *The Foundation Stage Learning and Development Network has brought educators together from the different sectors in a constructive and learning environment. All of the educators, from teaching and childcare, realised that they shared similar concerns and there was a feeling of all of us being in the same boat. People understand each other more now.*
> EARLY CHILDHOOD TEAM LEADER

Networks can be informal, where individuals with common interests and goals meet on a regular basis to share information and to plan action. They can also be formal, where committees or working parties are formed with official representation from professional associations, institutions or agencies. The advantages of establishing and participating in networks are that isolation is broken down, awareness of others' interests and activities is increased, barriers to communication are decreased, and misunderstanding and miscommunication are diminished.

> *Our group of local directors initiated informal meetings once a month to talk over work issues, concerns and problems, study, anything really. Alex wrote letters explaining the need for a 'Directors Support Group' and invited all of the local directors. Most accepted. We take turns, holding the meetings at different centres, so as well as talking, we can see if they are doing anything different. We can discuss things that we can't talk to our staff about or need personal help with.*
> DIRECTOR, PRE-SCHOOL CENTRE

Professional networks are learning communities through which experience and insights can be accessed (Osborne, 2008) and in which, through networking, early childhood educators offer others access to new understandings about early childhood (Meade, 2011). Successful networking—that is, engaging the cooperation of others—takes time, communication skills and good interpersonal relationships.

## Reflections on leadership in practice

While there is usually a defined position of leader, it is important to recognise that other positions in services have elements of leadership that, if supported by the leader, can allow for effective cooperation and networking between different professionals and agencies. Cooperation and networking between educators and different professionals enhances quality service provision and develops leadership capacity.

HEAD TEACHER, EARLY EXCELLENCE CENTRE

The strength of networking is in the development of trusting relationships, where allies and supporters can be called upon when required to add impact to activity. Early childhood educators who establish strong networks with colleagues from other professions can draw upon them to help raise the credibility and status of early childhood in the community. Networking is another way of reaching out to and engaging communities to enhance understanding of and support for early childhood's vision, mission, goals and concerns.

## Research and writing

The role and advantages of research as a source of information for decision-making and change are outlined in Chapter 11. However, research is also important for leadership in the community because it is a recognised means of gathering the facts and information that carry weight in arguments for change. The use of research findings gives substance and credibility to issues, and helps decision-makers to focus on key concerns and to consider different alternatives. Professional associations have specific research interests and can provide support for and access to relevant research findings. However, it is no longer acceptable to be a consumer of other people's research. Leadership in early childhood requires that commitment be made to engage in research that has been identified from intimate understanding of current professional needs and concerns.

*After visiting the Reggio Emilia pre-schools, we were interested in researching the impact of changing the way we organise lunchtime for the children and the team had an opportunity to access funding from the Education Action Zone. We planned how we would undertake the action research, then carried it out over a term and wrote a report. Doing a*

*systematic investigation of a change and writing it up really clarified our understanding of the impact of the change.*
EARLY CHILDHOOD TEACHER

Competent research includes the articulation and dissemination of research findings, ideas and concerns in ways that will reach and be understood by intended audiences. Something as simple as writing about current concerns in a newsletter is a way of leaders informing families and activating interest, support and continued effort to address issues. Many associations, agencies and government departments have websites where early childhood leaders and educators can share examples of leading practice and become involved in discussion groups. Writing letters to politicians, government ministers and the editors of newspapers and magazines displays leadership and advocacy on behalf of children, families and the profession. Publication in a professional journal requires greater effort and skill, which may need to be acquired through further study, but it is not outside the capabilities of many early childhood educators. The real purpose of writing is to express an informed opinion on a critical issue in clear, understandable and accurate ways.

## Reflections on leadership in practice

When the kindergarten was under threat of closure, the director was required to convince the funding body that the kindergarten and its activities were worthy of retention. It was the responsibility of the director to prepare and answer questions about an extensive written report that represented the setting and its activities in a positive light.
DIRECTOR, EARLY LEARNING CENTRE

Whereas writing can be undertaken during or outside work hours, public speaking—an alternative means of communicating a point of view—requires specific time commitments, usually away from services. This may be more difficult for early childhood educators who are bound by strict regulations during working hours, and who may find the extra demands on their personal time too burdensome. However, this activity should not be avoided.

*I was invited to do a presentation about my approach to numeracy for three- and four-year-olds to my local network that meets in the late afternoon a couple of times a term. At first, I didn't want to do it;*

*I thought people would know more than I do. But the adviser was really encouraging and gave me some tips. There were fifteen people there and it went really well, they asked lots of questions and I could answer them! It was challenging but a really worthwhile experience and I feel more confident about talking to others now.*

EARLY CHILDHOOD TEACHER

Opportunities to express a point of view arise informally with families and friends, educators and colleagues, in local neighbourhoods and communities, and formally at meetings, seminars and conferences and with employers. Speaking formally or informally helps inform others and engage support for issues and concerns, and should not be overlooked by early childhood educators—especially those with leadership responsibilities.

## Becoming politically aware and active

While early childhood educators increasingly act as advocates for children and families, continuing disregard of the role of power in politics and reluctance to become involved in politics means that they have not made as much of a difference to early childhood as they potentially could have. Steering clear of politics has constrained professional credibility and status. However, in order to meet the challenges of changing times, today's early childhood educators must become politically aware and active so that they make a positive contribution to the well-being of children and families.

Becoming politically aware and active benefits early childhood in a range of ways. First, politically active educators work proactively to inform and influence governments about the needs and requirements of children and families. Second, politically active educators reinforce the crucial role that early childhood plays in promoting child and family welfare. Third, politically aware educators highlight emerging issues and important concerns for those who are responsible for making decisions that support children and families in communities and society.

Becoming politically aware and active in early childhood entails understanding the process of democratic government and legislature; knowing the local and national public representatives and their platforms on issues of concern to early childhood; knowing who their counterparts are; being able to identify the public servants who administer the government departments responsible for early childhood services; and a willingness to lobby appropriate government officials by expressing an opinion personally or in writing. Lobbying is having a voice, speaking out and being heard as a way of stimulating action.

*We've tried to get the local politicians interested in early childhood issues by asking our members to send a standard letter that we provided to their local member; we've asked a couple of politicians to open new buildings or speak at annual general meetings; and we've invited them to tour selected services and speak with families.When we have this type of close personal contact with them, they seem to appreciate our concerns more.*
EARLY CHILDHOOD TEACHER AND ASSOCIATION REPRESENTATIVE

Lobbying is the process of informing public officials and relevant others about the issues that confront early childhood educators on a daily basis. It involves getting the right information to the right person at the right time. If politicians and government officials are ignorant of such issues, they are unlikely to take any action. If they are only partly informed or misinformed about issues of concern in early childhood, they cannot be expected to make decisions that will be appropriate. There are many groups with loud voices and well-organised campaigns who will capture the attention of the policy- and decision-makers in government. Early childhood educators need to exercise their political voice, to ensure their views are heard and understood by those who have the power and responsibility for making decisions that affect children and families.

Determined persistence to make meaningful contact with public officials is essential. Those who are easily fobbed off will make little progress in getting a hearing.The long history of reticence by early childhood educators to speak out and articulate their contribution and concerns has led to a weak power base. Becoming empowered through having a voice and being heard is a starting point for influencing the actions of public officials on behalf of children, families and early childhood. Given that early childhood has a distance to go in becoming politically powerful, one of the best ways of gaining the support of public officials is to invite them into early childhood services and begin to establish personal relationships with them. In this way, early childhood educators will be seen as professional and community leaders and experts on relevant issues, and their opinions will have more influence on government decisions.

Becoming politically aware and active means contributing to decision-making on issues that affect children, families and early childhood. It means appreciating the political dimension of early childhood and acting to ensure that issues command attention and priority within communities and society.

The media are increasingly powerful when it comes to shaping public opinion in society. Most people—particularly women—are interested in news related to children and families, especially in local communities. Many media reporters are interested in the issues that are of concern to early childhood because they are topical and capture people's attention. However, early childhood educators need to become more skilled in using the media to communicate and disseminate information and opinion to the public and to highlight other concerns critical to early childhood service provision.

*I was invited to appear on a current affairs television program to comment on the value of play in early learning. The program unit spent a day filming at the service and interviewing me. When the program was shown, they had cut out a lot of the pertinent comments I made and showed mainly gender-stereotyped play. The segment lasted about three minutes. I suppose even a short opportunity to talk about play helps the public understand its importance.*
DIRECTOR, EARLY LEARNING CENTRE

Regardless of the format chosen—a letter to the editor, a short article focusing on a particular issue for the local newspaper or an interview for television or radio— early childhood educators need to use the media to keep critical issues in front of the public eye and to build up community awareness.

## Bringing it together

Early childhood educators can increase the status of children, families and early childhood if they reach out to and engage the community as part of their leadership role and responsibility. When families are willing to contribute as a resource, they enhance their children's learning and educational outcomes and the viability of early childhood services, and benefit themselves from membership of a community network of families. Becoming politically aware and active contributes to successful advocacy on behalf of children and families. Politically astute and active contact with local, national and even international communities can take a variety of forms, from working with families, other professionals and agencies to accessing all the available channels of communication. Continued politically aware and motivated action by early childhood leaders and educators within the community can foster change in community openness to understanding about the fundamental importance of, and the vital role played by, early childhood services to benefit children and families.

# CHAPTER 13

## LEADING ETHICAL PRACTICE

*There is a strong ethical dimension in early childhood educators' daily work. We have to make fast decisions that sometimes are in conflict with our values. Sometimes, meeting the needs of one child can impinge on the needs of another, leading to unsatisfactory outcomes for children, families and educators. It isn't an easy job at times because there may be no right answer.*
EARLY CHILDHOOD TEACHER

### THIS CHAPTER EXPLORES

- promoting and protecting children's well-being and rights
- championing children and families
- the ethics of providing quality services
- the role of a profession's ethical principles
- ethical choices and dilemmas
- the benefits of an early childhood codes of ethics

New understanding about contemporary leadership has challenged early childhood leaders and educators to reconceptualise their thinking, ideas, perspectives and approaches. For those working with and for young children and families, the intricate interplay between pedagogy, research, policy and ethics guides how leadership is framed and enacted. In rapidly changing times, early childhood leaders are responsible for ensuring that practice in early childhood services benefits the well-being of children, families and the community. Therefore, they must be prepared to meet changing attitudes, needs, expectations and demands in ways that embody early childhood's enduring professional values. Early childhood leaders are professionally obliged to lead quality services that are underpinned by ethical practice. The significance, importance and complexity of the moral or ethical dimension of contemporary leadership cannot be under-estimated.

### Morality and ethics in leadership

The terms 'morality' and 'ethics' often are used interchangeably but in fact they have different meanings. Morality refers to a system or doctrine of values and principles that generally is externally imposed and used to distinguish between right and wrong and good and bad intentions, decisions and conduct. It is a code of interpersonal behaviour that is considered acceptable by individuals, cultures and societies, where conforming to values and principles leads to right and good behaviour.

Ethics refers to a codified philosophy of moral values that addresses questions of morality and describes the internally defined and adopted moral values and principles of a particular individual or professional group that are used to judge and govern conduct. Ethics often is applied to guide decision-making about more subtle concerns, such as rightness, fairness and equity. In early childhood, ethics should guide decision-making and policy development at all times (Barblett, Hydon and Kennedy, 2008).

The overwhelming majority of people who are attracted to working with and for children want to make a positive difference in the lives of children, families and communities, and act in accordance with their society's accepted morality. Because early childhood leaders and educators are intimately involved with and influential in the lives and welfare of children and families, they also have a professional obligation and duty to act ethically and to lead team members to do likewise. They understand and accept that they have a responsibility to become politically aware and active, and to advocate for the rights of children and families. This means that they are required to comply with and integrate professional ethical principles into daily practice.

Ethical practice requires early childhood leaders to develop considerable self-awareness about who they are, what values underpin their morality and ethics, how these affect their behaviour, and how their choices and decisions impact on others. Effective early childhood leaders are able to identify professional values and visibly personify (or live) their personal and professional values in their enactment of leadership. They define their own standards according to society's moral values as well as professional values, expectations and obligations, and put those standards into practice. Conscientious early childhood leaders who understand themselves are aware of the values that are most important to them—that is, the values in which they believe and that define them as people and as professionals. They proactively reflect about, choose and then embody their key values through their choices, decisions and actions.

Early childhood leaders who live out their values in their personal life and professional work are trusted, respected and perceived as 'having character' by colleagues. When early childhood leaders identify, share and live their values in their day-to-day work, team members, families and other professionals regard them as genuine, honest, having courage and integrity, doing the right thing, leading legitimately and authentically, and generally doing their best personally, professionally and ethically.

Transformational leadership has become synonymous with ethical leadership because it is underpinned by values and morality. Transformational leaders display strong values and work to raise others' consciousness in order to transcend self-interest. Their priorities and goals focus on the betterment of others and life in general. Today, early childhood educators wholeheartedly endorse the inclusion of ethics in their definition and enactment of leadership. Indeed, many would agree that leadership is essentially an ethical action that is guided by personal and professional values and principles about what is right and wrong, and in the rights and best interests of young children, families and early childhood services.

However, it must be remembered that all leaders are ordinary people who have chosen to take up or been given leadership roles and responsibilities. People are not always perfect, altruistic, good or moral. Sometimes, in trying to get the job done, leaders may abuse their position and power, make mistakes and wrong or imperfect choices. This does not mean that they should relinquish their leadership aspirations. Leaders who display humility when they fail to meet professional expectations and standards, but who then learn from mistakes and past experience, demonstrate capacity for learning and growth. In workplaces that have a transparent code of conduct and ethics, including standards for leadership, leaders are more likely to live up to professional expectations (Yaverbaum and Sherman, 2008). A professional code of conduct or ethics helps early childhood leaders and educators to understand core values, act in accordance with ethical principles, and make better choices and decisions about complex ethical issues, as well as routine matters.

An understanding of ethics is fundamental to leadership in early childhood because ethical principles help set high professional standards, build value-led workplace cultures, focus attention on what is right rather than what is expedient and guide decision-making. Ethics helps everyone in early childhood to understand:

- what they truly value
- how to connect values with daily life and early childhood practice
- influences on individual and professional choices and decisions, and
- standards and policies developed for early childhood services.

Ethical decision-making is a product of open dialogue when faced with problematic choices (Barblett, Hydon and Kennedy, 2008), characterised by empathy, fairness, equity, objectivity, learning from history and previous mistakes. It is based on information and facts from a range of perspectives and consultations. In early childhood, its aim is to protect and support children and families by arriving at facilitated, harmonious and just solutions to thorny issues.

In early childhood services, leaders hold social responsibility for enhancing the potential of the children and adults with whom they interact, for protecting their welfare, for laying the foundations for lifelong learning, and for providing quality services that are relevant and responsive to local communities. They are charged with moral and ethical responsibility to advocate for children, families and the sector (Engle, 2006)—that is, to be articulate, organised and skilful in acting as a voice for individuals and groups who may be vulnerable and powerless.

It has been suggested that every early childhood educator should become a children's champion and make a difference to the quality of children's and families' lives (National Association for the Education of Young Children, 1996; Championing Children, 2006) by:

- speaking out on behalf of children at every opportunity—for example, with colleagues, family members, friends, politicians and in the community
- doing something to improve the life of one child beyond their own family—for instance, volunteering at an out-of-school service, or supporting learning by, for example, taking a less advantaged child on an outing to a zoo, children's farm or museum
- holding public officials accountable for making children's and families' well-being and learning a national commitment in terms of actions as well as words—for example, investigating how public officials stand on issues affecting young children, families, early learning and education; supporting those who give priority to key issues for early childhood; challenging the status quo if it is not considered to be in the interests of children's well-being
- encouraging relevant associations to make a public commitment to children and families, perhaps by sponsoring a children's service, purchasing needed equipment, helping to create inviting public spaces for children and families or establishing a neighbourhood watch group, and
- urging others to become children's champions—to voice their opinions regarding the quality of children's lives, to participate in learning experiences and to release staff to give time to early childhood services.

## Leading ethical practice in early childhood services

Early childhood leaders and educators who engage in ethical practice base their day-to-day activities on core professional values directed at achieving high standards, securing ethical conduct, and advancing family and community understanding of quality service provision. Ethical practice refers to the ways in which early childhood educators understand and implement moral values and principles in their daily work (Hydon, 2009), and reflects professional ethical responsibilities for the protection of young children's and families' well-being in four key areas:

1. the promotion and protection of children's rights
2. ensuring quality services that affirm children's rights
3. administration of services in accordance with ethical values and obligations, and
4. using the profession's code of ethics to guide the resolution of ethical dilemmas.

Ethical practice in early childhood services results from the complex integration of leaders' understanding of, reflection about and decision-making in these four areas. Ethical values and principles determine how people ought to behave, treat one another and the obligations they have to one another; consequently, acting ethically in these areas means living by example and behaving professionally at all times.

## Promoting and protecting children's rights

One of the primary and significant responsibilities of any adult—but especially leaders of early childhood services—is to make decisions and behave in ways that promote and protect the rights of young children, who generally are considered to be dependent, vulnerable and voiceless in contemporary society. The concept of children's rights is a cultural construction about children's essential entitlements in society that still provokes some resistance and hostility when its use in advocacy is raised (Smith, 2008). It appears that where resources are limited, young children are the first and biggest losers. Although limited political and public interest and support for children's rights continues to be conspicuous, the vast majority of countries today give at least tacit recognition of and respect for their importance.

Families, local communities and most societies agree that, in principle, children have a universal right to survival and development, although whose responsibility it is and the level to which such rights might be promoted and protected still cause some debate. The term 'development' refers not only to physical health, but also to the 'mental, emotional, cognitive, social and cultural development' (Franklin and Hammarberg, 1995: x) in which the principle of equality is inherent. Although equity and social justice for children generally are endorsed globally, the rhetoric does not necessarily translate into action, with insignificant and unacceptable budgets invested in quality early childhood services by governments of some poorer and developing economies. However, early childhood service provision in more prosperous countries currently attracts more financial recognition than ever before, signalling and confirming its vital contribution to human success throughout life.

Contemporary understanding about children's essential entitlements distinguishes the traditional needs-based approach, where children were viewed as passive subjects, from the current rights-based approach, where children are viewed as legitimate citizens and active agents in their own development (Smith, 2008). Today, children's rights determine and prescribe how professionals define and meet identified entitlements and needs. Early childhood educators hold key positions, and are obliged professionally to actively articulate, protect, promote and educate others about the principles, requirements and stipulations relating to children's rights.

Early childhood leaders are cognisant of children's rights and entitlements because their work with and for children and families is built on intimate knowledge and extensive experience with them. Therefore, early childhood leaders have an ethical duty and responsibility to work as protectors, advocates, facilitators, negotiators and champions to ensure that children's rights are fully understood and embedded in practice in early childhood services. Given that young children are vulnerable and do not have a voice, they need special support to ensure that their rights are realised. Consequently, early childhood leaders and educators need to be aware of, sensitive to and respectful of the rights and best interests of children and families, and act to enable, enhance and empower them.

In the 1990s, the development of a professional code of ethics (or standards of practice) for early childhood was seen as a means of guaranteeing children's rights. In early childhood, the code of ethics provides clear statements about professional values, vision, mission and goals. Early childhood educators should refer to it:

- when faced with challenging ethical conundrums and choices
- for guiding decision-making, and
- for governing interpersonal interaction with young children and families.

In some countries, an early childhood professional code of ethics was developed by consensus, then endorsed and adopted by the sector in acknowledgement of the importance of raising ethical awareness, encouraging engagement in ethical thinking, conversations and reflection, and strengthening advocacy. It is easier for everyone who works with and for children and families to work ethically if practice is guided and supported by an ethical framework or code.

Early childhood leaders need to model and champion ethical practice because those who work with and for young children and families frequently are confronted with ethical choices and dilemmas about values, goals, practice and relationships. Therefore, they have a responsibility to promote and protect young children's rights. On a day-to-day basis, early childhood leaders and educators should act to guarantee, extend, educate about and advocate for the rights of young children and families.

## Ensuring quality services that affirm children's rights

The provision of quality and economically viable services that affirm children's rights is another ethical challenge for early childhood educators. The portrayal of families as consumers of services whose purchasing power can influence the type of provision offered within a community continues to raise considerable concern. Research indicates that a number of factors influence choice of service, and that quality of service is a high priority only for those families who appreciate its importance and influence. As well as variety and flexibility in service provision, issues of quality assurance and improvement, the rights of consumers and value for money in service provision need to be addressed.

Such issues can be incompatible with the rights and needs of young children in early childhood services. The trends towards privatisation, entrepreneurship and responsivity to competitive markets mean that consideration of children's rights may be overlooked when developing new and transforming existing services. While it is essential that early childhood services be affordable and cost efficient, these factors must be balanced against the ethical responsibility to protect children's rights. Ultimately, early childhood service provision cannot afford to sacrifice children's rights in order to meet short-term priorities and pressures because this will have long-term effects on children's development as productive citizens.

Clearly, explicit values and ethical principles are essential to affirm young children's rights to quality early childhood services that foster development and learning, and engage and support their families. Quality is not a finite goal that, once attained, can be checked off a list of things to do. The quest for quality is the pursuit of a complex vision and goal. Understanding of quality evolves and matures over time as early childhood educators' understanding about young children's rights, development and learning expands.

Quality in early childhood is related to professional practice where the rights and interests of children are given the highest priority. Unfortunately, statements about values, vision and goals, and written documents such as codes of ethics, are professional guidelines or reference points that can be used only to assist in decision-making and conflict resolution. In early childhood, these documents hold no legal status, and behaviour that breaches or does not conform to the guidelines, and is not illegal and unlawful, is not subject to mandatory legal or professional sanction. The power of such documents is derived from ethical obligations inherent in early childhood educators' professional identity, roles and responsibilities to promote and protect the rights of young children.

Many sets of indicators for assessing quality in early childhood services are available where quality is defined and underpinned by values and visions. Most incorporate the following principles that inherently and implicitly affirm children's rights before any other considerations:

- *Children come first.* Every child has the right to depend upon adults to provide the conditions that will enable them to reach their full potential. All adults bear responsibility for children, and it is essential that families receive the necessary support to ensure that their children receive the best possible start in life.
- *Children have the right to be recognised as people with views and interests.* Children have the right to a voice, to be listened to and to participate in decision-making about issues that affect their lives.
- *Children should have the opportunity to be part of a family and community,* to experience stable environments that enhance their esteem as individuals, their dignity and autonomy, self-confidence and enthusiasm for learning, and respect for others that ensures they are free from discrimination.
- *Families and communities need to be supported in promoting the interests and welfare of children.* Children need strong, dependable adults who provide love, security and the financial resources to ensure they can access an adequate standard of living. Early childhood services must be grounded in local communities and provide relevant and real choices for families.
- *Children have the right to safe play environments* that offer a range of opportunities for autonomy, social development and recreational activity.
- *Children and families have the right to participate in the services provided for them.* Service provision must address issues of access and equity.

The services provided for children should start with, and be based on, the rights and interests of children, not emerge from the interests of families (although their common interests must be acknowledged), or from those of governments, professionals, agencies and organisations, finances and pedagogical fashions.

### Ethical administration of early childhood services

Effective administration and management of early childhood services are traditional indicators of quality and considered to be necessary, but not sufficient, elements of leadership. Nevertheless, effective administration requires early childhood leaders to refer to and act upon ethical principles that are accepted and endorsed by the early childhood sector when making decisions. For early childhood, this means transforming traditional power relationships into collaborative, consultative, communicative, respectful and just decision-making.

Ethical administration of early childhood services involves applying moral values and principles to their planning, implementation, operation and evaluation. Values, vision, mission and goals, leadership style and collaborative contributions by others should underpin planning. Ethical decision-making and creative problem-solving, as well as aspects of motivation, team-building and professional development, should guide implementation. Operation should be conducted from a professional knowledge base, ethical choices made about issues such as facilities, resources, the use of space, room arrangement and scheduling, as well as sound financial management and trustworthy record-keeping. Evaluation should promote ongoing learning through processes that provide information about service effectiveness and inform the management of change. Each of these key functions involves ethical issues and choices, especially when decision-making cannot be settled by reference to pedagogy or statutory regulations.

Examples of ethical choices and dilemmas commonly encountered by early childhood leaders and educators include:

- requests from families that their toddlers be kept awake during the day because they say they can't get them to sleep at night
- requests that boys not be permitted to play with dolls, dress up in female clothes or play in the role-play area
- demands that three-year-old children be 'taught' reading and writing skills
- informing families about their child's behaviour, knowing that they are likely to punish the child for it at home
- 'permission' from a family member to smack their child when misbehaving in the service
- overhearing a child discuss with a friend the petty shoplifting he and his siblings were encouraged to do by their family
- informing families that their 'vegetarian' child ate a ham sandwich from another child's lunchbox
- overhearing a child discuss abusive behaviour within the family
- ignoring non-compliance with statuary staff:child ratios
- treating children differently because of their families' non-traditional values
- confronting a colleague about a breach of confidentiality, and
- implementing any practice or policy that is considered to be harmful to or not in the best interests of children.

Early childhood leaders who appreciate the delicate nature and complexity of such matters refer to and are guided by professional values and principles to ensure that any decision or action they take meets professional expectations about and standards of quality. This can be difficult for leaders, especially where the needs of individuals and services conflict (Reynolds, 2011). Effective leaders explicitly acknowledge their professional obligation to lead quality practice and services, so they refer to and are guided by an early childhood code of ethics and standards of practice when making decisions about complex ethical matters.

Staff recruitment and selection, development and evaluation are other areas that are critical to the ethical administration of early childhood services. Safe recruitment and selection are core responsibilities because children have the right to be protected from those who might harm or are unsuited to work with them. It is important that those charged with employment of staff appreciate recruitment and selection as an ethical responsibility, and as part of protecting the rights and needs of young children.

The quality of staff in terms of appropriate training and experience is essential for ensuring high-quality service provision in early childhood. Professional training and development opportunities need to be offered to all adults associated with early childhood services because the better the understanding that everybody has about what constitutes quality in early childhood services and the values, vision and goals of early development, learning and education, the more responsive early childhood services can be to the interests and needs of children and families. This is related to the ethical responsibility to provide quality early childhood services that affirm children's rights.

In addition to training opportunities, early childhood educators regularly need to evaluate their performance and professional goals. Evaluation is an essential part of the ongoing learning process in which all professionals engage. Reflective practice, as a basis for evaluation of educators, services and level of quality achievement, is central to the professional development of early childhood educators.

Reflection involves thinking about daily practice in order to identify gaps in knowledge, understanding and skill as a basis for improvement. Becoming reflective is part of being a lifelong learner. Reflective leaders and educators pursue and consider new theories, information and ideas, draw on the opinions of others and use these resources to develop new approaches in practice. Early childhood practice can be enhanced and extended through professional conversations and dialogues (Kuh, 2012) with colleagues, supervisors, mentors and coaches, as well as through training and other professional development opportunities. The use of professional portfolios and journals has been very effective for structuring, gathering evidence and documenting learning, professional growth and improvement in practice.

The ability to be reflective is grounded in thinking about learning and understanding yourself as a learner (Claxton, 2002). It means becoming more strategic about learning by planning in advance what changes might be needed, revising and adapting those plans in the light of insight gained from monitoring and learning from experience. Reflective educators take stock of themselves and the constraints of their working circumstances, seek out and use available resources, prioritise their learning challenges, review progress, make required modifications and ponder over how they can transfer or generalise their learning to other areas of their work. They reflect about their professional roles, values and goals, and feel confident to discuss and debate issues of practice and ethics with colleagues, other professionals and families. Becoming a reflective educator essentially involves evaluating professional practice through a process of thinking about earlier work, judging its effectiveness and developing an action plan for improvement in the future.

However, reflection and evaluation are not value-free processes. Perceptions of what is important in early childhood services are based on professional and personal values. Attributes, attitudes and behaviour are judged on the basis of such values. Early childhood leaders need to appreciate the value basis of reflection and evaluation, and ensure that procedures and processes are consistent with the early childhood sector's professional values, philosophies, ethics and pedagogies. Evaluation of personnel, practice and services must be conducted within the context of children's rights, social responsibility and ethical decision-making.

Where early childhood services are administered from an ethical perspective, positive interaction and collaborative teamwork will be evident. Early childhood leaders' ethical decision-making is marked by transparent values and principles that underpin administrative structures, processes and procedures. This helps team members to understand and appreciate the validity of administrative policies and operations.

## The code of ethics and courageous ethical choices

Being a competent early childhood educator in contemporary society means more than being trained, qualified and experienced in the provision of services for young children and families. It involves adopting a particular mental set or attitude towards one's work. Early childhood educators increasingly regard themselves as professionals, with a distinct professional identity and growing professional self-esteem and confidence.

Professionalism continues to be a valued in early childhood throughout the world. The adoption of a professional code of ethics is part of the definition of what it is to be a professional. Insightful early childhood educators appreciate that achieving professional status and credibility in the eyes of the community carries additional moral obligations and responsibilities to children, families, colleagues, services, local communities and society.

A professional code of ethics is a set of statements about appropriate and expected conduct of members of a professional working group that reflects agreed and adopted values. Such statements help professionals avoid temptation, poor choices, improper decisions and wrongdoing by providing guidelines for determining what is right and courageous rather than expedient or avoidant, what is good rather than practical, and what behaviour may never be engaged in or condoned under any circumstances. According to Barblett, Hydon and Kennedy (2008), a code of ethics offers a framework for identifying professional expectations and standards, a vehicle for advocacy, a mechanism for uniting the sector, a scaffold for reflective practice, a guide to decision-making and a challenge for action.

A code of ethics is a vehicle for protecting the rights and welfare of those who may be dependent and vulnerable, as well as a means of protecting members of the profession themselves from making unsuitable decisions or engaging in unacceptable behaviour in relation to young children and their families. While early childhood leaders might argue that they are guided by altruistic values, vision and goals, and naturally would act in accordance with children's rights and their best interests, a code of ethics provides a focus for debate about values and ethical issues, philosophy and pedagogy, guiding the complex decision-making faced in day-to-day work.

Early childhood educators benefit from a code of ethics because they have considerable autonomy and independence over their decisions and behaviour. Decisions have to be made quickly, often without discussion with or reference to others. Such pressures may result in inappropriate decisions, or decisions that do not protect children's rights or that are not in their best interests. In extreme cases, they may even be harmful illegal or unlawful.

*The family of a child with additional needs challenged an educator about the way she managed her child's behaviour. The family didn't understand that their child was just one child in a group of children, all of whom have needs and rights. The educator couldn't permit their child to continue with that behaviour because it could have resulted in injury to another child. She made the best decision she could at that time; in hindsight, she had other options but sometimes decisions have to be made fast.*
MANAGER, DAY NURSERY

In addition, a decision that can be rationalised and justified by reference to a code of ethics carries more weight and credibility, and as such is less likely to be challenged than one that does not have such a solid underpinning. A code of ethics can guide, support and enhance confidence in the demanding responsibility for courageous decision-making and problem-solving.

*Some aspects of the government guidelines for improving literacy have not been appropriate for four-year-olds. We need to have credible reasons for implementing the guidelines differently. There is research evidence we refer to but we want our professional values and insight into what works with children recognised by people like inspectors and advisers.*
EARLY YEARS TEACHER

A professional code of ethics is helpful because many situations and incidents that occur in day-to-day work with young children contain inherent conflicts of value or interest, or pose ethical choices, conundrums or dilemmas. Ethical choices that create quandaries, discord or dilemmas for early childhood educators arise from incidents that involve conflict between core values and difficult, uncomfortable options that result in less than satisfactory outcomes.

*Some families put a lot of pressure on us to teach the children to read and write in the nursery. They don't understand that many children are not ready for this and we don't want the children to experience failure. But if we don't respond to the families' expectations, they remove the children and enrol them at a service that will try to teach them those skills. What do we do? If we teach reading and writing too early, it is not in the best interests of some children. If we don't, the families get upset and threaten to find a nursery that does. The viability of our service could be jeopardised.*
NURSERY OFFICER

Early childhood leaders ultimately are responsible for deciding on or supporting courses of action that will affect the lives of other people. Where a decision is required but where no mutually acceptable or satisfactory options appear to exist, sensible leaders refer to the professional code of ethics to determine overriding values and principles to help them work towards an optimal resolution.

*There has been a lot of discussion among the staff about management's decision to accept three-year-olds who are still not toilet trained. The key issue here is not to disadvantage any child. We have policies about inclusion and equal opportunities so they need to understand that the decision was based on the values endorsed in the policies.*
DEPUTY SUPERVISOR, DAY NURSERY

Finally, a code of ethics is necessary because the early childhood's infrastructure incorporates certain features that increase the likelihood of ethical quandaries occurring in daily practice, such as low status and power, a multiplicity of clients with potentially conflicting needs and interests, and role multiplicity and ambiguity. A code of ethics can assist early childhood educators, including leaders, to have the courage to make decisions and behave in ways that do not compromise children, themselves and other parties and groups associated with early childhood services. While a code of ethics cannot, and is not, intended to solve the individual and complex situations faced by early childhood educators in their daily work, it does offer a tool for guiding reflection, decision-making and action.

Unfortunately, most professional codes of ethics are of limited benefit because they are powerless to enforce standards or apply sanctions to members who choose not to endorse or comply with—or even flagrantly breach—the principles and values accepted by and for the profession. Behaving in accordance with a profession's code of ethics usually is a voluntary undertaking by individual members of that profession. For the early childhood sector, a code of ethics signposts the moral obligations and responsibilities of educators to individuals and groups who are associated with services, and highlights moral issues related to working for and with those who are vulnerable.

Effective early childhood leaders act as a role model for others by using the code of ethics to raise and explore issues that emerge in practice and work to gain acceptance of and support for ethically appropriate rules and guidelines with team members. Although they cannot impose sanctions over non-compliance with or breaches of the principles reflected in the code of ethics by colleagues, ethical leaders accept the moral responsibility for identifying and raising such issues for discussion, and working towards greater understanding and positive resolution.

Thoughtful leaders appreciate that a code of ethics—even without sanctions—plays an important role in improving professional practice in early childhood services. It challenges educators to keep abreast of developments, and focuses collaborative and reflective thinking and debate, thereby increasing understanding of, and unity of purpose within teams and services. It directs advocacy—especially in relation to change—and raises early childhood's professional standing within the community. An early childhood code of ethics is a valuable resource for addressing the increasingly complex ethical challenges faced by leaders and educators in day-to-day practice.

## Bringing it together

Conscientious leaders in early childhood appreciate their moral obligation to act with professional integrity in all aspects of their work. In exercising ethical leadership, they clarify both personal morality and professional ethics. A professional code of ethics is a valuable tool for this process. Effective early childhood leaders clearly articulate and embody personal and professional value systems in their practice and, as a consequence, they are perceived as more predictable and credible. The leader's value system should be accessible, transparent and understood by everyone associated with early childhood services as the rationale for and foundation of services' vision, mission and goals, educators' ethical choices and decisions, and reflective practice, as well as the basis for administrative and operational structures and procedures. The ethics of leadership lie in early childhood leaders' attitudes towards the involvement and participation of others in issues that affect their lives. Ethical leadership stems from inclusive collaboration with people to achieve specific goals, and is founded on empathy, trust, respect, fairness, communication, cooperation and empowerment.

# CHAPTER 14

# LEADING FOR SUCCESSION: BUILDING LEADERSHIP CAPACITY

*Every early childhood educator has the potential to become a leader if they want to because most of the skills and qualities can be learned and developed. Leadership comes to some naturally but most of us learn to become leaders.*

MANAGER, DAY NURSERY

## THIS CHAPTER EXPLORES

- leadership and quality in early childhood services
- professional preparation for building capacity
- approaches for building leadership capacity
- distributed leadership for building capacity
- planning for succession

Competent leadership is a significant contributor to the quality of early childhood services, and early childhood leaders need to acquire specific dispositions, knowledge and skills to lead educators, children, families and other professionals, and address the complexity of issues and concerns that arise in practice (Reynolds, 2011). The style and standard of leadership exercised by formal leaders of early childhood services is a key factor in determining their quality, in terms of positive outcomes for children, families and services. The manner in which early childhood leaders personify and enact leadership sets the tone, expectations, standards, boundaries and culture of services.

All sustainable organisations need continual access to new leaders, and it is more cost efficient to draw on those who have been socialised within their own workplace cultures (Osborne, 2008). Regrettably, very few early childhood educators enter the sector with aspirations to take up leadership in the future and, perhaps because of the high-level demands and responsibilities implicit in leadership, not enough display ready willingness to engage in such roles. In order to build sustainable, flexible and inclusive early childhood service provision, it is essential that the early childhood sector, as well as individual leaders, invest in leadership recruitment, capacity-building and succession planning. These functions focus on

building and renewing both the sector's and services' leadership capacity by identifying, recruiting and developing a pool of high-potential individuals for meeting
current and future leadership needs (Fink, 2011).

Whether they aspire to, default into or are thrust into leadership roles and
responsibilities, most early childhood educators find the transition to leadership
demanding, daunting and overwhelming. Until recently, few early childhood leaders
had access to focused, relevant preparation or training prior to taking up leadership
positions and little on-the-job support has been available. Given the inherent transient and temporary nature of leadership, even newly appointed early childhood
leaders need to focus on identifying leadership aspiration, potential and talent in
team members, and plan for succession at the same time as progressing their own
professional expertise and leadership competence.

The need to stimulate the willingness of potential leaders to come forward is
even more crucial if workplace cultures openly or subtly discourage individuals
from expressing honest and valid interest in leadership aspiration, skill acquisition and enactment. Some early childhood leaders report having being teased and
ridiculed by peers and colleagues for displaying such ambitions and scorned for
their endeavours to acquire leadership skills or contribute as an informal leader.
The consequence of such short-sighted attitudes is that too few early childhood
educators gain the necessary knowledge, skills, perspectives and expertise to lead
early childhood, children and families in communities, governments and societies
of the future (Maxfield et al., 2011). For this reason, it is no longer acceptable
for early childhood educators to rely on individual leaders and be unprepared to
assume and exercise leadership responsibility.

Because of the complexity and multiplicity of leadership roles as well as the
variety of early childhood services, the creation of a pool of diverse leaders who
can take the lead in different facets and various contexts of leadership is essential.
Holistic leadership in early childhood for the twenty-first century is grounded in the
fundamental aspects outlined by Kagan and Bowman (1997):

- *administrative*—day-to-day operation and financial management
- *pedagogical*—theory, research and practice of teaching and learning
- *community*—understanding and responding to local realities and contexts
- *conceptual*—vision for change in the context of broader social policies,
  and
- *advocacy*—representing and bringing early childhood to public attention.

However, contemporary leadership in early childhood is expected to address
the following additional aspects:

- *ethical*—applying moral values and principles to decision-making and practice
- *cultural*—promoting and securing the commitment of educators, families and local communities to shared values, vision, mission and goals
- *performance-led*—promoting technical expertise, efficient performance and leading practice
- *capacity-building*—investing the future by identifying the leadership potential, qualities and contributions of aspiring, emergent and nascent leaders
- *career development*—enabling educators to see and follow progressive and fulfilling career pathways, and
- *entrepreneurial*—proactive, forward-looking, informed risk-taking, new and improved services, customer, market and business-minded.

Clearly, novice and poorly prepared leaders, as well as some experienced leaders, will find themselves unable to meet all of these additional expectations. However, if all early childhood educators view leadership as a collective responsibility, it can be distributed validly and appropriately among and within teams, thereby drawing on and extending the available pool of expertise for leadership. When formal leaders have the courage to step aside and share or disperse leadership, they create opportunities for leadership potential to emerge in others. When others display interest in or potential for such opportunities, responsible leaders build capacity by actively engaging and mentoring their efforts.

## Professional preparation for building capacity

Leadership in early childhood is a critical and complex role and responsibility, requiring conceptual and practical expertise in child development, pedagogy, organisational theory, fiscal and legal issues, and family, professional and community relationships. While quality early childhood services are associated with experienced leaders, it is evident that professional preparation makes a difference, with leaders who access specialised rather than generic training and other opportunities performing their roles and responsibilities more effectively.

Current research reveals a need for the creation of more integrated professional preparation and development systems that are tailored to the needs of early childhood's diverse workforce (Douglas, Heimer and Hagan, 2011). When aspiring and emerging early childhood leaders are appropriately prepared and skilled, they are more able to support young children and families, and shape and deliver quality services more efficiently and effectively. However, a study of several international approaches to leadership development concluded that little information was available about the skills required for leaders of children's services (National College for Leadership of Schools and Children's Services, 2010). Considerable research is needed to establish the requisite knowledge and skills for effective leadership in children's services, and the preparation and development opportunities that best develop them.

Although in the past very little preparation, training and support was available for those who aspired to or held leadership positions in early childhood, a variety of development opportunities are available now, with some tailored specifically to respond to varying qualifications, professional backgrounds and experience. Although recently qualified educators—especially those with university qualifications—enter early childhood today better prepared to take up leadership roles and responsibilities (Mistry and Sood, 2011), the inclusion of leadership as a core element and the promotion of early identification with leadership in preservice training is vital. Fortunately, 'learning on the job' with support from some generic training is no longer considered adequate for transitioning to leadership positions. The early cultivation of identity with and capacity for leadership in all early childhood educators will help uncover hidden interest or undeveloped potential, thereby expanding the human resources that can be drawn upon for leadership purposes.

In order to build leadership capacity as part of succession planning, every early childhood educator needs to develop the expertise required for effective leadership in services and communities. Given that early childhood is dynamic and driven by growth, change and responsiveness, every early childhood educator needs to embrace a lifelong learning perspective towards professional development, and to regard leadership as a key aspect of this development. Leaders are learners and learners become leaders. If leaders stop learning, they will lose their legitimacy. Effective leaders appreciate that learning is fundamental for competent leadership, and that collaborative learning with colleagues is a productive experience for both individuals and teams.

Thornton et al. (2009: 13) summarise some of the beneficial strategies associated with learning about leadership in professional preparation opportunities with peers, including:

- learning activities based on problem-solving in real-life situation
- reflection on real experiences based on feedback from leaders and peers
- challenges that stem from new ideas, and from confronting dilemmas and choices
- coaching to improve performance, and
- building communities or networks of practice to support learning.

Evidence indicates that the building leadership capacity and preparation of leaders are enhanced where a culture of inquiry (Watson and Williams, 2011), collective learning (Garavan and McCarthy, 2008) and reflective practice (Furman, 2012) is supported. Such processes encourage the creation of learning networks and communities of practice that:

- stimulate and support a culture of leadership based on conversations, intellectual engagement and shared professional understanding
- promote open dialogue within services about relationships between improvement, quality and leadership, and
- develop and articulate explicit visions of effective leadership in early childhood, its characteristics and standards, and strategies for capacity-building and succession planning.

Such learning processes are more than investments in the identification, nurture and professional development of aspiring, emergent and novice leaders. They help motivate, revitalise and reinvigorate experienced and mature leaders, and encourage workplace cultures that value leadership aspiration, engagement and progression.

## Approaches to building leadership capacity

The pressing need to build leadership capacity and plan for succession in early childhood has been acknowledged by the expanding and diverse professional opportunities that are available for broadening identification with and capacity for leadership in early childhood educators. The most effective opportunities are tailored to and build on individual qualifications, experience and baseline under-standing about and agendas for leadership in early childhood.

Different training and capacity-building opportunities need to be developed for those with little or basic training, those with vocational qualifications, those with degree qualifications and those with postgraduate qualifications. Tailored training opportunities help individuals to transition from naïve to better-evolved concep-tions of leadership.

To build leadership capacity and motivate aspiring, emerging and potential leaders achieve a more evolved understanding about leadership and its role, it is important to begin with where people are by pinpointing early childhood educators' entry level of understanding and matching individualised, challenging development opportunities that foster strengths and work on overcoming weaknesses. As they begin to expand their appreciation of leadership and its role in early childhood services, most educators will start to display attitudes, behaviour and skills associ-ated with a more advanced understanding of leadership.

**Table 14.1:** Relationship between conceptions of leadership and training and qualifications

| Conception of leadership | Training/qualifications/focus |
| --- | --- |
| Little focus on or awareness about leadership | On-the-job training, novice, least qualified, focus on survival |
| Leader as a guide—warm, knowledgeable, assertive, goal-oriented, supervisor, mentor | Basic or vocational qualification, focus on day-to-day tasks |
| Leader as a motivator—warm, confident, empowering, proactive, planner | Further education or vocational qualification, focus on practical competence, team membership |
| Leader as a strategist—visionary, influential, proactive, empowering, systematic planner, risk-taker, advocate | University undergraduate degree, professional qualification, focus on leading practice, role model, supervisor, mentor |
| Leader as an entrepreneur—visionary, influential, professional authority, advocate, informed risk-taker, business-minded, market-competitor | University postgraduate degree, professional qualification, focus on excellence, growth, change, role model, mentor, coach |

Although individual improvement is important, the sustainability and responsiveness of early childhood services are linked closely to teams' collective capacity for leadership. Consequently, early childhood leaders also need to focus on igniting, inspiring and engaging their teams with leadership (Fink, 2011). Shared and distributed styles of leadership offer teams a variety of opportunities to uncover and build leadership potential.

Preparation for and training to build leadership skill and capacity do not happen through one-off in-service events. Rather, improvement in leadership skills and enhanced capacity originate in and are produced through early childhood leaders' and educators' substantial engagement in a range of learning and development experiences over a period of time. Currently, the range of longer-term opportunities available for building leadership skill and capacity include:

- a series of workshops with some workplace reflection, action and support
- workplace-based action research projects, sometimes inspired and supported by local communities of practice

- leadership development programs that are longer-term, practice-based, tailored to individual needs and may permit specialist accreditation
- specialist higher degree qualifications for those who aspire to or have demonstrated potential for leadership
- mentoring of emergent and newly appointed leaders
- coaching for experienced leaders, and
- accelerated professional development opportunities, sometimes in related sectors, for advanced leaders who aspire to contribute to structural and system development.

Unfortunately, access to some opportunities may be limited by geographical restrictions and follow-up support may not be available or sustained over a sufficient period of time.

In some countries, longer-term preparation opportunities offer access to recognised national professional qualifications for leadership in early childhood— for example, England's Early Years Professional Status qualification and the New Leaders in Early Years pilot program. These training opportunities offer professional accreditation to help early childhood educators become graduate leaders and graduate leaders to become strategic leaders in the sector (Children's Workforce Development Council, 2011).

Opportunities for building leadership capacity within multi-agency services in the early childhood sector incorporate an ethos of community partnership when exploring the expertise and experience required for leading across professional boundaries, and focus on:

- engaging service and community partnerships to connect with community resources and to respond to leadership opportunities through active involvement with a wide range of community services, agencies and bodies
- responsivity to cultural and community context to collaborate in developing initiatives that meet the needs of diverse but related cultural and community contexts
- responsivity to diverse contexts to develop generic leadership competencies that ensure success in diverse services and contexts
- mentoring and coaching to learn about the processes for and mutual benefits of one-to-one relationships for personal and professional development, and
- opportunities to transition to more advanced leadership through opportunities to put theory into practice.

Those who participate in leadership training opportunities generally report experiencing an increased sense of empowerment, a heightened sense of self-esteem and increased feelings of self-efficacy and confidence, especially in communication and interpersonal relationships, team-building, decision-making, responsiveness to change and professional development. However, in order to sustain advances in leadership capacity, early childhood leaders need to ensure that their newly acquired skills and competencies are practised daily and that, through observed positive outcomes for children, families and services, they remain motivated to practice, refine and assimilate them into their leadership skill repertoire.

## Reflections on leadership in practice

Leadership capabilities are best developed through mentoring and modelling, involving support of reputable and experienced colleagues at every level and at any stage of a person's career.
ASSOCIATE PROFESSOR, EARLY CHILDHOOD

The provision of suitable training opportunities that are designed specifically for early childhood educators can accelerate leadership capacity-building and planning for succession. Currently, early childhood as a sector appreciates that, through the provision of relevant, specialised, comprehensive, intensive, sustained professional development opportunities, it can grow its own leaders from within.

### Distributed leadership for building capacity

Building leadership capacity is about creating a culture of leadership where leadership is valued over management, where spontaneous and informal leadership, as well as action indicative of potential, is recognised, respected and reinforced. Experienced leaders advocate the benefits of distributed leadership for investing in, supporting, mentoring and coaching the professional development of aspiring and emergent leaders (Harris and Spillane, 2008; Talan, 2010). Distributed leadership can encourage early childhood educators to gain broader experience and perspectives that shift them from a management and positional perspective to a distributed and more holistic conception about leadership.

Building leadership capacity begins with the creation of conditions and opportunities that promote team learning by bringing early childhood educators together so that they can construct and negotiate shared understandings, meanings, language, goals and purposes of leadership. To make a start, such conversations could explore:

- what leadership means in and across contexts (to begin developing shared understanding, meaning and language)
- what roles and responsibilities are central to enacting leadership in and across contexts (to begin defining the parameters of leadership practice), and
- how authentic leadership might be exercised in and across contexts (to begin stimulating team acceptance of and commitment to distributed leadership in action).

Ryder et al. (2011: 62) pose two key questions for early childhood educators regarding the development of leadership development programs underpinned by a distributed leadership perspective.

- Why do we need to develop leadership and how will this development occur?
- Which leadership practices best align with early childhood practice?

In practical terms, early childhood educators need time, resources and opportunities that encourage and value a culture of distributed leadership in order to:

- try out and experience a range of delegated, supervised and mentored leadership roles and responsibilities
- model effective leadership practice
- be mentored for leadership aspiration
- engage in shared and team leadership throughout services, and
- access specialised professional preparation for transition to more advanced leadership roles.

When a culture of leadership is built, valued and embedded in early childhood services, educators are encouraged to aspire to and take on more complex roles and higher levels of responsibility. Thornton et al. (2009) conclude that to prepare leaders and build capacity, professional opportunities need to build in and resource:

- support for distributed leadership practice
- mentoring by experienced leaders
- reflection on real and practical experiences and situations

- problem-focused and contextually specific scenarios
- tailored opportunities that address individual and assessed needs
- the inclusion of teams in relevant issues
- networking and collegial dialogue, and
- longer-term options and sustained follow-up support.

Where leadership capacity is grown through customised preparation opportunities, the emerging leaders will be instrumental in raising the quality of leadership, thereby improving the quality of outcomes and services for children and families and enhancing early childhood's profile with local communities and the public.

## Planning for succession

At some point, every leader moves on, either to another position or to a different lifestyle or life choice. The promotion or resignation of a leader can leave a gaping hole in workplaces where leadership has been invested in one position or person, where little attention has been paid to building leadership capacity in team members and where scant thought has been put into succession planning. Because of the inherent transient nature of leadership, confident leaders are not threatened by the need to plan for succession. Rather, they view succession planning as a part of their responsibility to manage transition and change in ways that minimise disruption to quality service provision.

Planning for succession is a means of preparing early childhood teams and services for the inevitable transfer of leadership. It is a rational approach for identifying, developing and retaining those early childhood educators who display interest in, as well as potential and talent for, leadership. It increases the availability of diverse, capable and experienced educators who are prepared to embrace leadership roles as and when they become available. It guides targeted recruitment and induction of new staff who can supplement existing leadership capacity. It can be a means for career development where those with the most potential are supported to advance more quickly in their professional development and career. It is a proactive strategy for managing the careers of those with advanced leadership potential and ambition. Succession planning in early childhood is an intentional strategy that ensures continuity in key leadership roles, functions and responsibilities, and stability of service provision.

Succession management empowers individuals and teams because it incorporates learning opportunities for analysing, evaluating and discussing strengths and weaknesses, gaps and surpluses, people and positions, and finding ways of supporting personal and career development. It ensures that everyone develops the knowledge, skills and expertise needed to meet changing expectations and requirements for early childhood service provision. For early childhood leaders, it involves identifying who will be staying and who might be leaving, who are the shining stars, who might be burnt out, who is not performing or contributing satisfactorily, who has leadership potential, who needs to be challenged and stretched, who needs additional mentoring and leadership experience to achieve their potential, and who is competent, able, ready and willing to assume leadership roles and responsibilities.

Effective succession planning depends on:

- a culture of professional leadership development and progression
- shared definitions of leadership dispositions, competencies, functions, roles and responsibilities by team members
- willingness of all team members to engage in open and collaborative dialogue about perceived leadership needs
- the ability to diagnose current and future gaps, surpluses and needs in leadership capacity
- a range of strategies for building leadership capacity that contributes to realising vision, managing transitions and change, and
- regular review and revision of its impact in relation to the identification, development, recruitment and retention of a supply of capable leaders.

Both early childhood leaders and services for children and families benefit from thoughtful succession planning because:

- a pool of diverse leadership talent is created
- leaders pinpoint and target people with potential for taking up key roles
- individual services and agencies assess and match their leadership needs with qualified talent from within or outside the organisation
- audits or inventories of employee history can inform future staffing decisions
- accessible career pathways at different levels are clarified
- employee attrition and subsequent retraining needs are reduced, and
- it is a means for motivating, recognising and rewarding leadership effort.

Succession planning has positive outcomes for leadership continuity and transition as well as staffing and service stability. It embeds the prerequisite conditions for organisational growth, sustainability and renewal, thereby averting potential decline in effectiveness and relevance. It is a fundamental contributor to the close relationship between the quality of leadership and the quality of early childhood services.

## Bringing it together

The ongoing attention to leadership in early childhood has grown out of research evidence indicating that it contributes to the quality of early childhood services and that specific preparation, training and professional development opportunities for leadership are essential in order to enact this complex role successfully. Given the demands for quality and accountability in early childhood, there is a pressing need for effective, professional leadership. Increasingly, able early childhood leaders contribute to enhancing the professional competence, confidence and status of the sector in the eyes of local communities and the public, which in turn has generated greater awareness about and support for early childhood services. However, in order to build sustainable leadership capacity and plan for succession, early childhood leaders need to think about how to structure, make space and offer opportunities for others to assume suitable leadership roles and responsibilities, and to find the resources that underpin distributed leadership. Focusing on embedding shared, collaborative and distributed leadership helps to identify, prepare and support emergent leaders in early childhood services. Leadership capacity-building and planning for succession support the transition to leadership when required.

# POSTSCRIPT: AN AIDE-MEMOIRE FOR ASPIRING LEADERS IN EARLY CHILDHOOD

Leadership is subtle, complex, multi-faceted, multi-dimensional and essentially holistic. It is a personal expression of values and vision that is constructed through the interrelationship of and interaction between many elements. Its effective enactment creates synergy, where leadership becomes more than the sum of its parts. Deconstructing leadership into its various components can be helpful, but ultimately leadership is a personalised, integrated activity.

It is important to remember that there is no established profile of an ideal leader in early childhood; nor is there a stereotype about who or what a good leader is in any particular context. Authentic, genuine leaders learn from but do not emulate others. They develop their own personal qualities and individual styles out of awareness about and assessment of their own strengths and personalities and their work context. As a result, well-rounded leadership grows out of certain features that are recognised as key contributors to effective leadership in early childhood:

- *choice*—your options, courses of action, preferences, decisions
- *character*—your personality, dispositions, conduct, identity, ethics, willpower
- *credibility*—your trustworthiness, integrity, believability, reliability, dependability
- *charisma*—your inspiration, appeal, presence, style
- *courage*—your fearlessness, bravery, intrepidness, boldness, daring
- *calibre*—your merit, excellence, talent, capability, competence
- *commitment*—your responsibility, dedication, loyalty, duty, obligation
- *context*—the circumstances, situations, environments, conditions and factors that influence how you choose to personify and enact leadership
- *communication*—your conversations, dialogues, relationships, liaisons
- *collaboration*—your connections, cooperation, partnerships, consensus
- *challenge*—the tests, demands and risks you meet and face
- *championship*—what you advocate, support, promote, stand up, lobby and fight for
- *creativity*—your curiosity, imagination, innovativeness, vision, inspiration

- *change*—what and how you transform, modify, adapt and evolve, and
- *cultivation of capacity*—how you identify, recruit and build leadership capacity.

All leaders are human—imperfect, incomplete and flawed, with the potential to make mistakes, poor choices and improper decisions. Ancona et al. (2011: 179) encourage us to 'end the myth of the complete leader: the flawless person at the top who's got it all figured out'. None of us is perfect! However, every early childhood educator can make a positive difference to children, families and services by striving to be the best leader that they can be through their commitment to learning about, developing and refining their personal leadership capabilities in the contexts within which they work.

# REFERENCES

Adler, A. 1958, *What Life Should Mean to You*, G.P. Putnam's Sons, New York.

Alred, G. and Garvey, B. 2010, *The Mentoring Pocketbook*, 3rd edn, Laurel House, Alresford.

Ancona, D., Malone, T., Orlikowski, W.J. and Senge, P. 2011, 'In praise of the incomplete leader', in *Harvard Business Review* (ed.), *On Leadership*, Harvard Business School Press, Boston.

Anning, A., Cottrell, D., Frost, N., Green, J. and Robinson, M. 2010, *Developing Multi-professional Teamwork for Integrated Children's Services*, Open University Press, Maidenhead.

Australian Early Childhood Association Inc. 1991, 'Australian Early Childhood Association Code of Ethics', *Australian Journal of Early Childhood*, vol. 16, no. 1, pp. 3–6.

Australian Government Department of Education, Employment and Workplace Relations 2009, *Being, Becoming and Belonging: The Early Years Learning Framework for Australia*, Council of Australian Governments, Canberra.

Australian Institute of Family Studies 2011, 'Part B: Does collaboration benefit children and families? Exploring the evidence', in *Interagency Collaboration*, AFRC Briefing No. 21, Australian Family Relationships Clearinghouse, <http://aifs.gov.au/afrc/pubs/briefing/b021/b021-bb.html> (accessed 20 October 2011).

Baldock, P., Fitzgerald, D. and Kay, J. 2009, *Understanding Early Years Policy*, 2nd edn, Sage, London.

Barblett, L., Hydon, C. and Kennedy, A. 2008, *The Code of Ethics: A Guide for Everyday Practice*, Early Childhood Australia, Canberra, <http://www.early childhoodaustralia.org.au> (accessed 20 October 2011).

Bennis, W. 1989, *On Becoming a Leader*, Hutchinson, London.

Cameron, C. and Moss, P. (eds) 2011, *Social Pedagogy and Working with Children and Young People: Where Care and Education Meet*, Jessica Kingsley, London.

Campus Kindergarten, University of Queensland n.d., *Philosophy Values Statement*, <http://www.uq.edu.au/campuskindy/Our%20philosophy.htm> (accessed 20 November 2011).

Carnall, C. 2007, *Managing Change in Organisations*, 5th edn, Prentice Hall, Hemel Hempstead.

Caruso, J.J. and Fawcett, M.T. 2007, *Supervision in Early Childhood: A Developmental Perspective*, 3rd edn, Teachers College Press, New York.

Championing Children 2006, *Championing Children: A Shared Set of Skills,*

*Knowledge and Behaviours for Those Leading and Managing Integrated Children's Services*, 2nd edn, Department for Education and Skills, Nottingham.

Children's Services Central 2011, *Policy Development. Resources and Publication*, Children's Services Central, Sydney, <http://www.cscentral.org.au/publications/policy-development.html> (accessed 20 November 2011).

Children's Workforce Development Council 2010, *Everyone Working Together: Setting Up Multi-Agency Services*, Children's Development Working Council, Leeds.

—— 2011, *Developing Early Years Leaders is Central to Workforce Development and Improving Outcomes for Children and Young People*, Children's Development Working Council, Leeds, <http://www.cwdc.org.uk/early-years/graduate-leaders-in-the-early-years> (accessed 20 November 2011).

Claxton, G. 2002, *Building Learning Power*, Henleaze House, Bristol.

Cohen, L., Manion, L. and Harrison, K. 2011, *Research Methods in Education*, 7th edn, Routledge Falmer, London.

Collett, A. 2010, *The Multi-agency Team. Does it Really Work?* Centre for Education Policy in Practice, Bath Spa University, Bath.

Collins, J. 2001, *Good to Great: Why Some Companies Make the Leap . . . and Others Don't*, Harper Collins, New York.

de Bono, E. 2004, *Six Thinking Hats*, Penguin, Harmondsworth.

Department of Children, Schools and Families 2010, *Working Together to Safeguard Children: A Guide to Inter-agency Working to Safeguard and Promote the Welfare of Children*, Department of Children, Schools and Families, London.

Douglas, A., Heimer, L. and Hagan, W. 2011, *The Massachusetts Early Education and Childcare Professional Development System Study, Year 1 Report*, University of Massachusetts, Boston, <http://www.mass.gov/Eoedu/docs/EEC/profdevelopment/20110208umbinterimrpt.pdf> (accessed 20 October 2011).

Draper, L. and Wheeler, H. 2010, 'Working with parents', in G. Pugh and B. Duffy (eds), *Contemporary Issues in the Early Years: Working Collaboratively for Children*, 5th edn, Paul Chapman, London.

Duffy, E. 1995, 'Horizontal violence: A conundrum for nursing', *Collegian Journal of the Royal College of Nursing*, no. 2, pp. 5–17.

Dunlop, A. 2008, *A Literature Review on Leadership in the Early Years*, <http://www.ltscotland.org.uk/Images/leadershipreview_tcm4-499140.doc> (accessed 20 October 2011).

Early Childhood Australia, *Mission Statement*, <http://www.earlychildhoodaustralia.org.au> (accessed 20 November 2011).

Ebbeck, M. and Waniganayake, M. 2003, *Early Childhood Professionals: Leading Today and Tomorrow*, MacLennan and Petty, Sydney.

Elliot, A. 2008, 'Mentoring for professional growth', *Every Child*, vol. 14, no. 3, p. 7.

Engle, P. 2006, 'Comprehensive policy guide of child rights', in *A Guide to General Comment 7: 'Implementing Child Rights in Early Childhood'*, United Nations Committee on the Rights of the Child, Bernard van Leer Foundation, The Hague.

Fink, D. 2011, 'Pipelines, pools and reservoirs: Building leadership capacity for sustained improvements', *Journal of Educational Administration*, vol. 49, no. 6, pp. 670–84.

Fitzgerald, D. and Kay, J. 2007, *Working Together in Children's Services*, Routledge, London.

Franklin, B. and Hammarberg, T. 1995, *The Handbook of Children's Rights: Comparative Policy and Practice*, Routledge, London.

Frière, P. 1972, *Pedagogy of the Oppressed*, Penguin, Harmondsworth.

Frost, N. 2005, *Professionalism, Partnership and Joined-up Thinking: A Research Review of Front Line Working with Children*, Research in Practice, Totnes.

Furman, G. 2012, 'Social justice leadership as praxis: Developing capacities through preparation programs', *Educational Administration Quarterly*, vol. 48, no. 2, pp. 191–229.

Garavan, T.N. and McCarthy, A. 2008, 'Collective learning and human resource development', *Advances in Developing Human Resources*, vol. 10, no. 4, pp. 451–71.

Gardner, H. 1983, *Frames of Mind: Theories of Multiple Intelligences*, Basic Books, New York.

Gasper, M. 2010, *Multi-agency Working in the Early Years: Challenges and Opportunities*, Sage, London.

George, B., Sims, P., Mclean, A.N. and Mayer, D. 2011, 'Discovering your authentic leadership', in *Harvard Business Review* (ed.), *On Leadership*, Harvard Business School Press, Boston.

Goffee, R. and Jones, G. 2011, 'Why should anyone be led by you?' in *Harvard Business Review* (ed.), *On Leadership*, Harvard Business School Press, Boston.

Goleman, D. 1996, *Emotional Intelligence: Why It Can Matter More than IQ*, Bloomsbury, London.

—— 2011, 'What makes a leader?' in *Harvard Business Review* (ed.), *On Leadership*, Harvard Business School Press, Boston.

Goleman, D., Boyatzis, R. and McKee, A. 2002, *Primal Leadership: Realising the Power of Emotional Intelligence*, Harvard Business School Press, Boston.

—— 2004, *Learning to Lead with Emotional Intelligence*, Harvard Business School Press, Boston.

Gowrie Queensland n.d., *Philosophy Statement*, <http://www.gowrie-brisbane.com. au> (accessed 20 November 2011).

Gowrie South Australia n.d., *Vision Statement*, <http://www.gowrie-adelaide.com. au/cms> (accessed 20 November 2011).

Gowrie Tasmania, *Mission and Values Statements*, <http://www.gowrie-tas.com.au/ about-gowrie> (accessed 20 November 2011).

Gowrie Victoria n.d., *The Gowrie Australia Mission Statement*, <http://www. gowrievictoria.org.au/AboutUs/GowriearoundAustralia> (accessed 20 November 2011).

Gowrie Western Australia n.d., *Vision, Mission and Values Statements*, <http://www. gowrie-wa.com.au> (accessed 20 November 2011).

Hand, L.M. 2006, 'Horizontal violence in early childhood education and care: Implications for leadership', *Australian Journal of Early Childhood*, vol. 31, no. 3, pp. 40–8.

—— 2009, 'Why bullying is an issue in the early childhood workplace', *Every Child*, vol. 15, no. 2, p. 24.

Harris, A. and Spillane, J. 2008, 'Distributed leadership through the looking glass', *Management in Education*, vol. 22, no. 1, pp. 31–4.

Hartley, D. 2009, 'Education policy, distributed leadership and socio-cultural theory', *Educational Review*, vol. 61, no. 2, pp. 139–50.

*Harvard Business Review* 2011, *On Leadership*, Harvard Business School Press, Boston.

Hedges, H. 2011, 'Connecting "snippets of knowledge": Teachers' understandings of the concept of working theories', *Early Years*, vol. 31, no. 3, pp. 271–84.

Heikka, J. and Waniganayake, M. 2011, 'Pedagogical leadership from a distributed perspective within the context of early childhood education', *International Journal of Leadership in Education*, no. 1, pp. 1–14.

Hopkins, D. 2008, *A Teacher's Guide to Classroom Research*, 4th edn, Open University Press, Philadelphia, PA.

Hunsaker, P.L. and Hunsaker, J.S. 2009, *Managing People*, DK Publishing, New York.

Hydon, C. 2009, 'The quest for ethical practice', *Every Child*, vol. 15, no. 4, p. 8.

Johnson, D.W. 2008, *Reaching Out: Interpersonal Effectiveness and Self-Actualisation*, 10th edn, Allyn & Bacon, Boston.

Johnson, D.W. and Johnson F.P. 2008, *Joining Together: Group Theory and Process*, 10th edn, Pearson, New York.

Kagan, S. and Bowman, B.T. (eds) 1997, *Leadership in Early Care and Education*, National Association for the Education of Young Children, Washington, DC.

Katz, L. 1995, 'The nature of professions: Where is early childhood education?', in L. Katz (ed.), *Talks with Teachers: A Collection*, Ablex, Norwood.

Koenig, A.M., Eagly, A.H., Mitchell, A.A. and Ristikani, T. 2011, 'Are leader stereotypes masculine? A meta-analysis of three research paradigms', *Psychological Bulletin*, vol. 137, no. 4, pp. 616–42.

Kouzes, J.M. and Posner, B.Z. 2007, *The Leadership Challenge*, 4th edn, Jossey Bass, San Francisco.

Krotoski, A. 2010, 'Linked out?' *Royal Society for the Arts Journal*, Autumn, pp. 28–31.

Kuh, L.P. 2012, 'Promoting communities of practice and parallel process in early childhood settings', *Journal of Early Childhood Teacher Education*, vol. 33, no. 1, pp. 19–37.

Lloyd, E. and Hallett, E. 2010, 'Professionalising the early childhood workforce in England: Work in progress or a missed opportunity?' *Contemporary Issues in Early Childhood*, vol. 11, no. 1, pp. 75–88.

MacNaughton, G. and Hughes, P. 2008, *Doing Action Research in Early Childhood Studies: A Step by Step Guide*, Open University Press, Buckingham.

MacNaughton, G., Rolfe, S. and Siraj-Blatchford, I. (eds) 2010, *Doing Educational Research: International Perspectives on Theory and Practice*, 2nd edn, Open University Press, Buckingham.

Marrin, J. 2011, *Leadership for Dummies*, John Wiley & Sons, Chichester.

Maslow, A. 1970, *Motivation and Personality*, Harper & Row, New York.

Maxfield, C.R., Ricks-Doneen, J., Klocko, B.A. and Sturges, L. 2011, 'Developing and supporting early childhood teacher leaders: A leadership project connecting university, community and public school resources', in B. Alford, C. Perreault, L. Zellner and J. Ballenger (eds), *Blazing New Trails: Preparing Leaders to Improve Access and Equity in Today's Schools*, Proactive Publications, Lancaster, PA.

Maxwell, J. 2011a, *5 Levels of Leadership*, Center Street, New York.

—— 2011b, *How Successful People Think Workbook*, Center Street Hachette Book Group, New York.

McNiff, J. 2010, *Action Research for Professional Development: Concise Advice for New (and Experienced) Action Researchers*, September Books, Dorset.

Meade, A. 2011, 'Centres of innovation: Gaining a new understanding of reality', *Early Education*, vol. 50, Spring/Summer, pp. 7–10.

Mistry, M. and Sood, K. 2011, 'Challenges of early years leadership preparation: A comparison between early and experienced early years practitioners in England', *Management in Education*, vol. 12, no. 26, pp. 28–37.

Moyles, J. 2006, *Effective Leadership and Management in the Early Years*, Open University Press, Maidenhead.

Mukherji, P. and Albon, D. 2010, *Research Methods in Early Childhood: An Introductory Guide*, Sage, London.

National Association for the Education of Young Children 1996, *After the Stand: Be a Children's Champion*, <http://www.naeyc.org/ece/1996/06.asp> (accessed 20 November 2011).

—— n.d., *Mission, Goals and Objectives Statements*, <http://naeyc.org/about/mission> (accessed 20 November 2011).

National College for Leadership of Schools and Children's Services 2010, *International Approaches to Children's Services Leadership and Leadership Development*, National College of Leadership in Schools and Children's Services, Nottingham.

National Day Nursery Association n.d., *Vision, Mission and Goal Statements*, <http://www.ndna.org.uk/about-us> (accessed 20 November 2011).

North American Reggio Emilia Alliance n.d., *Mission Statement*, <http://reggio alliance.org/downloads/narea10.1.pdf> (accessed 20 November 2011).

Osborne, C. 2008, *Leadership*, DK Publishing, New York.

Pascal, C. 2011, 'Practitioner research: An intellectual and adventurous narrative at a tipping point?' Keynote presentation, British Early Childhood Education Research Association Conference, Birmingham, February.

Pen Green Centre 1983, *Vision Statement 1983*, <http://www.pengreen.org/pen greencentre.php> (accessed 20 November 2011).

Peterson, S.M. and Baker, A.C. 2011, Readiness to change in communities, organisations and individuals, in J.A. Sutterby (ed.), *The Early Childhood Educator Professional Development Grant: Research and Practice—Advances in Early Education and Care*, Emerald Group, Cambridge, MA.

Poole, J. 2011, *Leadership in Easy Steps*, Easy Steps Limited, Southam.

Pratt-Johnson, Y. 2006, 'Communicating cross-culturally: What teachers should know', *TESL Journal*, no. 2, February, <http://iteslj.org/Articles/Pratt-Johnson-CrossClutural.html> (accessed 20 November 2011).

Redding, S., Murphy, M. and Sheley, P. (eds) 2011, *Handbook on Family and Community Engagement*, Academic Development Institute, Lincoln, IL.

Reynolds, B. 2011, 'Between a rock and a hard place: Leadership dilemmas in Tasmania early childhood education and care centres', *Journal of Educational Leadership, Policy and Practice*, vol. 26, no. 2, pp. 26–34.

Roberts-Holmes, G. 2011, *Doing Your Early Years Project: A Step by Step Guide*, 2nd edn, Sage, London.

Rodd, J. 2006, *Leadership in Early Childhood*, 3rd edn, Allen & Unwin, Sydney.

Rogers, C. 1961, *On Becoming a Person*, Houghton Mifflin, Boston.

Ryder, D., Chandra,Y., Dalton,J., Homer, M. and Passingham, D. 2011, 'The development process of an early childhood leadership programme: A distributed leadership perspective', *Journal of Educational Leadership, Policy and Practice*, vol. 26, no. 2, pp. 62–8.

Schulz, K. 2010, 'Making good mistakes', *Royal Society for the Arts Journal*, Autumn, pp. 16–17.

Semann, A. and Waniganayake, M. 2010, 'Courageous acts', *Rattler*, Autumn, pp. 92–3.

Sinclair, A. 2007, *Leadership for the Disillusioned*, Allen & Unwin, Sydney.

Siraj-Blatchford, I. and Manni, L. 2006, *Effective Leadership in the Early Years Sector Study*, Institute of Education, University of London, London.

Small, M.L. 2010, 'Human resources', *Royal Society for the Arts Journal*, Autumn, pp. 18–21.

Smith, A.B. 2008, *Children's Rights and Early Childhood Education: Links to Theory and Advocacy*, Early Childhood Australia, <http://www.earlychildhoodaustralia. org.au> (accessed 20 November 2011).

Staffordshire Children's Trust 2010, 'Parent and carer engagement toolkit', in *Involving Parents and Families*, Children's Workforce Development Council, Leeds, <http://www.cwdcouncil.org.uk/working-with-parents-and-families> (accessed 20 November 2011).

Talan, T. 2010, 'Distributed leadership: Something new or something borrowed?', *Leadership Exchange*, May/June, pp. 8–10.

Thornton, K., Wansborough, D., Clarkin-Phillips, J., Aitken, H. and Tamati, A. 2009, *Conceptualising Leadership in Early Childhood Education in Aotearoa New Zealand*, Occasional Paper No. 2, New Zealand Teachers Council, Wellington.

Thornton, L. and Brunton, P. 2010, *The Parent Partnership Toolkit for Early Years*, Optimus Education, London.

Vander Ven, K.1991, 'The relationship between notions of caregiving held by early childhood practitioners and stages of career development', in B. Po-King Chan (ed.), *Early Childhood Towards the 21st Century: A Worldwide Perspective*, Yew Chung Education Publishing, Hong Kong.

Vygotsky, L.A. 1978, *Mind and Society: The Development of Higher Psychological Processes*, Scribner, New York.

Walker, G. 2010, *Working Together for Children: A Critical Introduction to Multi-agency Working*, Continuum, London.

Watson, B. and Williams, B. 2011, 'Leadership: Leveraging the benefits of professional learning', *Early Education*, vol. 50, Spring/Summer, pp. 22–4.

Wilson, V. and Pirrie, A. 2000, *Multi-Disciplinary Teamworking: Beyond the Barriers? Review of the Issues, Research Report No. 96*, Scottish Council for Educational Research, Edinburgh.

Wooden, J. and Jamison, S. 2009, *Coach Wooden's Leadership Game Plan for Success*, McGraw-Hill, New York.

Yaverbaum, E. and Sherman, E. 2008, *The Everything Leadership Book*, 2nd edn, F+W Publications, Avon, MA.

Zachery, L. 2009, *The Mentee's Guide: Making Mentoring Work for You*, Jossey-Bass, San Francisco.

# AUTHOR INDEX

# SUBJECT INDEX